Parents and Professionals Alike
Give High Praise to *Facing Autism*

"Patients and parents have often been among the best teachers in my quest to become a better doctor. This has been especially true of families facing autism. In *Facing Autism*, Lynn Hamilton has created a book that is both a practical primer for such families and a wonderful tribute to parents as the best teachers of other parents."

—JOHN BOHN, M.D.
Ryan Hamilton's pediatrician, U.W. Health Physicians Plus
Middleton, Wisconsin

"*Facing Autism* is a book I would eagerly share with families of children newly diagnosed with PDD/autism. It is, as the title implies, proactive and positive. It is written by a remarkable woman who would have loved to have access to such a book just a few short years ago when her son was diagnosed with autism. Parents of young children with autism will glean a direction for intervention from this comprehensive compendium of diagnostic issues and intervention options."

—MARJORIE A. GETZ, PH.D.
developmental specialist, Lutheran General Children's Hospital
Park Ridge, Illinois

"I heartily recommend *Facing Autism*. Lynn Hamilton has done a superb job of assessing the many treatment options offered to parents of autistic children. She describes them clearly and engagingly. An excellent book!"

—BERNARD RIMLAND, PH.D.
director, Autism Research Institute

"Lynn Hamilton does a very good job of summarizing the medical and nutritional therapies available for people with autism and PDD. Therapists and parents will be very pleased with this book."

—DR. WILLIAM SHOW
author of *Biological Treatments for Autism and PDD*

"Reading Lynn's book is like having a long, friendly, and supportive conversation with someone who understands. The research is meticulous and expansive, yet the book is a delight to read. After reading *Facing Autism,* you will feel that you have gained a new friend and valuable insights into treating your child's condition."

—SUSAN K. WALLITSCH
mother of child with autism

"Lynn Hamilton shows a clear understanding of Applied Behavior Analysis and its role in the treatment of children with autism. Her writing should be most helpful to parents who must make their way through the maze that autism presents."

—JOSEPH E. MORROW, PH.D.
president, Applied Behavior Consultants
Sacramento, CA

"In *Facing Autism,* Lynn has endeavored to be as accurate as possible in describing the several approaches that she felt were helpful in Ryan's treatment and has had experts review what was written. The book is therefore somewhat unique in that it represents the input of a variety of experts who think quite differently about autism, but whose collective work contributed to a positive outcome for one little boy. Both parents and professionals working with autistic children will find this interesting reading."

—DR. GLEN O. SALLOWS
psychologist and director, Wisconsin Early Autism Project
Madison, Wisconsin

"*Facing Autism* is a book that every parent of an autistic child should read, particularly those parents whose child has been newly diagnosed with the disorder. Lynn weaves together personal accounts and the different treatment modalities used with her son, Ryan. The book is both a resource guide and a compelling narrative of one family's courageous journey."

—JEAN MUCKIAN, RN, BSN
U.W. Health Physicians Plus
Middleton, Wisconsin

FACING
AUTISM

GIVING PARENTS REASONS FOR
HOPE AND GUIDANCE FOR HELP

LYNN M. HAMILTON

WaterBrook
PRESS

FACING AUTISM
PUBLISHED BY WATERBROOK PRESS
5446 North Academy Boulevard, Suite 200
Colorado Springs, Colorado 80918
A division of Random House, Inc.

This book is intended as a resource to provide a summary of current autism research and treatments and to point the reader to the source materials that contain a more thorough treatment of the subject. None of the information presented in this book is meant to be a prescription for any kind of treatment, medical or otherwise, and reference to other organizations and materials is for convenience only and is not intended as an endorsement. No therapy should be initiated unless recommended and supervised by a qualified professional. The medical professional and the parent or guardian of the child needing treatment are responsible for weighing the risks before beginning any of the therapies described in this book. The author has made every effort to present the current research accurately and assumes no responsibility for inaccuracies, omissions, or errors contained in the source materials. The author and publisher are not liable for misuse of information provided. The author and publisher are neither liable nor responsible to any person or entity for any loss, damage, or injury caused or alleged to be caused by the information in this book.

Scripture taken from the *Holy Bible, New International Version*®. NIV®. Copyright © 1973, 1978, 1984 by International Bible Society. Used by permission of Zondervan Publishing House. All rights reserved.

ISBN 1-57856-262-7

WATERBROOK and its deer design logo are registered trademarks of WaterBrook Press, a division of Random House, Inc.

Library of Congress Cataloging-in-Publication Data
Hamilton, Lynn M.
        Facing autism : reasons for hope, guidance for help / Lynn M. Hamilton.
            p.   cm.
        Includes bibliographical references and index.
        ISBN 1-57856-262-7
        1. Autism in children—Case studies.   2. Parents of autistic children—Case studies.
    3. Autistic children—Care—Case studies.   I. Title.

RJ506.A9 H246   2000
618.92'8982—dc21   99-047754

Printed in the United States of America

2000—First Edition

10 9 8 7 6 5 4

This book is dedicated to our precious children

— Ryan and Tori —

for whom we would climb any mountain.

CONTENTS

FOREWORD

A book you like becomes your friend. If you are the parent of an autistic child, *Facing Autism* will quickly become a good and close friend—a friend you admire and trust and consult often. *Facing Autism* is Lynn Hamilton's personal story of her encounter with autism. Her diligent, intelligent, and very often successful search for answers will captivate you, as it did me. Beyond that it will inform you, as she presents solid, well-researched, useful information.

When my autistic son was born in 1956, I was already three years past my Ph.D. in psychology. I had never seen or heard the word *autism,* nor had I seen an autistic child. Nor had our pediatrician, Dr. Black, encountered an autistic child in his thirty-five years of medical practice.

Autism was then a very rare disorder, occurring in only one of every three to four thousand children. As I write these words, in mid-1999, we see evidence of an enormous upsurge in the incidence of autism. Some studies report figures as high as one child in 150. While the reality of the upsurge in autism is indisputable, the cause is the subject of increasingly heated controversy. The sharp-eyed reader may discern a pattern in the pages of this book that suggests what many, including me, believe to be the most plausible cause. But the underlying cause, or causes, is not the thesis of Lynn's book. Her main thrust relates to treatments—treatments that work.

To appreciate how significant and helpful her coverage of treatments is, you need to understand what you would have faced just a few years ago. In the '50s and '60s and early '70s, when our son was growing up, the treatment options were limited and far from positive. The psychiatrists of that era had been taught that autistic children were biologically normal youngsters who had somehow discerned that their mothers, "refrigerator mothers" they were called, did not really love nor want them, so the children had simply tuned out the world and become autistic. (My 1964 book *Infantile Autism* is credited with having destroyed that myth, but that is another story.) So the treatment strategy was to give the children tranquilizers or antipsychotic drugs to make life more bearable for the adults who were forced to deal with the children and to place the children and their mothers in psychoanalytic-type therapies, which would supposedly unearth the subconscious traumas or conflicts believed to be the root cause of autism. The children were given paper or clay dolls representing their mothers and were encouraged to express their sublimated hostility by shredding or smashing the symbolic evil mothers. The mothers who could afford it were required to reveal their most private thoughts to the psychiatrist, who assured them that until they acknowledged their repressed hatred for the child, the child would never recover. Denial was greeted with a smirk. It was virtually an admission of guilt—so said the textbooks.

After *Infantile Autism* was published, I began looking for more rational—and more effective—treatment options. When our son, Mark, was five, my wife and I were told he was a hopeless case and should be immediately placed in an institution. At age eight and a half, Mark was still in diapers and had never asked or answered a question. But we started him on the two forms of therapy I perceived as most promising—behavior modification and megavitamin B$_6$ therapy—both of which were derided and ridiculed by those in the medical profession. We quickly began seeing excellent results. Mark's progress continues to this day. Perhaps you've seen him interviewed on CBS, PBS, or CNN, but that, too, is another story.

In the past decade there has been an enormous upsurge in treatment options available to parents of autistic children, which parallels the upsurge in the incidence of autism itself. But not all of these options are worthwhile. Parents, once faced with too few choices, are now confronted with too many.

As you can see, my desire that parents be accurately informed about autism and its treatment is both professional and personal. That's why I heartily recommend this book to you as a great friend and invaluable resource in facing your child's autism. Lynn Hamilton has done a superb job of examining, evaluating, and explaining the major treatment options available to parents, including behavior modification, now relabeled ABA, and megavitamin therapy, along with many newer therapies. She also has filled the book with practical help on everything from whom to call for help, how to get funding, what foods to avoid, and how to work with the schools and doctors.

If you can buy only one guidebook on autism, *Facing Autism* is the one to get!

BERNARD RIMLAND, PH.D.
Director, Autism Research Institute

ACKNOWLEDGMENTS

Though one name is listed on the cover, scores of people had a hand in making this book a reality. I have to begin by thanking my family. Roger, you are the most wonderful husband and father, and I love you more than words can express. Together we have climbed this mountain, and together we will conquer any challenge that may lie ahead. Thank you for your love, support, encouragement, and strength. Tori, I thank you for being such a loving, caring daughter. You have played a major role in Ryan's life and his learning process, though you are too young to know it. I look forward to seeing how your life unfolds.

To my parents, Dave and Joyce Nolte: Thank you for your love and support through the years and especially for all the baby-sitting and meals as I spent long hours writing this manuscript. It *is* a joy living next to you, and I love you both! And to my sister, Gail Bothum: Your generosity and constant encouragement have blessed us all along the way.

To Russ and Barb Hamilton, Roger's parents: I am very grateful for your encouragement and loving concern. And to my sister-in-law and her husband, Carol and Rob Schmidt: You know more than anyone else in our families what we've gone through. Thanks for your generosity and frequent, expert medical advice as you've traveled this road with us. We're glad Roger's parents have been there to lift the load for you, as my parents have for us.

And to the rest of Roger's and my family: Thanks for all your encouragement, compassion, and help. There are too many of you to list, but I thank you all!

To all the "Operation Rescue Ryan" prayer partners around the world, those I know and those I've never met: I thank you for standing and kneeling with us for the life of our son. I especially want to thank those at High Point Church and the women of Tapestry for the consistent prayer intervention on our behalf. Things happen when God's people pray!

To Dr. Glen Sallows and Tamlynn Graupner, with the Wisconsin Early Autism Project: I thank you from the bottom of my heart for all you have done in rescuing our son as you have guided us through every step of ABA. We're grateful you started this therapy in Madison, and we are deeply indebted to you.

To all the therapists and educators along the way: There are more than I can mention by name, but I especially want to express my gratitude to Michelle Sherman, Bohdanna Popowycz Kvam, Chrissy Brennan, Dawn Rasinske, Jennie Zimmers, Liz Dyer, Kristina and Patrick Carlin, Becky Spellman, Jen La Luzerne, Kim Wroblewski, Jennifer Valaskey, Katherine Clark, Dave Merz, Michelle Benjamin, Jill White, Carin Swanson, Eileen Hamele, Marge Blanc, and Martha Bowhan. We are fortunate to have had the best.

In addition, my deepest thanks to—

Dr. John Bohn and Jeanie Muckian—for looking and going beyond the obvious in Ryan's medical care.

Mary Alice Sicard and Susan Wallitsch—for your knowledge, experience, friendship, and support. Either one of you could have written this book.

Ruth Ann Ebsen—for listening, supporting, and being there when I needed you.

Dave Frahm—for prompting me to write this book. It was not my dream to write, but you made me see the need and encouraged me to fill it.

Dan Rich, my publisher—for giving me this opportunity and making it happen.

Carol Bartley, my editor—for making these words come alive. What a gift you have! Thank you for using it on this book.

Dr. Bernard Rimland, Dr. William Shaw, Dr. Bruce Semon, Dr. Sidney Baker, Dr. Sudhir Gupta, Dr. Glen Sallows, Dr. Joseph Morrow, Gay Langham-McNally, and many more—for lending your expertise in checking the accuracy of the material in your respective fields.

Sherry Mears, Earl Leyda, Karen Evans, Jennie Zimmers, and Sandy Schelthelm—for helping behind the scenes so I could sit in front of my computer to write.

Our colleagues at the Navigators and its leadership—for your prayers, encouragement, and understanding in giving us the freedom to put extra time and energy into Ryan's life. What an honor it is to be partners in the gospel with all of you.

While all these people have worked very hard to make this book and Ryan's rescue from autism possible, no one has worked harder than our dear son. Ryan, Dad and I are so proud of you. We painfully watched as you regressed into autism, and we worked alongside you as you fought your way out. Your inner strength and courage, along with your loving heart, have brought you back. You are such a precious boy, and I know you will grow to be a remarkable man. I am so proud to be your mom!

Most important, I would like to thank the Lord for guiding us each step of this journey. It would be easy to take credit for the battles won, but the glory rightfully belongs to the Lord. It is only through Christ and His strength, grace, love, and mercy that we have come this far.

Chapter 1

The Early Days

The field cannot well be seen from within the field.

RALPH WALDO EMERSON

In a month we would be leaving for a summer in Siberia. The work Roger and I do in Christian ministry had taken us there for the summer of 1991, and now two years later we were anxious to return. But this time we were going to Russia with a thirteen-month-old child. We were excited about showing Ryan off to all our friends, but taking a child to Russia wasn't an easy task. Items that could be easily purchased in the States, like diapers, weren't available in Siberia, so we would have to pack everything Ryan needed for the summer. What toys should we take? What kind of food would they have for Ryan, and what additional food should we carry with us? And just how many diapers *does* a toddler use in nine weeks? The questions and the preparations were different this trip.

I began making careful lists of what we used each week in caring for Ryan, from diapers and wipes to shampoo. I also watched Ryan closely as he played and noted which toys and books he liked best. The toys needed to be small enough to carry easily but exciting enough to keep his attention on the long flights to and from Moscow.

In preparation for our travels we discussed medications and vaccinations with our doctor. Ryan had already had several ear infections, so we wanted to take along some antibiotics. We also wanted to have him vaccinated before we left since we didn't know how commonly vaccines were used in Russia. He was current on all his shots, but he would soon need the MMR (measles, mumps, and rubella), so we gave it to him at twelve and a half months old.

With everything ready, we left for Russia. Overly prepared for the trip, we checked nine bags and carried three on the plane. After arriving in Russia, we faced a three-day journey on the Trans-Siberian Railroad. Ryan enjoyed the train and its constant rocking, but he seemed fussy and cried more often than normal. I remarked that we had hit the "terrible twos" at only thirteen months old.

Once we arrived and settled in, Ryan did better. He liked exploring the apartment that we had rented. Our bedroom had white lace curtains, and Ryan would hide behind them and play peekaboo with us. Or he would play outside in a sandbox, digging in the sand and sifting it through his fingers. He also loved petting the dogs in the neighborhood, especially a little brown puppy that two children upstairs owned. He would chase it and giggle when it jumped on him and licked his face.

Ryan enjoyed his days in Siberia. Although I had brought a lot of packaged food from home, like tuna and macaroni and cheese, Ryan liked the Russian food and ate and drank everything offered, except the milk. He learned to wave good-bye when spoken to in English or Russian and understood whatever we said to him. Although he spoke only a few words, I attributed it to the confusion of hearing two languages and was certain his vocabulary would blossom once we returned home.

All in all, it was a typical summer, except we spent it in Siberia.

Signs of Change

When we returned from Siberia, my parents met us at the airport to drive us back to Madison. Mom had brought us our favorite soda and snacks, which made Roger and me extremely happy, but Ryan was only interested in some balloons he saw. He kept saying, "Bbboom, bboom," and reaching out to the balloons. With this new word, *balloon,* he now had six or seven words.

When we got home to our apartment, we went to visit our close friends Dawn and Scott. They had two children: Zac, who was a couple of years older than Ryan, and Lynsey, who was only eight days older. Unlike Ryan, Lynsey was quite a talker. Over the summer she had learned many new words and was even putting them together in phrases. This caught my attention, but I brushed it aside. After all, girls generally talk earlier than boys.

But as I watched Lynsey learn new words in the following weeks, I realized that not only was Ryan *not* learning new words, but the words he had previously spoken were gone. Was I imagining things? I dug out Ryan's first-year calendar and flipped through the months. Yes, I had written down some words, so he had said them. Where were they now? Perhaps Ryan had become confused in the transition between Russia and America, I thought, but as I continued to compare Ryan to Lynsey, Ryan fell further behind each day.

One day we had friends over for a cookout in our backyard. While Sarah and I were in the kitchen preparing the food, Ryan came in and began to scream. As usual, I tried to figure out what he wanted. I pulled out cereal from the cupboard, but he kept screaming. I opened the refrigerator and took out the milk, then juice and then water. Ryan's screaming increased. He didn't point to anything or give me any clue as to what he wanted, but since we were in the kitchen, I assumed he was hungry or thirsty. I continued to pull out items one by one, until I finally stumbled on what he wanted—a cookie. Taking the cookie, he calmed down and left the room.

Seeing my stress, Sarah shared how she required her children from an early age to speak to her either in words or in sign language to get what they wanted. She stressed the importance of not giving in to children until they communicate their desire clearly. I didn't feel as though I was giving in to Ryan, but she had four talking children and I had none, so I tried. The next time Ryan came to the kitchen and screamed, I tried to get him to say what he wanted. I gave him words to choose from, but I didn't show him anything from the cupboards. This made him scream more. In my determination to help him learn to talk, I pushed even harder until another friend, Marie, approached me with her answer to my problem.

Marie felt I was pushing Ryan too hard. If I would only relax about his language and allow him to develop at his own speed, he would speak. I liked this better and it was a lot easier on my ears, but still the language didn't come.

One week when I picked him up from Sunday school, I mentioned my concern about his language delay to the teacher. He didn't seem concerned, saying, "Einstein didn't speak until he was four." I had heard that many times.

Our concern about Ryan's language skills kept us from realizing that other skills and behaviors were deteriorating as well. Daily, Ryan became more difficult to handle.

Strong-Willed or Out of Control?
Late in November, when Ryan was about eighteen months old, we went to walk the mall with three friends, Dawn, Linda, and Heidi, and their kids. All the Christmas decorations were up, and the kids

were excited. We started our excursion at the food court. I put Ryan in a chair and set some food in front of him, but he wouldn't sit still. He immediately got out of his chair and ran away. I called after him, but he didn't stop. I chased him down and brought him back, and again he scurried away. "No" and "stop" seemed to have no meaning to him at all. Never did he look back to acknowledge my commands. In fact, it was as if he didn't hear me. The other mothers enjoyed their lunch with their kids, while I just tried to contain my son in the area. As my frustration grew, I wondered, *Can't he sit long enough for me to eat?*

Feeling bad for me, my friends finished their food quickly, and we began walking around the mall. Ryan, of course, led the way with me in close pursuit. He was driven to touch everything. When I told him no or disciplined him, he would turn right around and do it again. When Lynsey touched something she wasn't supposed to, Dawn told her "no, no" in a calm, gentle voice, and, lo and behold, Lynsey stopped! Why wouldn't Ryan? The other children, all about the same age as Ryan, stayed close to their moms and enjoyed the decorations with childish glee while my child ran wild.

As Linda's son, Isaac, said something cute, Linda commented, "Isn't this a wonderful age?" I looked at her as if she had just landed from another planet. I thought, *No! This is not a wonderful age. I hate it! I can't control my child. I can't eat in peace. I can't talk to my friends. All I do is chase this child, and he won't listen to a thing I say! Why am I such a bad mom? Why can't Ryan behave like the other kids? What am I doing wrong? Why do I even try to leave the house? I hate this!*

Within moments Ryan was getting into the decorations again, and I couldn't get him to stop. I'd had enough. Breaking down in tears, I picked up Ryan, who was screaming in defiance, and excused myself to go home.

Ryan wasn't always out of control. He was normally happy, playful, and affectionate—if things were done his way. He loved to cuddle and hug and run and laugh. But if demands or limits were put on him or if I told him to do anything other than what he had chosen, he would let loose a bloodcurdling scream and throw a tantrum as if he were terribly hurt. His body would shake, sometimes as he stood, other times as he lay on the floor.

Believing Ryan was a strong-willed child, I read every book about raising a strong-willed child that I could get my hands on and tried every technique, but none worked. Again I thought I must be a bad mom. Having been given the techniques to tame my child's behavior, I couldn't make them work. It *had* to be my fault.

The blame I felt for Ryan's behavior may have been partly due to my insecurity, but it was confirmed by the stares and comments of those around Roger and me. Looks of disapproval were commonplace. When Ryan would stand on the chairs at McDonald's and make noises, adults stared openly. If our eyes met, they would shake their heads and look away. One man in the Denver airport swore at us as Ryan screamed because of the loud noises, and another time a man grabbed Ryan by the arm and yanked him off the ground during a tantrum. It was open season for judging our parenting skills, and with no other explanation for his behavior, we accepted the blame.

We weren't the only ones who couldn't handle Ryan. At one point I joined a Bible study for mothers of young children. They provided childcare filled with wonderful activities for the kids while the moms got a break and had a chance to learn. Each week I would go, looking forward to the day's speaker and Bible study time, but each week ended the same. About a half-hour into the lecture, someone would come find me to let me know they were having a hard time handling Ryan. Apologetically, they would ask me to come get him. Often I would hear comments like, "He sure is all boy." After several failed attempts, I dropped out.

Dietary Changes

One area in which Ryan was no different from his friends was eating. He seemed hungry all the time. As a toddler he had eaten any food we gave him, but somewhere along the way things began to change. While in Russia, Ryan drank water from a cup and milk from his bottle. But as he was closing in on two years old, we felt it was time to make the bottle disappear. When we moved from an apartment to a house, we decided to "lose" his bottles in the move. In our apartment, he knew where we stored them and would point and scream until we would give him a bottle, even if the bottles weren't there. But in the new house, there would be no cupboard assigned to them. They would just disappear.

When the move came, we put our plan into action. The bottles were gone and the cups took over. What we didn't count on was that Ryan refused to drink milk from a cup. To him, milk came from a bottle and water from a cup. Every time we gave him a cup of milk, he would throw a tantrum and refuse it. Eventually we gave up. Refusing to bring back bottles, we settled on allowing him to drink just water for the time being, assuming that one day he would be willing to drink milk in a cup. We were wrong.

Besides his drink limitations, his eating habits were also changing. This child who used to eat everything was becoming a very picky eater. He used to eat cottage cheese, but now he wouldn't touch it. The same was true for most vegetables and fruits. One by one Ryan began refusing foods, and the foods he would eat became more defined. I had grown up eating chocolate-chip pancakes, and we passed this tradition on to Ryan. He loved them, but he began demanding extreme consistency. When we made pancakes, there had to be two of them and they had to be the same size. If we gave him just one pancake, he would tantrum uncontrollably. To him, pancakes came in twos.

Other foods began to follow suit. He liked to eat fish sticks, but now they had to be Fisher Boy square fish patties. He would accept no other brand and no other shape. The same was true with chicken nuggets and fruit-grain bars. Ryan's once varied repertoire of food was whittled down to just a few items. He would eat pancakes, waffles, and French toast—all of them plain, without butter or syrup. He would eat grilled cheese but only with mozzarella cheese. He ate chicken nuggets, corn dogs, and Doritos. In fact, he loved Cool Ranch Doritos and would have been content to live on Doritos alone or on most other junk food, like chips, cookies, ice cream, and cake, but he refused to eat any fruits or vegetables or to drink juice or milk.

The strangest thing was that Ryan was still growing well, and despite occasional ear infections or bouts of diarrhea, he looked healthy. Since he was still at the upper end of the chart for height and appeared healthy, our doctor told us not to worry. "Kids are often picky eaters," he said. "Just keep offering him healthy food, and someday he will eat it."

A Place for Everything

Ryan's rigidity with food transferred over into other areas of his life. Ever since Ryan was little, he had loved to watch movies while rocking on his horse. He rocked on it so much that he actually wore through the thick metal rings connecting the springs to the horse.

To him, the rocking horse and movies went hand in hand. He

would watch movies every waking hour if he were allowed. And he didn't like to vary the movies but repeatedly watched the same ones. Disney's *Snow White* was one of his favorites, and he knew it so well he would often imitate the dwarfs' actions before they happened. At certain parts he would squeal and wiggle with delight. It was fun seeing him enjoy these movies, but there was a nagging feeling that he was unusually attached to them. Did all children respond to movies like this?

In Ryan's world everything had a place where it should stay, including his movies. Our two-story home had a finished basement, which we made into three rooms: a playroom, a laundry room, and an office for Roger. The basement playroom had the TV and many of Ryan's toys. In most playrooms toys lie on the floor until Mom or Dad comes to put them away. However, Ryan insisted we leave certain things on the floor. He would place his *Pinocchio* video in the middle of the floor, just to the left of his rocking horse. Whether he was watching *Pinocchio* or not, the video cover had to remain there. When I would pick it up and put it away, Ryan would throw himself into an extreme tantrum. His hands would shake, and he would scream as if he were being tortured until he could return the video to its designated place on the floor. This behavior bothered us, but discipline didn't seem to correct it. He wasn't acting out of defiance. He seemed to need the video in its spot to have peace within himself.

Ryan also liked order in objects that surrounded him. When outside, he would find rocks and line them up by size. Inside, he would take stuffed animals or cars and place them in straight lines or perfect semicircles. Since Roger and I like order in our lives, his behavior didn't bother us. We just figured he was a bright, organized child.

Daily Life

With Ryan more difficult to understand and handle all the time, the stress in our daily lives grew. With each regression, Ryan screamed more and my nerves became more strained. I was now pregnant with our second child, so my tolerance was probably lowered by all the changes in my body.

Although I loved my little boy more than I ever thought I could love a child, I was fearful of having another one like him. It took everything I had to keep up with him and survive each day. How could I handle the stress if my second child acted the same way? Bathing and diapering Ryan required two people—one to hold him down while the other tried to change the diaper. Being kicked by Ryan in the process wasn't unusual. Dressing him wasn't any easier. He would run around the house with us trying to catch him long enough to get a shirt or pair of pants on him. Having raised five children, my mother often wondered why it took two of us to do such simple tasks like bathing or dressing Ryan.

I've always considered myself a strong person with a high tolerance for stress, but this was getting the best of me. Each day I would feel ready for the battles, but by the time Roger came home from work, I would literally be shaking. Why was this so hard? Was I not cut out to be a mother? The very thought made me feel guilty.

A Hearing Problem?

When Ryan was about two years old, we took him to our pediatrician to have his ears checked because we were becoming increasingly concerned about his lack of language. We thought that perhaps his ears were plugged with wax so he wasn't hearing properly. If we could get his ears cleared, maybe his speech would develop.

When we arrived for the appointment, Ryan seemed anxious.

As we waited in the examining room, Ryan, with his usual high level of energy, opened every cupboard door and drawer he could find. He would take out the dressing gowns, and I would put them back. He would grab the doctor's equipment, and I would frantically try to pry it out of his little hands. It amazes me how strong little hands can be when they want something they aren't supposed to have. I tried to redirect him with books and toys, but it didn't work. He had his own agenda.

When the doctor arrived, Ryan was turning the lights on and off. It drove me nuts, but at least he wasn't breaking anything and he was happy. The doctor tried to examine him while Ryan sat on my lap, but Ryan wouldn't cooperate. I held his head with one hand, wrapped my other arm around his stomach, and tried to contain his legs with mine. The doctor looked into his ears, but he really couldn't see much because there was too much wax. *Great,* I thought. *Let's get the wax out and fix this.*

When I released Ryan, he fell to the floor in a tantrum. I looked at our doctor and asked, "Is this normal?" He commented that it wasn't, but he didn't know what to make of it. We flushed out Ryan's ears with a warm water solution and waited to see if things improved.

Unfortunately, they didn't. Over the next few weeks we noticed more strange characteristics of his "hearing" problem. Sometimes he appeared to hear well; other times he seemed deaf. One day when he was in the bathtub, I called his name but he didn't respond. Trying again, I called out, "Ryan!" but he didn't answer. I spoke louder and moved closer, but he didn't bat an eye. Finally I got within five inches of his face and called his name again. Nothing. He wasn't trying to look around me; it was as if I didn't exist. How could this be? Ryan loved to be affectionate with us. He loved to run into our arms and laugh. He enjoyed being chased in circles around our living room. How could he then, at other times, so totally ignore us?

We decided to try our own hearing test. One day while Ryan had a movie on but was facing away from the TV, we muted the sound. He instantly noticed and turned around to see if the TV was turned off. Then we tried making a variety of sounds around him in the room. He seemed to notice all those sounds, too. We called his name and got no response. We tried again. No response. We tried a third time. This time he looked at us. Did he focus so intensely that he could tune us out? We doubted it. Then what was wrong?

Sleep Disorder

Ryan was never a very good sleeper; I, on the other hand, was extremely gifted in sleeping. I could sleep anywhere, anytime, and I needed a whole lot of it. When Ryan was first born, his sporadic sleep was not unusual, but as he got older and still didn't sleep through the night, it became more noticeable. By the time Ryan was two and a half and was still not sleeping though the night, I'd had it. My nerves were raw, and my sleep deprivation was affecting other areas of my life.

We had heard many methods of training a child to sleep through the night, so we began to explore them. We read a good book called *Solving Your Child's Sleep Problems*, which gave us some understanding of why Ryan might not be sleeping through the night, as well as practical solutions. They helped for a while, but we still hadn't solved the problem.

As Ryan got older, not only did he not sleep through the night, but he also needed me to lie down next to him to get to sleep. I was his comfort. When he awoke at night, he needed me beside him to fall back asleep. One night I got so frustrated that I grabbed a baby blanket and threw it across the room. "I can't take this anymore! I need to sleep!" I said as I broke down in tears. "We have to find an answer!" Roger agreed, but where to look for those answers?

Uneven Skill Levels

Although the volunteers at the moms' group were unable to handle Ryan, Roger and I were able to leave him with the Sunday-school teachers. Each week we would drop him off before the worship service, nervous about how he would do. Some days they would come and get us, but often they were able to keep him the whole hour. Since volunteer teachers ran our Sunday-school class with parents rotating as helpers, I welcomed my turn in the classroom. Then I'd be able to watch other two-year-olds in action and, hopefully, prove to myself that I was worrying about nothing.

When the week came for me to help, Ryan and I eagerly went to the classroom. We were the first ones there, so I began to set up the room with puzzles, books, and toys. Ryan liked puzzles, so he chose some to do. The kids trickled in and the class began.

First on the agenda was craft time. All the kids sat around the table to color and make a special craft about our lesson. Ryan refused. He wouldn't sit down or color. In fact, I realized that he had *never* colored. Our neighbor's children loved to color, but when Ryan didn't, I just thought he wasn't old enough. Yet he was the only child in the class who couldn't color.

Next we had circle time. All the kids came running over to the circle and started singing songs with the teacher. One shy little girl wanted to sit right next to me, but as I sat there with her, my eyes were glued on Ryan. He wouldn't come to the group. Even when another parent tried to bring him over, he screamed and refused.

He preferred to wander around the back of the room looking out the window or staring into space. During story time we again tried to get Ryan to come listen to the story. After all, he used to love having stories read to him at home. But no luck. Ryan would have nothing to do with story time.

Next was snack time. Surely Ryan would want the snack. I was wrong. Ryan drank the water but wouldn't eat the apple slices or cheese. He used to love fruit and cheese. When had he stopped? We tried to get Ryan to sit at the table with the other kids for the snack, but he threw a tantrum. In order to maintain peace in the classroom, we gave in, and he went back to his wandering. Now I knew why they were able to handle him in Sunday school. As long as he wasn't expected to participate in anything, he was happy.

For the first time I really knew something was wrong with Ryan. I leaned up against the wall and slid to the floor, weeping. I didn't know *what* was wrong, but I knew deep in my heart that Ryan was different. One of the other parents came over to console me by reminding me that boys develop later than girls and that I shouldn't compare him with other kids. That sounded nice, but I knew better. Ryan couldn't do anything that came so naturally to the other children. What confused me was that Ryan could do some things much better than these children. They were struggling with simple puzzles, putting a circle into a circle opening and a duck into a duck opening. Ryan, on the other hand, worked complex, interlocking puzzles with thirty or more pieces. What was going on?

When Roger came to get us after the service was over, I shared with him what I was feeling. He took me in his arms and tried to console me. "Give Ryan some more time. He'll catch up." But I knew the problem went deeper than that.

Chapter 2

Seeking Answers

*Between the idea and the reality, between
the motion and the act, falls the shadow.*

T. S. ELIOT

In June of 1994—now seven months pregnant—I was not only deeply concerned about Ryan, but I began having problems with my pregnancy and was put on bed rest. Ryan had been a big baby, and I had been huge when I was pregnant with him. With this pregnancy I was rather small, and our baby didn't appear to be growing. My doctor became concerned and sent me to a specialist, who performed a detailed ultrasound to check for abnormalities. She also gave me a non-stress test that day and twice a week for the next two weeks. None of these tests revealed a problem. However, a second ultrasound revealed that there was still no growth, so three weeks prior to my due date the doctors decided to induce me.

The doctor warned us ahead of time that our baby might have Down syndrome or another disorder. Although Roger and I knew we would love this child regardless, we were worried about having a child with special needs. How would we handle it?

During the birth a variety of specialists filled the room, ready to act. As soon as Victoria drew her first breath, they whisked her to the other side of the room to examine her. Within moments a collective sigh came from the doctors. Tori, as we nicknamed her, was small but healthy. In fact, this baby they had expected to weigh only four pounds eleven ounces surprised us all by topping the scales at five pounds nine ounces!

That afternoon Ryan came to the hospital with my mother and father. At first he seemed angry when we showed him his new sister. He ran around the room and crawled under the bed. But when he returned the next day, he was much different. This time he smiled and gently petted her and wiggled with excitement. I don't know what went on in Ryan's head that night, but from that day forward, Ryan has loved his sister freely. Never have we been concerned when they are together. Ryan is always gentle and loving with her.

Answers Postponed Again

In the fall, when things calmed down after Tori's birth, we again sought answers for Ryan, only to be sidetracked once more when my appendix ruptured in October. As soon as I recovered, we set out with greater determination than ever. A friend named Sandy told me about a government agency set up to aid children from birth to three years old. She said this agency, called Bridges for Families, could test Ryan's language skills. If the tests showed he had significant delays, they would give him speech therapy at no cost. That piqued my interest, and I set up an appointment to discuss my concerns about Ryan.

When Bonnie came from the agency, we talked at length about Ryan's strengths and weaknesses. She took me through a long checklist, asking what he could do in terms of language as well as other daily skills. I was so concerned about his language, I really wasn't worried about the other areas.

Over the next few weeks, the agency sent several people to examine Ryan's skills, including a speech therapist, a physical therapist, and a third specialist whose field wasn't mentioned. When they had finished their observations, the agency called to set up a time to discuss the findings. Roger was going to be out of town for a few days, so I asked, "Do you think I'll need my husband with me when I hear the results?" She assured me that I would be fine, that there was nothing I didn't already know. So we scheduled the appointment for December 2.

When the day arrived, I was nervous but not frightened. After all, there was nothing I didn't already know, right? Bonnie and the two therapists who had run most of the tests on Ryan came in and, after some small talk, began to read their report. The first three pages did, in fact, recount things I already knew—our concern for his development and our unsuccessful attempts to test his hearing. As they covered language comprehension, expressive language, sensory-motor observations, and play, they described him accurately, and the language they used made everything seem normal, even positive.

Then came the fourth page—the summary and recommendations. "Ryan, at thirty months of age, exhibits significant delays in the areas of speech and language and sensory-motor development."

Significant delays? Now I began to worry.

They went on. "Age range levels were assigned for specific areas within Ryan's communication development.... Skills were often scattered across age ranges, which may indicate a difference in terms of his language development." Each developmental area was followed by an age range to indicate his progress:

"Interaction-Attachment: 15-18 months."

"Language Comprehension: 9 months."

"Language Expression: 9 months."

As they read these first items, I could feel the tears coming and I fought to hold them back. My throat tightened and began to sting as I tried to maintain my composure.

They went on.

"Gesture: 12-15 months."

"Pragmatics: 9-12 months."

I didn't even know what pragmatics meant, but he was delayed in that too.

I needed Roger. How could anyone think that this news was no big deal, that I didn't need support?

"Play: 9-12 months."

I was stunned. How could they say my two-and-a-half-year-old was like a toddler? They tried to encourage me by pointing out that some fragmented skills went as high as eighteen or twenty-one months, but that was no comfort. His overall development was severely delayed. Since they weren't in a position to make a diagnosis, they recommended we set up appointments with three specialists: an audiologist, a neurologist, and a developmental specialist.

Near the end of the visit someone referred to Ryan as a "special-needs child." With those words my hurt turned to anger. When I closed the door behind them, I hit my fist on my hand. "How dare they call him a special-needs child!" I had never put Ryan in that category, and I would fight anyone who did! Then I broke down and cried.

Pulling myself together, I found the phone numbers of the doctors they had recommended and began calling for appointments. The first two came easily—the audiologist on December 7 and the neurologist on December 19. But the developmental specialist said I couldn't get an appointment for at least two months. I wasn't giving up that easily. "Please," I begged, "I need to know what's going on. I'll take any appointment or cancellation. Give me fifteen minutes' notice, and I'll be there." The nurse said she would keep that in mind, but the doctor had a limited schedule and she was booked.

The Audiologist

When Roger returned after the weekend, we talked a lot. While we had more questions than answers, we agreed that we weren't going to label Ryan without even knowing what was wrong. Maybe his hearing was impaired and could be fixed with a hearing aid.

Our appointment with the audiologist came quickly. We were ushered into a sound room, which had a small table and chair, speakers throughout the room, and a window into the control room. Ryan refused to wear headphones, which didn't surprise us, so they checked his hearing in a more general manner. As Ryan did a puzzle at the table, they brought up a sound somewhere in the room and watched for Ryan to acknowledge it in any way. Sometimes he did; other times he didn't.

When the audiologist finished, he said Ryan didn't appear to have any major hearing loss that would contribute to his speech delays. The answers lay elsewhere.

Insight Offered

As Christmas approached, our church held its annual Christmas cantata. Though I had been actively involved with the production in the past, I wasn't this year. However, they did need help backstage with quick costume changes, so I volunteered. As I sat in the changing room with several of the performers, tears welled up in my eyes. Peggy, one of the mothers, asked me what was wrong, so I shared with her Ryan's strange behavior and our struggles to find answers. Without hesitation, she asked if I'd ever considered that he might have autism.

"No!" I blurted out in disbelief. Peggy had a daughter with autism, but Ryan was nothing like her daughter. How could she even suggest such a thing? I was already on edge emotionally, so her question released a flood of tears.

"Does that scare you?" she asked.

"Yes," I replied, not knowing what to say. She talked about autism and how it isn't something to fear, but I wasn't listening. I was too afraid.

The Neurologist

On the nineteenth we headed off for the hospital to meet with the neurologist. Once there we followed a series of red stars on the floor to the neurology waiting area. Ryan led the way with us, as always, trying to keep him in check. Fortunately, they had a play structure to crawl in and a large fish tank in the waiting room. Ryan loved watching fish and climbing, but his attention span was short. The nurse saw we were having trouble occupying him, so she took us down to our room, which was located next to a shelf full of toys. Ryan found a toy with many pieces and proceeded to organize them on the floor.

Before long the neurologist and a resident physician came in to examine Ryan and ask us some questions. They recommended a series of blood and urine tests to check for metabolic disorders and an EEG (electroencephalogram) to check for Landau-Kleffner Syndrome. The neurologist said Ryan had autistic *symptoms* but that didn't necessarily mean he had autism, so he wanted to check for other possibilities. For instance, a child who is deaf may exhibit autistic symptoms such as delayed language and tantrums, he explained, but when the child regains hearing or learns to communicate in an alternate manner, the autistic symptoms disappear. We had already ruled out a hearing problem, but we held on to the hope that some other factor could be detected and resolved.

Though we were afraid of the word *autism,* we weren't overcome. After all, it was only a possibility, and possibilities often don't happen.

Before we left, we had to get Ryan's blood and urine samples. I knew I couldn't handle watching them draw blood, so Roger went with Ryan. It took four people to hold Ryan down as they took the necessary vials of blood. Sitting in the lobby, I could hear Ryan cry, and my stomach ached. Did we really have to do this to our little boy? I looked at the other children waiting for blood draws, knowing that each one had something wrong. *Children shouldn't have to be getting blood drawn and scheduling EEGs,* I thought. *They should be playing in the snow and enjoying being kids.*

As soon as the medical staff was finished, Ryan ran to my arms, crying. I held him so tight, wanting him to know that I felt his pain and was so sorry we had to put him through that. He continued to cry on my shoulder as I carried him to the car.

Once again we would have to wait for answers.

The EEG

Just two days before Christmas we found ourselves back at the hospital for the EEG. Again we followed the red stars to the prep room, where they read the consent form. I know consent forms are a necessary precaution, but for parents the possibilities are absolutely devastating to consider right before a procedure.

Next was sedation. I know that many people go under sedation and do fine, but since this was Ryan's first time, I was afraid my little boy might not wake up. We did the only thing we could do—we prayed for God's protection over Ryan and trusted Him with his life.

The sedation went well, and within a few minutes they began to glue the electrodes on Ryan's head. He fussed a couple of times, but they eventually got all of them on, and we walked alongside Ryan as they wheeled his bed into the EEG testing room.

During the test Ryan slept as they shined different lights or strobes in his face and watched his readings for signs of change. I asked the technician if it looked good or bad, but he said that only the doctor would know after he saw the whole graph.

The procedure didn't take long, although it seemed like forever to us. When Ryan woke up, a woman was walking through the halls, giving each child toys for Christmas. Ryan was given a car and a stuffed pig wearing a party hat. He looked at them and put them down. Even though he wasn't interested, we were grateful that someone cared enough about the children in the hospital so close to Christmas that she took the time to come and bring some cheer.

Christmas

Christmas has always been a favorite time of year for Roger and me because there are constant reminders of God's love—how He sent His Son into the world to bring us to Him. This Christmas we wrapped ourselves in those truths more than ever. God loved Ryan more than we did, more than we could even comprehend. He would guide us, He would care for Ryan, He would be there, no matter what path we had to walk.

We celebrated Christmas Day at my sister Gail's house, as always, along with our other three siblings, their spouses and children, our parents, Gail's in-laws, and a couple of friends from Russia. Despite the mounting worry and uncertainty, we had a great time talking, eating, and ice-skating on their pond in the backyard. Six-month-old Tori didn't require much, but Ryan had to be monitored at all times—unless he was watching a movie. Then he would focus on the television for a while, and we could catch our breath. While other children played with their new toys, Ryan had no interest in toys or in playing with his cousins; instead, he cried off and on all day.

The family knew about all the testing we'd just done, and the consensus of the house was that Ryan couldn't have autism. It had to be something else. We just needed to find out what.

More Waiting

New Year's came and went as we waited for the results of the EEG. I called the clinic numerous times over several days, but no one returned my calls. I was trying to be patient, but it was getting harder to wait. After all, this was my son, and I needed some answers.

In the midst of that frustration, the office of the developmental specialist called the first week of January to advise us they had a cancellation on the twelfth. Would we like to take it? "Yes!" I responded immediately and thanked her profusely for getting us in so fast.

By January 9 we still had not received Ryan's EEG or lab results. Each time I called I added another *please* to the message, so the ninth call had nine *pleases* in front of the "Call me." By now I was anxious and angry. Didn't anyone have the courtesy to call me back? Did they have any idea what it's like to sit day after day waiting to hear test results on one's child?

Since I needed the results before the appointment with the developmental specialist, I went to the neurologist's office on the tenth, determined not to leave until I had spoken with the doctor directly. When I arrived, I explained the situation to his secretary.

After a short wait, the doctor came and apologized for taking so long to get the results to me. I asked him why no one had returned my phone calls. His response? They had misplaced Ryan's file, so they didn't know the results. However, he had them now, and he went on to tell me the EEG was normal and they found no abnormalities in the blood or urine tests. He had hoped Ryan had a rare disease called Landau-Kleffner Syndrome, but the results were negative. I wasn't sure why he wanted Ryan to have this rare disease because that didn't sound good either. Silly me, I thought a negative EEG would be a positive thing!

"Do you think Ryan's problems are due to our being in another country recently and will go away with time?" I asked.

"No," he replied coldly. "He probably has infantile autism, and that won't go away."

Fighting my anger about his insensitive statements and feeling the tears forming, I thanked him for his time and left—quickly.

Finally, an Answer

Two days later we were back at the hospital, this time to see the developmental specialist. After my experience with the neurologist, I was uptight. Could Ryan really have autism? Was this doctor going to be as cold as the last one? Could we trust her? Roger and I talked about the possibility of Ryan having autism and decided we were not going to accept this label unless we were fully convinced, and that would take a lot.

As we were waiting, a friend walked by. Cyd is a doctor, and I believe God sent her to us at that moment. Cyd had done part of her residency under this specialist and respected her and her opinions. A huge weight was lifted off my shoulders. I trusted Cyd, and if she trusted this doctor, then I could too.

Soon the doctor called us into her office—a small room with a couch on each side, a small table, a chair, and several toys scattered on the floor. Ryan sat there sorting the toys, taking the puzzle pieces one by one and putting them upside down in a pile. When he had all the pieces in a pile, he would take the top one and, again one by one, put them in another pile, this time right side up. He did this for quite a while before moving on to some letters, which he arranged in a row on the floor.

While Ryan contentedly sorted the toys and letters, the doctor sat next to Roger and me on the couch and asked us many questions. She smiled often and listened well. Although I felt very comfortable with her, I was terrified of what she might tell us.

Two hours into our appointment the words came out. "I'm sorry to have to say this," she said gently, "but Ryan has autism."

The finality of the statement hit us with the force of a speeding train.

"But he can't," I blurted. "He looks at us! People with autism don't make eye contact!" This time I couldn't hold back the tears, and Roger was in tears now too.

"What you don't realize, Lynn," she responded, "is that, for the two hours I have been with him, he has not once acknowledged my existence. A typical child will notice when a person is present and then decide to draw closer or back away. Ryan doesn't even know that I'm here."

She was right. Ryan didn't acknowledge her at all. He was content to sit and line up the toys and puzzles in the room. He had become a very organized child, demanding that things be in certain places and in a particular order or row. We had been proud of his ability to order his world, since we also like things orderly, but that extreme need for order had been just one more symptom of autism.

Realizing our need to understand her pronouncement, she walked us through the diagnostic chart step by step. For each criterion she would ask, "Do you think this describes Ryan?"

"Yes," we would agree.

With each yes the reality of his autism sank in. Roger and I sat close to each other and sobbed. Every glance at our precious little boy brought another round of tears.

Still resisting the diagnosis, I clung to the hope that Ryan might actually have what is called Pervasive Developmental Disorder–Not Otherwise Specified (PDD–NOS), which seemed to me less frightening than autism. "Don't you think that he might have PDD–NOS instead? Isn't he just mildly affected?" I asked. *Perhaps I exaggerated my answers. Maybe he really hasn't regressed. Perhaps we're being too picky about his delays. He might catch up.* Even as these thoughts raced through my head, I knew what she said was true. I had seen the chart and Ryan fit it to a tee. It made sense of what we had experienced—the lining of toys, the regression in skills, the lack of language, the screaming and tantrums, the lack of play or pretending. Everything pointed to autism. Everything fit.

Although we were overwhelmed with grief, a part of me was relieved that at least we knew what was going on. He wasn't acting the way he did because I was a bad mother. Ryan couldn't help it; he had autism. We finally had our answer.

Hope in the Midst of Grief

With that diagnosis, so many of the hopes and dreams we had for Ryan flew out the window right there in the doctor's office. I didn't know much about autism, but I had seen *Rain Man,* and I knew that my dreams for Ryan didn't include watching Judge Wapner and counting toothpicks. I had dreams for him to succeed in school, have lots of friends, go to college, get married, and enjoy life. I had often prayed that Ryan would someday be a missionary to help people know about the Lord. Now I wondered if he would ever be able to understand God at all.

At that moment the Lord reminded me of a verse I had memorized months earlier: "I am the LORD, the God of all mankind. Is anything too hard for me?"[1]

No, Lord, nothing is too hard for You, I thought. *You knew that Ryan had autism before we did, and I know that You cause all things to work together for good to those who love You. I don't understand how this can be good, but I trust You. Lord, You can help us through this. You can do anything that You please. Lord, help us. Heal our son! Direct us to what we need to do.*

In the middle of the doctor's office, through our tears and in our sorrow, the Lord gave us hope. Hope that would drive us to find more answers, this time to help our son. Hope that we could overcome this or learn to live within it. We would work and pray for the former, but we would trust God if He chose the latter.

Chapter 3

Operation Rescue Ryan

"Perseverance": to continue on with a knife in your heart.
CHINESE LANGUAGE

Within minutes of coming home from the clinic that Thursday, I was on the phone, beginning to pursue Ryan's recovery. I called a family we knew at church whose son has autism, and they invited us over for dinner the next night to begin orienting us. Next I called the Autism Society of America, followed by the Autism Society of Wisconsin. Unable to stop crying, I asked them to send me any information that might help.

Then I made the most important call, though I didn't know it at the time. At the recommendation of the developmental specialist, I called Dr. Glen Sallows, who was just beginning to treat autism with a therapy that was new to our area. According to the developmental specialist, some people were benefiting from the Lovaas therapy he was doing, but it wasn't for everyone. Since Roger and I were very structured people, she thought we might be good candidates. Not knowing anything else about the Lovaas treatment, I called Dr. Sallows and left a tearful message on his machine.

On Monday our friend Sandy came over to visit. I sat in the rocking chair, looking vacantly across the room, and worked through my thoughts aloud with her. When I mentioned I had called Dr. Sallows about the Lovaas therapy, Sandy immediately grabbed some books she had brought. Over the weekend she had checked out several books on autism and its treatment from the library. Since she had already read two of them and was in the middle of a third, she knew more than I did at the time. What a gift. I was so emotionally drained I couldn't even think of reading a book, but she stepped in and did it for me.

She opened one of the books to pages that compared behavioral programs with horse training, with therapists yelling at the children or spraying them in the face with water.[1] I was appalled! How could anyone treat a child like that, like an animal? I had no idea yet what course to follow, but it certainly wouldn't be this.

However, Dr. Sallows called me back that day. When we talked on the phone, he shared with me that many children were showing impressive results from this treatment and some were actually recovering. Although that sounded encouraging, I remained leery and skeptical. He urged me to get Catherine Maurice's book *Let Me Hear Your Voice,* which relates her experiences with this form of therapy. I told him I'd think about the treatment, although I had no intention of calling him back or pursuing it. But I did decide to purchase the book—just in case it had something I needed to know.

Dr. Sallows must have sensed my skepticism because within a couple of days a parent called me. Kathy and her husband, Chris, had been doing Lovaas therapy with their son Bryan for a year. When I asked her about the punishments inflicted on the children, she said that was no longer a part of the therapy. I also asked if the kids actually learned or if they were just being trained like animals. She answered all my questions and explained more about Dr. Lovaas and the real nature of his treatment. Then she suggested that I actually watch a session. They were having a therapist recruitment night at their house in a few days, so she invited me to come and learn. Figuring I had nothing to lose, I accepted.

Beginning Operation Rescue Ryan

Another step we took in those first few days was to send out a newsletter. Since Roger and I work with a Christian organization, we have about five hundred people on our mailing list who pray for us regularly. Eight days after Ryan's diagnosis, I sat down at our computer and typed a letter. It wasn't well thought out or polished; it was merely my broken heart on paper, pleading for prayer support. We needed direction and strength, which we knew wouldn't come without prayer. This would be the first of many letters over the next several years titled "Operation Rescue Ryan."

In response, our friends called and sent letters, faxes, and e-mails from around the country and around the world. We were humbled by the outpouring of love and support for our precious little boy, and the results of their prayers would become clear over time.

Investigating Therapy

When the day came to visit Chris and Kathy's house, Roger stayed home with the children and I went alone. Chris and Kathy were joined by Michelle, a senior therapist, and Kristie, a lead therapist, as well as three prospective therapists. We watched a video about Dr. Lovaas and his research, which explained the treatment succinctly and showed some children who had been in the research program. It was impressive, but I wasn't convinced.

After the video Chris gave a short presentation and explained more about this in-home therapy, which is now called Applied Behavior Analysis or ABA. While the therapist prospects were filling out applications, Chris turned to me and commented, "When you start therapy, you will need to hire about four or five students as line therapists."

My response was polite but abrupt, "*If* I start therapy."

Michelle then led us into the therapy room, where Kristie proceeded to work with Bryan. She called him to the table and told him, "Touch cow." When he didn't do it, she told him again. When he didn't do it a third time, she picked up his hand and helped him touch it. Then she gave him a spoonful of ice cream and told him what a good job he had done. They tried the drill again, and he did better this time. When he later responded without any prompts, we spontaneously applauded. Glancing up, I saw the pride in his parents' faces.

I watched him work for about fifteen minutes, noting it was all positive reinforcement. The therapist was gentle and kind; there certainly was no hitting, yelling, or spraying water in his face. In between the drills, they played on the floor with a couple of toys.

When I asked Chris what benefits he saw with this therapy and why they chose it, he shared some of the changes in Bryan since they had begun treatment. Bryan, although still nonverbal, was beginning to say sounds. That night he made a cow sound for us when Kristie asked him what a cow said. Bryan also had changed tremendously in terms of affect, he said. One of the hardest things for Chris and Kathy had been that Bryan didn't show any affection. "It was so bad that I could leave and he would never notice," explained Chris. But now Bryan hugged and cuddled with his parents. As Kathy sat in a rocking chair, Bryan climbed up in her lap and my heart melted. Chris added how he and Bryan could now for the first time cook pancakes together for breakfast. Bryan was still affected by autism, but he had blossomed and his life had been greatly enhanced. Chris and Kathy had found this type of therapy to be the most effective for Bryan, and they planned to continue it as long as he needed it.

Considering this treatment more seriously now, I made an appointment with another family to observe their therapy session. From what the mother, Susan, told me, their son Clayton was a lot more like Ryan than Bryan was—an active boy, full of affection, but impeded by the autism.

Clayton, in fact, amazed me. When I entered his room, he was bouncing on his bed during a break between drills. When I greeted him, he acknowledged me. I joined him near the bed where he was looking at a quiltlike hanging that had the alphabet on it. Clayton read the letters aloud to me while he jumped. As I watched the therapist proceed with some drills, I was impressed by the amount of positive reinforcement Clayton was getting and how happy he was. He seemed not only to be learning but enjoying it! His drills were more complex than Bryan's, as he was learning his alphabet, building with blocks, and learning to say, "I want..."

Yes, Clayton was more like Ryan, and that gave me hope. Ryan couldn't talk and he surely didn't know his alphabet, but maybe this therapy could unlock those doors. Maybe this *would* be the best thing for him.

When I went home that night, I picked up Catherine Maurice's book, and from the first page her book captivated me. I could relate to her struggles, her fears, and her ambition. Each turn of the page increased my hope for Ryan. In three days I had finished it and was convinced. Roger read it next, and he concurred. Here was the hope we'd been praying for. Whatever it took to get this treatment, whatever sacrifice was required, nothing would stop us from getting Ryan into this therapy.

God's Provision

I called Dr. Sallows the next day and asked about beginning therapy. He said a research group was starting, and if Ryan qualified, we could participate. However, some tests needed to be performed beforehand, which would cost $1,050. This was our first roadblock, but we believed that if God was in this, He could take care of it.

A few days after my talk with Dr. Sallows, I was sitting upstairs on our bed reading more about autism when the phone rang. On the other end was a friend we seldom get to talk to. Since receiving our letter, she and her husband had been praying for us, and as they were praying, the Lord laid it on their hearts that we might need money. Independently, each clearly sensed God saying, "Here is a thousand dollars. Give it to the Hamiltons." She was calling to ask if we might need a thousand dollars.

Though I was crying, I was grinning from ear to ear. We hadn't told anyone about needing money, yet God made sure we had the amount necessary to get started. As I shared with our friend what the Lord was doing through their generosity, she wept with me.

Pre-Therapy Testing

On February 6, Tamlynn Graupner and Dr. Sallows came to our house to evaluate Ryan. In order to qualify for the research, Ryan had to have an IQ of 35 or above, which I felt confident he did. After they explained what the research would include, we went to the basement playroom to do some preliminary tasks before the official testing. We tried a series of commands with Ryan like, "Go to Mommy" or "Get the bear," but Ryan did none of them. He wanted to watch a movie, and when we refused, he let out a shriek. Of all the commands we tried, Ryan did none.

Tammy then took Ryan upstairs to his room to run a variety of tests, including the Cattell Infant Intelligence Scale, the Merrill-Palmer Scale of Mental Tests, the Reynell Developmental Language Scale, and the Vineland Adaptive Behavior Scale. Though Ryan was now thirty-three months old, on the Cattell "Ryan achieved a developmental age of 17 months...yielding an IQ equivalent of 53," which is considered in the mildly retarded range. However, on the Merrill-Palmer Scale, which includes both verbal and spatial tasks, Ryan showed an IQ of 100. Although Ryan's verbal abilities were delayed, his spatial abilities were advanced.

The Reynell scores indicated Ryan understood language at the level of a sixteen-month-old, while his expressive language was lower. In their report they mentioned that "he does not currently demonstrate expressive communication in the form of language; however, he does function at the pre-language level in expressive communication as is evidenced in his nonverbal communication behaviors of pointing and directing others."

Last, the Vineland scale showed that Ryan's communication abilities were equivalent to a ten-month-old child, his daily living skills were at the level of a fourteen-month-old, his socialization was at eleven months, and his motor skills were at nineteen months.

Although it hurt to hear that his development was so delayed and that his IQ fell in the retarded range according to one test, this time I was not devastated. Dr. Lovaas's tape showed children who had increased tremendously in their IQs, and I knew Ryan could change as well. But these tests showed we had a lot of work ahead of us.

The First Step Forward

On March 5 we began. Because we were in the research project, Dr. Sallows helped us find volunteers from our local university who could earn credit in their degree program through their work with Ryan. Michelle Sherman, the woman I'd met at Chris and Kathy's house, became our senior therapist. She had been trained in California by Dr. Lovaas and his institute, and though she had worked with several families under the supervision of Dr. Lovaas, we were her first workshop on her own. Our other therapists included Bohdanna, Chrissy, Liz, Kristie, and Sandi, who were university students, and Dawn, a friend of ours who volunteered. Dr. Sallows and Tammy were there to supervise the training, while my parents, our speech therapist, Roger, and I were there to learn alongside the therapists.

The workshop took place in our living room where we set up a small table and two chairs in the middle of the room so everyone could see. After introductions and a viewing of the Lovaas video, our training began. Dr. Sallows explained that we would work on things that came easily to Ryan so he would feel successful, but he would probably still scream at first because we were directing him.

Dr. Sallows was right. Ryan's first experience with ABA etched itself deeply in our memories.

Michelle began the first drill by calling Ryan over to the table, saying, "Ryan, come here." Then she picked him up and took him to the chair and praised him. She told him to sit and put him in his chair. Ryan fought with every ounce of energy he had, but Michelle got him into the chair and positioned her body so he couldn't get away. Dr. Sallows sat behind Ryan and put his arm around his waist. Though Ryan would have run away had he thought it possible, Dr. Sallows's arm was obviously relaxed; no force was used to keep Ryan in his chair.

Michelle said, "Do this," and then grabbed a block and dropped it into a bucket. As Ryan screamed, she took his hand and helped him pick up a block to drop into the bucket. Ryan kept his hand as rigid as possible to avoid participating, but that didn't stop Michelle. She put her hand over Ryan's and made him pick up the block and release it into the bucket, while Ryan continued screaming.

We sat in stunned silence. Michelle called out, "Somebody clap!" We did so timidly, unsure of what to think even though we had been told beforehand to clap and reinforce Ryan's actions. After one more repetition of this drill, Michelle told Ryan, "Go play." Ryan jumped out of his chair and ran into my arms, where I hugged him and told him it would be all right.

After a minute of explanation to us, Michelle again called him over and sat him down. While tears ran down his face, he screamed and reached out to me. What they asked of Ryan was not difficult for him. He had done it on his own hundreds of times, but he refused to do it on anyone else's terms. He looked at us through his tears and screams as if to say, "Why are you letting them do this to me?" For the first few hours of the workshop, Ryan screamed whenever any demand was made of him.

Although it was extremely painful to watch, I had peace in my heart since I knew that this was what he needed. Roger, however, couldn't stand to see him hurting, so he went downstairs to his office and sobbed. My dad also left in tears, but my mom and I stayed. Though Ryan screamed, they *weren't* hurting him. He just wanted to be left alone. Michelle was always gentle yet assertive. I knew that we were doing the right thing and that Ryan needed to obey his therapists if he was going to improve. I knew this was his best chance.

As they continued the drills, Dr. Sallows suggested I wait in the kitchen where Ryan couldn't look to me for help. I walked out of sight and prayed that God would give us a breakthrough—even a small one—that day. At the end of each drill, I returned and held Ryan until it was time for the next one.

Each person, including Roger and me, took turns doing drills with Ryan. We tried using chocolate ice cream as a reinforcer when he did the drill correctly, but he spit it out and continued screaming. We had a bit more success using cookies, but his resistance and screaming continued. Ryan mostly wanted his mommy and daddy to hug him, so we did.

At one point Ryan began to feel successful and started to smile, but he caught himself and stopped. It was as if he didn't want us to know that he was proud of what he had done.

As the day went on, Ryan relaxed and his screaming diminished to a whimper. Since Ryan loved to have us bounce him up and down on the foldout bed in the living room, we pulled it out to use as a reinforcer. Soon after, another reinforcer came quite unexpectedly. Because Ryan loved movies so much, we would often make him laugh by repeating a line of which he was especially fond. Simply saying the words "Pea soup!" (from the movie *The Rescuers Down Under*) in a gravelly voice made Ryan laugh hysterically. So Roger and I started yelling "Pea soup!" every time we bounced him. As soon as Michelle chimed in with her rendition, they were friends for life. That was the reinforcer he needed.

This time when Michelle called Ryan back to the table, he actually came on his own! Then he sat in the chair and did the drill. The roomful of therapists had been cheering and applauding throughout the day to encourage him, but to no effect. This time, their thunderous applause and yelling brought a huge smile to Ryan's face. Tears again streamed down Roger's and my cheeks, but they were tears of joy for the first time all day. We were on our way.

After that drill, it was back to the couch for more "pea soup."

Michelle bounced him several times and then stopped. Ryan yelled out, "Ah-geh! Ah-geh!" Michelle responded, "Again! Again!" Ryan had just said his first new word in nearly two years! We yelled and jumped enough to shake the whole house. Our Ryan was not only enjoying the therapy, but he was saying words! God had given us our first step forward.

There would be many steps forward in the days and weeks to come but also a significant number of steps backward. Ryan would lose his new word the next day and go for days before saying another, but the words did come. Each successful drill laid the foundation for future successes as progress came one small step at a time. And each day God gave us a glimmer of hope to carry us through to the next.

Chapter 4

Understand What You're Facing

*Knowledge is of two kinds: we know
a subject ourselves, or we know where we
can find information upon it.*

SAMUEL JOHNSON

As Roger and I came to grips with the reality of Ryan's autism, we not only wrestled with our emotions, but we also struggled to understand what this disorder is all about. This was totally new to us, and we quickly found out how little people—including doctors—know about it. Unlike the manner in which so many childhood illnesses are handled, we couldn't just get Ryan a prescription of penicillin, wait ten days, and pronounce him cured. For two parents who like to have control in their lives and who love their son fiercely, this was especially hard to deal with. But if we were going to help our son, we had to accept it and learn as much as we could as quickly as we could.

What is this disorder that pulls children into a world of their own?

What Is Autism?

Autism is actually just one classification under the umbrella of Pervasive Developmental Disorders, which also includes Asperger's Disorder (also known as Asperger's Syndrome), Rett's, Childhood Disintegrative Disorder, and PDD–NOS (Pervasive Developmental Disorder–Not Otherwise Specified). Unlike other diseases, which can be diagnosed by their physiological symptoms and medical testing, autism is determined by how closely the child's condition fits certain criteria. Since children can vary so widely within these criteria, many professionals have recently begun using the term *Autism Spectrum Disorder* (ASD) to emphasize the variance. Those who are affected with ASD fit a number of descriptions in several categories, so labeling a child as having a particular disorder within this spectrum is highly subjective and far from an exact science. One doctor may label a child with autism while another may categorize the child in the PDD–NOS range. However, no matter which label a child receives within the spectrum, the treatment strategies are much the same.

Since autism is determined merely by subjective criteria and not by physiological testing, Dr. Bernard Rimland, director of the Autism Research Institute, strongly advocates referring to a child as having a *label* of autism, not a *diagnosis* of autism. A diagnosis gives people a false sense of having found the problem without truly knowing the underlying biological cause. Even though I agree with Dr. Rimland, *diagnosis* is a commonly used term and difficult to avoid, so I use it in the book with the understanding that *label* is more accurate.

What Are the Signs of Autism?
Autism can be recognized by its profound effect on a person's ability to relate to and function in the world. The fourth and latest edition

of *The Diagnostic and Statistical Manual of Mental Disorders* states that autism is characterized by "markedly abnormal or impaired development in social interaction and communication and a markedly restricted repertoire of activity and interests."[1]

According to this manual, a person could be labeled as having autism if he or she meets the following criteria:

A. A total of six (or more) items from (1), (2), and (3), with at least two from (1), and one each from (2) and (3):

1. qualitative impairment in social interaction, as manifested by at least two of the following:
   a. marked impairment in the use of multiple nonverbal behaviors such as eye-to-eye gaze, facial expression, body postures, and gestures to regulate social interaction
   b. failure to develop peer relationships appropriate to developmental level
   c. a lack of spontaneous seeking to share enjoyment, interests, or achievements with other people (e.g., by a lack of showing, bringing, or pointing out objects of interest)
   d. lack of social or emotional reciprocity

2. qualitative impairments in communication as manifested by at least one of the following:
   a. delay in, or total lack of, the development of spoken language (not accompanied by an attempt to compensate through alternative modes of communication such as gesture or mime)
   b. in individuals with adequate speech, marked impairment in the ability to initiate or sustain a conversation with others
   c. stereotyped and repetitive use of language or idiosyncratic language

   d. lack of varied, spontaneous make-believe play or social
      imitative play appropriate to developmental level

3. restricted repetitive and stereotyped patterns of behavior,
   interests, and activities, as manifested by at least one of the
   following:

   a. encompassing preoccupation with one or more stereo-
      typed and restricted patterns of interest that is abnormal
      either in intensity or focus

   b. apparently inflexible adherence to specific, nonfunctional
      routines or rituals

   c. stereotyped and repetitive motor mannerisms (e.g., hand
      or finger flapping or twisting, or complex whole-body
      movements)

   d. persistent preoccupation with parts of objects

B. Delays or abnormal functioning in at least one of the following areas, with onset prior to age 3 years: (1) social interaction,
(2) language as used in social communication, or (3) symbolic
or imaginative play.

C. The disturbance is not better accounted for by Rett's Disorder
or Childhood Disintegrative Disorder.[2]

As with Ryan, one of the first signs of autism may be a person's speech. Individuals with autism frequently have no speech at
all, or if they do speak, they may continually repeat the same
words (perseveration) or they may echo back what others have
said (echolalia). Normal give-and-take communication is generally absent or very difficult. Another red flag is a child who begins
to develop language and then loses it.

Not playing imaginatively or with peers, a rigid adherence to
routines, repeating behaviors over and over, spinning or lining up

objects, hand flapping, body rocking, severe oversensitivity or under-sensitivity to external stimuli, an inability to cope with any un-expected change in routine—all these can signal a developmental disorder. Although we hadn't understood the significance of his behaviors, Ryan had exhibited many of these patterns. In fact, most children exhibit one or two of these traits, so these signs of autism can easily be overlooked. However, with autism the traits are more numerous and severe. For example, many children throw tantrums when they don't get their way or a routine is broken, but a child with autism may have more extreme or longer-lasting tantrums.

How Early Can Autism Be Detected?

Establishing an accurate age for the onset of autism is difficult since children don't develop along rigid, uniform lines. Because Ryan was our first child, we didn't know what "normal" development looked like, and he met the developmental criteria during his rou-tine physicals. Since learning of his autism, we've gone back over scores of videotapes and, in hindsight, have picked up signs we missed before. The tapes show that Ryan definitely regressed.

Another factor that makes it hard to determine the onset of autism is that no two children are exactly alike in their characteris-tics and severity of impairment. With four criteria in each of three different categories and varying degrees of severity for each criterion, children with autism may appear quite different. Many are distant and unaffectionate; others are very affectionate and make eye con-tact. Some develop average or even above average speech; others never speak at all. Like snowflakes, no two are exactly the same.

Since an early diagnosis is crucial, tools have been developed to help doctors recognize warning signs in a child as young as eigh-teen months, though most physicians don't possess these tools.

published a
...hild Doesn't
...hecklist for
...rate tool for
...n.

...searchers to
...ow evidence
...ousand chil-
...n who failed
...iv). Ten out
...label. The
...ntal delay.
...y two other children failed some of the key points but not all of them. Of this group, fifteen were later diagnosed with a developmental delay, while the other seven developed normally. None of the children who failed only one or zero key items was ever diagnosed with autism or developmental delay.[3]

Checklist for Autism in Toddlers (CHAT)

Section A: ask parent

1. Does your child enjoy being swung, bounced on your knee, etc.?
2. Does your child take an interest in other children?
3. Does your child like climbing on things, such as stairs?
4. Does your child enjoy playing peek-a-boo or hide-and-seek?
5. Does your child ever PRETEND, for example, to make a cup of tea using a toy cup and teapot, or pretend other things?
6. Does your child ever use his/her index finger to point, to ASK for something?

Families for Early Autism Treatment (FEAT) has published a booklet and video for physicians called *Doctor, My Child Doesn't Talk,* which includes a variation of the following Checklist for Autism in Toddlers (the CHAT), a remarkably accurate tool for predicting which children will receive a label of autism.

The CHAT was developed by a team of British researchers to determine if children as young as eighteen months show evidence of autism. When they used the CHAT on sixteen thousand children in southeast England, they found twelve children who failed the key points of the test (A-5, A-7, B-ii, B-iii, and B-iv). Ten out of these twelve children later received the autism label. The remaining two received a diagnosis of developmental delay. Twenty-two other children failed some of the key points but not all of them. Of this group, fifteen were later diagnosed with a developmental delay, while the other seven developed normally. None of the children who failed only one or zero key items was ever diagnosed with autism or developmental delay.[3]

Checklist for Autism in Toddlers (CHAT)
Section A: ask parent

1. Does your child enjoy being swung, bounced on your knee, etc.?
2. Does your child take an interest in other children?
3. Does your child like climbing on things, such as stairs?
4. Does your child enjoy playing peek-a-boo or hide-and-seek?
5. Does your child ever PRETEND, for example, to make a cup of tea using a toy cup and teapot, or pretend other things?
6. Does your child ever use his/her index finger to point, to ASK for something?

objects, hand flapping, body rocking, severe oversensitivity or under-sensitivity to external stimuli, an inability to cope with any un-expected change in routine—all these can signal a developmental disorder. Although we hadn't understood the significance of his behaviors, Ryan had exhibited many of these patterns. In fact, most children exhibit one or two of these traits, so these signs of autism can easily be overlooked. However, with autism the traits are more numerous and severe. For example, many children throw tantrums when they don't get their way or a routine is broken, but a child with autism may have more extreme or longer-lasting tantrums.

How Early Can Autism Be Detected?

Establishing an accurate age for the onset of autism is difficult since children don't develop along rigid, uniform lines. Because Ryan was our first child, we didn't know what "normal" development looked like, and he met the developmental criteria during his rou-tine physicals. Since learning of his autism, we've gone back over scores of videotapes and, in hindsight, have picked up signs we missed before. The tapes show that Ryan definitely regressed.

Another factor that makes it hard to determine the onset of autism is that no two children are exactly alike in their characteris-tics and severity of impairment. With four criteria in each of three different categories and varying degrees of severity for each criterion, children with autism may appear quite different. Many are distant and unaffectionate; others are very affectionate and make eye con-tact. Some develop average or even above average speech; others never speak at all. Like snowflakes, no two are exactly the same.

Since an early diagnosis is crucial, tools have been developed to help doctors recognize warning signs in a child as young as eigh-teen months, though most physicians don't possess these tools.

7. Does your child ever use his/her index finger to point, to indicate INTEREST in something?

8. Can your child play properly with small toys (e.g., cars or blocks) without just mouthing, fiddling, or dropping them?

9. Does your child ever bring objects over to you (parent), to SHOW you something?

Section B: GP [General Practitioner] or health visitor's observation:

i. During the appointment, has the child made eye contact with you?

ii. Get the child's attention, then point across the room at an interesting object and say, "Oh look! There's a (name of toy)!" Watch the child's face. Does the child look across to see what you are pointing at?[a]

iii. Get the child's attention, then give the child a miniature toy cup and teapot and say, "Can you make a cup of tea?" Does the child pretend to pour out tea, drink it, etc.?[b]

iv. Say to the child, "Where's the light?" or "Show me the light." Does the child POINT with his/her index finger at the light?[c]

v. Can the child build a tower of blocks? (If so, how many?) (Number of blocks...)

[a] To record YES on this item, ensure that the child has not simply looked at your hand but has actually looked at the object you are pointing at.

[b] If you can elicit an example of pretending in some other game, score a YES on this item.

[c] Repeat this with, "Where's the teddy bear?" or some other unreachable object if child does not understand the word "light." To record a YES on this item, the child must have looked up at your face around the time you were pointing.[4]

If your child has *not* been labeled in the autism spectrum, yet you consider that a possibility, I urge you to find qualified professionals to give you an accurate evaluation. We began our search for answers with a program called "Birth to Three," which is available in every state at no cost to you, though the name of the program and the age treated may vary from state to state. To learn the name and phone number of the program offered in your area, call the National Information Center for Children and Youth with Disabilities (NICHCY) at 800-695-0285. Their Web site (http://www.nichcy.org/states.htm) also lists the program offered in each state.

The program evaluators will assess your child's skill levels and determine whether he or she has significant delays. If they find delays, they will then refer you to specialists, such as a pediatric developmental specialist, psychiatrist, or psychologist, who can make a diagnosis. *Make sure the professional you choose has extensive experience with autism.* You don't want to be given a label of autism if your child doesn't have it, nor do you want to have the label withheld if he does. Too often I have heard of doctors wanting to "wait a few months (or years) and see what happens" before they give a diagnosis. Waiting doesn't benefit the child. The earlier the diagnosis, the earlier treatment can be started and the better chance the child has for improvement.

How Common Is Autism?

Since autism was first labeled by Dr. Leo Kanner more than fifty years ago, estimates of the number of people affected by autism and related disorders have varied widely, though it is generally agreed that boys outnumber girls four to one. Typical estimates project that 4 to 5 people in 10,000 have autism, which means that approximately

360,000 individuals in the United States alone have this disorder.[5] The Autism Society of America estimates that 1 in 500 children has autism with over a half million people affected, while other reports suggest the percentage is even higher. In California, statistics show that autism may actually occur in 1 of every 312 children.[6]

The California Department of Developmental Services released a study in 1999 that showed an increase in the number of autistic clients from 3,864 in 1987 to 11,995 in 1998. This represents an average annual increase of 26 percent, while the increase for other disorders such as epilepsy, cerebral palsy, and mental retardation was only 3 to 4 percent annually.[7] "By the end of 1998, nearly half of the population of persons with autism consisted of children between birth and nine years of age. What is more important, during the eleven-year period between 1987 and 1998, the median age of the population of persons with autism drops from fifteen years to nine years. Clearly, more and younger children are entering the system."[8]

Some experts believe that the incidence of autism is significantly higher now than in previous decades. Dr. Rimland has been collecting data from parents of autistic children over the last thirty-four years. From 1965 through 1969, 919 parents (1 percent of the respondents) had children with autism who were under the age of three. By 1994–95, the number of children with autism under the age of three had risen to 3,916 (17 percent of the respondents). Rimland suggests three possible reasons for this apparent rise: increased use of antibiotics, reactions to vaccinations, and pollution. However, he quickly points out that this *apparent* increase in autism could also be due to increased awareness and better diagnostic criteria, although many questions are not addressed by the simple answer of increased awareness and media attention.[9]

Disorders Within the Spectrum

The other four disorders that fall under the PDD umbrella—Rett's Disorder, Childhood Disintegrative Disorder (CDD), Asperger's Disorder, and Pervasive Developmental Disorder–Not Otherwise Specified (PDD–NOS)—are similar to autism, yet there are distinguishing characteristics.

Rett's Disorder

Unlike autism, which occurs four times more frequently in boys than in girls, Rett's Disorder affects only girls. According to *The Diagnostic and Statistical Manual of Mental Disorders,* girls with Rett's Disorder develop normally at first but then experience a deceleration in head growth between five and forty-eight months. They lose previously acquired hand skills, which are replaced by stereotyped hand movements. They also are characterized by the loss of social interaction, poor physical coordination, and severe impairment in expressing and receiving language.

The criteria for Rett's Disorder are as follows:

A. All of the following:
  1. apparently normal prenatal and perinatal development
  2. apparently normal psychomotor development through the first five months after birth
  3. normal head circumference at birth
B. Onset of all of the following after the period of normal development:
  1. deceleration of head growth between ages 5 and 48 months
  2. loss of previously acquired purposeful hand skills between ages 5 and 30 months with the subsequent development of

stereotyped hand movements (e.g., hand wringing or hand washing)

3. loss of social engagement early in the course (although often social interaction develops later)

4. appearance of poorly coordinated gait or trunk movements

5. severely impaired expressive and receptive language development with severe psychomotor retardation[10]

Childhood Disintegrative Disorder

Childhood Disintegrative Disorder (CDD), also known as Heller's Disease, is much rarer than autism and differs from autism in that the child develops normally for at least the first two years. Then the regression occurs before the child is ten years old. With autism, any regression tends to begin between the first and second year of life.

The criteria for CDD are as follows:

A. Apparently normal development for at least the first 2 years after birth as manifested by the presence of age-appropriate verbal and nonverbal communication, social relationships, play, and adaptive behavior.

B. Clinically significant loss of previously acquired skills (before age 10 years) in at least two of the following areas:
1. expressive or receptive language
2. social skills or adaptive behavior
3. bowel or bladder control
4. play
5. motor skills

C. Abnormalities of functioning in at least two of the following areas:

1. qualitative impairment in social interaction (e.g., impairment in nonverbal behaviors, failure to develop peer relationships, lack of social or emotional reciprocity)
2. qualitative impairments in communication (e.g., delay or lack of spoken language, inability to initiate or sustain a conversation, stereotyped and repetitive use of language, lack of varied make-believe play)
3. restricted, repetitive, and stereotyped patterns of behavior, interests, and activities, including motor stereotypes and mannerisms

D. The disturbance is not better accounted for by another specific Pervasive Developmental Disorder or by schizophrenia.[11]

Asperger's Disorder

Many experts view Asperger's Disorder as high-functioning autism, though children with Asperger's Disorder have no significant delays in language or in cognitive development, self-help skills, and some adaptive behaviors. As with autism, the children will show significant impairments in social functioning as well as stereotyped behaviors and repetitive mannerisms.

Asperger's Disorder criteria include:

A. Qualitative impairment in social interaction, as manifested by at least two of the following:
1. marked impairment in the use of multiple nonverbal behaviors such as eye-to-eye gaze, facial expression, body postures, and gestures to regulate social interaction
2. failure to develop peer relationships appropriate to developmental level

3. a lack of spontaneous seeking to share enjoyment, interest, or achievements with other people (e.g., by a lack of showing, bringing, or pointing out objects of interest to other people)

4. lack of social or emotional reciprocity

B. Restricted repetitive and stereotyped patterns of behavior, interests, and activities, as manifested by at least one of the following:

1. encompassing preoccupation with one or more stereotyped and restricted patterns of interest that is abnormal either in intensity or focus

2. apparently inflexible adherence to specific, nonfunctional routines or rituals

3. stereotyped and repetitive motor mannerisms (e.g., hand or finger flapping or twisting, or complex whole-body movements)

4. persistent preoccupation with parts of objects

C. The disturbance causes clinically significant impairment in social, occupational, or other important areas of functioning.

D. There is no clinically significant general delay in language (e.g., single words used by age 2 years, communicative phrases used by age 3 years).

E. There is no clinically significant delay in cognitive development or in the development of age-appropriate self-help skills, adaptive behavior (other than in social interaction), and curiosity about the environment in childhood.

F. Criteria are not met for another specific Pervasive Developmental Disorder or schizophrenia.[12]

PDD–NOS

Pervasive Developmental Disorder–Not Otherwise Specified (PDD–NOS) is a very nebulous term used for children who don't fully meet the criteria for one of the other disorders. *The Diagnostic and Statistical Manual of Mental Disorders* states that "this category should be used when there is a severe and pervasive impairment in the development of reciprocal social interaction, verbal and nonverbal communication skills…but the criteria are not met by a specific Pervasive Developmental Disorder."[13] Though receiving a label of PDD–NOS for a child can be a good thing from a parent's perspective since it may fall on the mild end of the spectrum, it can also be problematic. If a child's condition isn't specified as autism or one of the other disorders, then he or she may be denied special services on the basis that the condition isn't severe enough to warrant them.

Other Illnesses with Similar Symptoms

Landau-Kleffner Syndrome

Landau-Kleffner Syndrome (LKS), or Acquired Childhood Epileptic Aphasia, is much less common than autism, with roughly only 170 cases of LKS reported from 1957 through the early 1990s,[14] though the rates are rising as information about it spreads. LKS can occur alone or with autism, especially along with Childhood Disintegrative Disorder. Although children with LKS demonstrate many behaviors similar to autism, in all cases children with LKS have an abnormal electroencephalogram (EEG), stemming from abnormal brain activity. In approximately 80 percent of the cases, seizures occur, although these seizures may only occur during sleep and are therefore best detected by an overnight EEG. Besides typical seizure symptoms, other types of seizures include staring spells, drooling, odd movements or smacking with the mouth, a metallic taste in the mouth, and abnormal nighttime behaviors, such as periods of night waking between periods of normal sleep, night terrors, or night euphoria. Some children experience head-drop seizures, where their heads fall forward and they appear to be asleep for a few seconds. Hyperactivity, anxiety, aggressiveness, and depression are often associated with LKS.

The most common scenario with LKS children is normal development until regression occurs between the ages of three and seven, causing an inexplicable difficulty in understanding what is said to them. This auditory agnosia can occur suddenly or gradually, and eventually it affects the child's spoken language as well, often resulting in a complete loss of speech.

To test for Landau-Kleffner, an overnight EEG *with no use of sedatives* is necessary since anesthesia, sedatives, and hypnotics will skew the results. When we realized our initial EEG was invalid, we scheduled a second one. It is important to go to a clinic with plenty of experience in handling children with autism, as they will have better results in keeping the electrodes on the child and more experience in reading the results for LKS. Having an overnight EEG isn't as hard as it sounds. For us, the most difficult part was getting the electrodes glued onto Ryan's scalp, which took about six minutes. He screamed through this part, but once the electrodes were on and the medical staff wrapped his head with gauze, he was fine. Some hospitals use a "cap" of electrodes that children can wear, but this method may give less accurate results.

After the electrodes were in place, Ryan was given a room where he was constantly videotaped and "plugged in" to the EEG monitor. The cord for the EEG was long enough that Ryan could walk around the room, use the bathroom, and play. Ryan's results came back normal with no signs of seizure activity.

If you have any cause to suspect LKS, contact a child neurologist as soon as possible. "Because LKS—which is often misdiagnosed as autism—is treatable if diagnosed in its early stages, B. G. R. Neville and colleagues stress the urgency of identifying the disorder."[15] Some patients are treated with medications while others opt for surgery for treatment. If medications are ineffective, it is important to have your child examined by a pediatric epileptologist to discuss other treatment options. Dr. Rimland points out that "some children can be cured completely while others show great improvement but remain disabled."[16] The cause of LKS is not known, and there have not been any studies on the long-term progress of LKS children.

Phenylketonuria (PKU)

In the United States, most children are screened immediately after birth for phenylketonuria, or PKU, a genetic disorder involving the inadequate metabolism of the amino acid phenylalanine. If a child is diagnosed with the disorder, a phenylalanine-free diet can be prescribed. If a special diet is not followed, brain damage occurs, resulting in mental retardation and some autistic behaviors. Most children are tested at birth, but if your child has not been tested for PKU, have your doctor order this test. It's a simple test that can rule out one possible cause for his behaviors.

Fragile X Syndrome

Fragile X Syndrome results from "an abnormality in the DNA molecules of the sex chromosome."[17] It often causes mental retardation, and roughly one-fourth of those with mental retardation would also be classified as autistic. Individuals with Fragile X Syndrome are often hypersensitive to sights, sounds, smells, and tactile stimuli, and like children with autism, they commonly engage in hand flapping, avoid eye contact, have tactile defensiveness and perseverative speech.[18] Many physicians will order a blood test to rule out Fragile X Syndrome during the early stages of autism diagnosis.

What If the Autism Label Fits?

When Ryan was first diagnosed with autism, I began looking for a pediatrician who could help us with the complex issues of autism. We heard about John Bohn, a wonderful doctor in our city who had several patients with autism. Dr. Bohn is one in a million—a man with compassion for children, a man who has made a special place in his heart and practice for children with autism and other special needs, and a man with a wealth of knowledge and experience.

When I first spoke with him, I mentioned that we have an autistic son. He interrupted me and said, "You don't have an autistic son; you have a son who happens to have autism." That stopped me in my tracks. Is autism part of who Ryan is, or is it something he has?

People within the world of autism differ on the answer. Temple Grandin is a well-known adult with autism who has received her Ph.D. in animal science and authored two books. She writes, "If I could snap my fingers and be non-autistic, I would not. Autism is part of what I am."[19] On the other hand, Donna Williams, another author with autism, says, "Autism is not me. Autism is just an information-processing problem that controls who I appear to be. Autism tries to stop me from being free to be myself. I CAN FIGHT AUTISM…I WILL CONTROL IT…IT WILL NOT CONTROL ME" (emphasis hers).[20]

We tend to see Ryan as Donna saw herself. In the beginning Ryan was controlled by the autism, but as we began treating it, he started to change and learn. He became free to express himself, and his personality blossomed. By combating his autism and helping him overcome it, we believe we have taken nothing away from who Ryan is; instead, we have opened the doors to let him be him.

Who Should Know of Your Child's Diagnosis?

During the first two years of Ryan's therapy, he made obvious progress, but he was still noticeably different from other kids his age. It wasn't until he passed his fifth birthday that people started to ask questions like, "What is supposed to be different about Ryan?" People had difficulty picking him out in a group of children.

One day in January of Ryan's kindergarten year, I gleefully returned from dropping Ryan off at school and recounted to Roger a conversation I had just had with a substitute aid. She had never worked with Ryan before, and as she entered the class, she tried to figure out which child she was there to help. After a few minutes, she had to ask the teacher to point out Ryan! Even when he was pointed out, she was unsure of what help he needed.

This incident gives us tremendous joy, but it also illustrates a dilemma faced by parents whose children have recovered or who are well on their way. Do we tell people that our child has autism, or do we try to keep it a secret? Both sides have merit. Your answer may depend on the circumstances surrounding your child's school situation, the kids he or she plays with, or the type of aid your child needs.

We struggled with this decision as we prepared to enroll Ryan in preschool. Following the advice of our clinic, we told his preschool teachers and the director about his diagnosis. Since Ryan still had significant speech delays and his behavior could be quite oppositional, we knew the school staff would realize Ryan had some differences. Telling them ahead of time allowed us to gain the trust of the teachers and staff and to work as a team to prepare Ryan for kindergarten.

As Ryan prepared to enter kindergarten in the fall of 1998, we faced the decision again. Ryan had been receiving early childhood occupational and speech therapy through our school district, as a supplement to his ABA therapy. In Wisconsin, if a child with special needs goes for one year without services, the law requires that the records be destroyed unless the parents sign a release form. Since Ryan was doing so well, we discontinued his school services in 1996 so we would be in a position to send him to kindergarten without a label. We had his records destroyed to keep our options open, but we kept copies of every school form, evaluation, and service record in case we decided to reveal Ryan's background.

We feared that if we told them of Ryan's autism, they might not require as much from him in the classroom. If he struggled with a concept or with a social situation, we didn't want him to be given excuses and not pushed to excel like a typical child. We also worried about misconceptions his teacher might have about autism. We wanted him to achieve to the best of his ability and not be held back by a label.

On the other hand, we didn't want the teachers thinking Ryan was disobedient or unruly if his behavior wasn't in line. He can easily get emotional over something that seems out of place or is handled in a different way than he is accustomed to. Other children may also get upset over such things, but not to the extent Ryan does.

When the time approached for his kindergarten screening, we decided to be completely open with the school personnel. Ryan still had a speech delay and lacked the social skills to blend in undetected, so we met with the M-Team (Multidisciplinary Team) for evaluations, then prepared an Individualized Education Plan (IEP) for Ryan. We wanted his teacher and the special-education teachers to work with us, but we made sure that no parents or children would know of his diagnosis and that Ryan wouldn't be pulled from class to receive therapy from special-education teachers. We agreed to have an aid in the class to help Ryan *only* when he needed assistance, and the children assumed the aid was there to help all of them equally.

Although there have been bumps along the way, Ryan's kindergarten experience has been wonderful. I believe we made the right decision for *our* family about revealing Ryan's past. The school has been excited to see Ryan's continual progress, and we have worked together to create a daily score sheet so we can evaluate Ryan throughout each school day. That way we know immediately if portions of the school day or certain tasks are particularly difficult for him. The aid has worked out great, helping every child in the classroom without smothering Ryan.

Currently we are discussing with the school the possibility of Ryan entering first grade without an aid and without an IEP. Since the aid who works with him deliberately stays away from him unless he gets into trouble or needs help, this may be possible. But there are still questions about his ability to handle a full day of school on his own, especially with large class sizes. In this school they combine first and second graders into large classrooms of forty to fifty students, with two teachers working as a team. With that many children in a class, the students are expected to work more independently while the teachers focus on fewer students at a time. Ryan has done well with his small class and one teacher, but how will he do with that many children and more unstructured time? The school feels that Ryan might do best if "paired" in a classroom with a child who needs much more special help than he. They would share an aid, but the aid would assist him only if he needed it, while focusing most of her attention on the other child. We are still unsure what is best for Ryan and what our decision will be.

In terms of making Ryan's history public, we wrestled with putting our real names in this book. Catherine Maurice chose to use pseudonyms for herself and her children in order to protect their identity in her book *Let Me Hear Your Voice,* while Julia Crowder used her name in her book about her son Drew, who recovered from autism. We know people have strong feelings on both sides.

Several factors guided our decision to make Ryan's autism known. Since his diagnosis, we have sent regular letters to nearly five hundred people who have committed to pray for us and for Ryan, so the word has already been out. Second, people seem to have a relatively short attention span; even those who have heard Ryan's story regularly ask questions that demonstrate their "amnesia." Third, we have been able to help many who desperately need answers and hope, so it would be difficult for us to hide from the opportunity to help others. Finally, given the nature of our work in ministry, we will likely move in the future. If there comes a time when we feel that Ryan needs anonymity in his school setting, we will trust the Lord to place us in a situation where we can give it to him. For now, we feel comfortable with our relative openness.

Each family needs to make this difficult decision for itself. Certainly you don't want your child to be a sideshow attraction, and I hope that won't happen to Ryan. Yet some people may need to know so your child can be adequately helped. It would be wonderful if every family who has a child with autism had to wrestle with this question, since that would mean those children had made miraculous progress.

Step by Step

As time goes on, you will find that everything related to autism tends to be a process—the process of finding the label and understanding it, the process of accepting the journey once you have begun, and the process of treating the autism. Over the next few chapters as we look at many avenues for treating autism, you could become overwhelmed. Explore what you can, when you are ready. Taking each process one step at a time, you may discover, as we have, the anxiety about the unknown transforming into new hope for your child's future.

Chapter 5

Ten Things to Do First

A journey of a thousand miles must begin with a single step.

CHINESE PROVERB

The day we learned of Ryan's autism I did the only thing I knew to get help—I called the Autism Society and Dr. Sallows. But after I left my tearful messages, I didn't know what else to do. Where were we to go from there? Should we wait until the information arrived? I knew Ryan needed help, but what kind and from whom? I felt an urgency to begin combating his autism, but how?

Fortunately we had friends who were willing to show us the ropes and walk us through the beginning steps of our journey. Since not everyone has that option, this chapter focuses on where to start. There are many avenues to explore and so much that will be done over time, but these "top ten" steps are practical ones you can *begin* to take the first month.

1. Understand Your Child's Diagnosis

Ironically, Ryan was diagnosed during National Autism Awareness Week, and although we had been told autism was a possibility, we really weren't aware of what autism is. My experience had been limited to watching *Rain Man* on TV and knowing casually some families from our church who had children with autism. But Ryan wasn't like Dustin Hoffman or their kids. If they each had autism, why were they so different?

Understanding the label your child has been given is an important starting point. Was your child diagnosed with autism, PDD–NOS, Asperger's, Landau-Kleffner Syndrome, or another related disorder? To learn more about the specifics of your child's disorder, begin with the professional who diagnosed your child. Ask the doctor to explain why that label fits. Our doctor took us step by step through the diagnostic criteria chart, explaining why autism fit and other disorders didn't. Feel free to call your doctor with questions.

If you haven't already, read chapter 4, "Understand What You're Facing," to learn more about autism. You'll find several diagnostic tools to familiarize you with each disorder. Use these tools to confirm in your mind that you have an accurate diagnosis. If you aren't sure, call your doctor back and discuss it further. If you still aren't convinced, make an appointment with a second doctor. Until you're convinced the diagnosis is accurate, you won't actively pursue treating it.

Reading a book by a person with autism provides excellent insight. Temple Grandin's books *Emergence: Labeled Autistic* and *Thinking in Pictures and Other Reports from My Life with Autism* are good ones to start with. Grandin is a remarkable woman with autism who has earned her Ph.D. in animal science. In *Thinking in Pictures* she explains how her thought process differs, how she thinks in pictures instead of words. She also describes her sensory problems, her struggle to learn empathy, and the challenges of developing relationships with people who don't have autism. Another book to consider is *There's a Boy in Here*, written by Judy Barron about her son Sean. Since Ryan couldn't speak, we didn't know what was going on inside him and couldn't understand things like why brushing his teeth was so painful. Books such as these gave us a rare insider's view that Ryan couldn't provide. (See the end of this chapter for an annotated list of suggestions.)

Talking to another family about their experiences can also be very helpful. The day after Ryan's diagnosis, Susie and Jeff, who have a child with autism, invited us for dinner. From the moment we walked in, we felt their empathy because they had walked in our shoes. We could talk honestly with them about the struggles we were just beginning to face. Through the course of the evening I realized that their son, Christopher, and Ryan were not so different. Like Ryan, Christopher was fascinated by movies and would watch them all day if allowed. When Susie showed me the hundreds of videos they had acquired, I even found myself laughing. I thought I was the only one who had a stockpile of movies! Both boys also had very limited diets. Christopher ate a total of five foods and drank only Sprite and citrus punch juice. Because he would eat only one breakfast bar and the company was discontinuing it, Susie and Jeff would drive hundreds of miles to buy as many as they could find. Although the following days would teach us more about Ryan's strengths and weaknesses, his needs and desires, and his autism, talking with Susie and Jeff that night and seeing the many parallels confirmed the diagnosis for me and allowed me to start moving forward.

2. Allow Yourself to Grieve

While this isn't an item to check off a "to do" list, it is important to give yourself permission to grieve. You haven't lost your child physically, but you may have lost many of your dreams and plans for your child, which can be extremely painful. In time you will develop new goals and dreams for him, but for now you need the freedom to grieve. For the first few days I couldn't look at Ryan without crying. I forgot to eat, had difficulty sleeping, and lost seven pounds in a week.

After that first week, my emotional meltdowns occurred about once a week, usually when I saw another child and realized that Ryan might never reach the typical milestones most parents take for granted. About three weeks after his diagnosis, Roger and I watched a grade-school choir perform. All I could think was, *Will Ryan ever be able to stand up front and sing with a group?* And the tears started to flow. Afterward, someone who knew our situation came up to me and said, "Are you still grieving?" I nodded politely but thought, *Of course I'm still grieving! Wouldn't you be?* Without intending any harm, people will say insensitive things because they really don't understand your grief. Trying to encourage us, one friend said to Roger, "Don't worry. You'll have other children." When such things are said— and it's usually at the worst possible time—try not to let their words or expectations upset you. Your friends have not walked in your shoes.

Each person grieves differently. Some grieve without tears, dealing with their pain by keeping busy. Some grieve for a short time and then are able to move on. Others need much more time to process their feelings. Susan is the mother of Franke, a seven-year-old boy with autism. For the first six months after his diagnosis, as Susan awakened each morning she would lie in bed in that half-awake state, thankful it was merely a nightmare. Her little boy didn't really have autism. Then reality would hit, and she grieved all over again.

Be careful not to judge your spouse or others for how they grieve; instead, take time to talk honestly with each other about how you're feeling. You may feel you have to be strong for your spouse or someone else, but in order to be strong you first need to be honest with your feelings. I am very grateful that Roger felt free to cry with me. It brought me into his grief and him into mine.

Roger and I have found many outlets to process our grief. Time with the Lord, our closest friend and confidant, has brought the greatest benefit. In those first days, we poured our hearts out to Him in our prayer journals, and we filled the pages, recounting how He gave us strength and comfort every step of the way. I am very grateful also to friends who let me talk openly without passing judgment. Roger, too, needed friends with whom he could release his feelings. One afternoon he went out with his close friend, Rick, and as they sat together talking, Roger couldn't stop crying. As every word brought more tears, Rick sat beside him, willing to listen and give support.

Find what will help you. Seek the comfort and support of your spouse, family, friends, a counselor, or clergy—not only for your sake but for the sake of your child who needs you now more than ever.

If you have other children, make sure that they, too, have outlets and support. Whether siblings are young children or teenagers, they may need help with their feelings. One family we know takes their four-year-old daughter to a therapist weekly, which they have found very beneficial. Although your thoughts and energies are naturally focused on your child with autism, take time to listen to your other children, realizing they need extra attention under the circumstances too.

In the midst of your grief, let me remind you of two things. First, autism is not a death sentence. Your precious child is the same today as he was before the diagnosis; you just didn't have the label before. You still have him and your family, and though you may not feel like it now, you will make it through this. If possible, take time in the first few weeks to do something fun as a family. Even if you cry during the outing, it will be good for you to be together and enjoy each other. Second, don't become paralyzed by your grief. Although Susan was overwhelmed anew by grief each morning for six months, it didn't stop her from seeking help for Franke; instead, she used her grief to spur herself on. Choose to use your grief as a motivator to action.

3. Contact the Autism Research Institute

The Autism Research Institute (ARI) is the hub of a worldwide network of parents and professionals concerned with autism. The only organization of its kind, ARI was founded in 1967 to conduct and foster scientific research designed to improve the methods of diagnosing, treating, and preventing autism. ARI also disseminates research findings to parents and others seeking help. The ARI databank, the world's largest on autism, contains over thirty thousand detailed case histories of children with autism from over sixty countries.

Dr. Bernard Rimland, the founder and director of ARI, is well known and highly respected in the world of autism. As the father of a grown child with autism, he brings not only professional expertise but also a parent's perspective. Dr. Rimland is also the founder of the Autism Society of America and the author of the book *Infantile Autism*.

One of my regrets in combating Ryan's autism is that I waited nearly two years to write Dr. Rimland and to subscribe to his newsletter. I was given his address and phone number in the beginning, but I left it tacked to my bulletin board untouched. Finally, after giving the information to someone else, I decided to subscribe to his newsletter myself. Since then I have gleaned a tremendous amount of information from his publications. His institute also takes calls weekdays from eight o'clock in the morning to noon (Pacific Time) at 619-281-7165. Although Dr. Rimland is an internationally recognized authority on autism, he still takes time to talk with parents and professionals who need his assistance. I've called on several occasions and have had the pleasure of learning directly from him.

ARI's quarterly newsletter, the *Autism Research Review International* (ARRI), provides the latest information. Often I first hear of a new idea through his newsletter, which spurs me to read the research article cited. Other times I look to Dr. Rimland's publication to explain in layman's terms a medical article I've already read.

Along with the ARRI newsletter, the institute offers many books, videotapes, and information packets. The organization is nonprofit, relying upon donations to cover day-to-day operating costs, and charges no fees except to cover the cost of materials and postage.

One of the many contributions Dr. Rimland has made is to initiate the DAN! (Defeat Autism Now!) project. In January of 1995 "the Autism Research Institute convened a group of about thirty carefully selected physicians and scientists...for the express purpose of sharing information and ideas toward defeating autism as quickly as possible."[1] Just three years later, in 1998, the DAN! Conference had grown to more than one thousand attendees. "One major goal of the DAN! Conference was to produce a document that could be used by physicians everywhere as a guide for the clinical assessment of autistic patients, leading to appropriate treatment. After a year of strenuous work, the document, representing a consensus statement of the state-of-the-art alternative medical approach to the diagnosis and treatment of autism, is now available. The forty-page manual is titled *Clinical Assessment Options for Children with Autism and Related Disorders: A Biomedical Approach* and costs $25.00 (U.S. Funds)."[2] This book soon became known as the DAN! protocol.

When we first received our copy of the protocol, we were overwhelmed, not by its size but by the amount of information. The book isn't long, but it covers numerous medical tests, ranging from testing gluten sensitivity to autoimmunity evaluations, that can be ordered through your physician. To have all these tests performed isn't realistic for most people due to the cost, some of which insurance may not cover. We've used several of them with Ryan, but we took them one at a time over a period of many months.

Since we're focusing on things that can be done the first month, I recommend that right now you tear out the ARI order form in the back of this book and order the newsletter, the DAN! protocol, and other information that pertains to your child. When you request the Parent Packet, you will receive many items, including the Diagnostic E-2 Checklist. If you fill out and return this checklist, ARI will score it and enter the results in their database, then send you the results and the interpretation—free of charge. This information could help you understand more clearly the label your child has received. ARI gives each child a file number to maintain confidentiality. If you have access to the Internet, check out ARI's Web site http://www.autism.com/ari. Don't wait two years as I did. Take advantage now of the work ARI has done in paving the way for us and our children.

4. Contact the Autism Society

Calling the Autism Society of America (ASA) is a simple but effective step in gathering information. Their national number is

800-3AUTISM. When you call, ask them to send you a copy of their newsletter and any information they make available on autism and its treatment. The ASA doesn't endorse any one treatment, so they provide materials on a variety of options.

Request from them the phone number of the Autism Society in your state. Next, contact them and ask for their newsletter and any available information. Each state has local chapters, so ask for the name and number of the local contact. Inquire about local services, therapy options and providers, agencies that provide financial assistance, and family support groups. You can't immediately read or follow up on all the information you'll receive, but you'll have it available when you are ready.

Later you may want to consider going to an Autism Society conference. The ASA holds a national conference every year in July in different locations around the country, and the Autism Society in your state may also hold a yearly conference closer to you. These conferences offer a wide variety of topics for parents and professionals and will give you additional direction and support.

5. Put Your Name on Waiting Lists
Help is available, but often there's a wait, so I recommend you put your name on several waiting lists right away.

The ABA List
In my opinion, the most important list to get on is for a professional consultant trained in Applied Behavior Analysis (ABA). I credit ABA for the majority of our son's tremendous progress, so I've dedicated a whole chapter to this therapy. Since you may have to wait several weeks or even as long as a year before you're assigned a consultant, you'll have time to learn about ABA and decide whether or

not you actually want to pursue it. I recommend that you turn to Appendix A, which lists consultants. Choose several that are close to you or interest you, call them, and put your name on their waiting lists. Ask them to send you information about their clinic, staff, treatment procedures, and costs, and find out how long the wait will be to begin treatment. Please note that I'm not recommending or endorsing the names on the list; I'm merely providing the names for your investigation. While you're waiting, you can learn more about ABA and narrow your choice to one provider to hire. If you change your mind after you've researched ABA, you can always remove your name from the list. But if you do choose to pursue this treatment, you will have bought your child more time, and time is precious. You cannot afford to waste any of it waiting unnecessarily.

Other Waiting Lists

After you've put your name on a waiting list for an ABA consultant, seek out other services in your area. You don't know what services you'll need in the future, and it may take months or even years to become eligible, so list yourself for all available help. For example, in our area an organization called Family Support and Resource Center offers, among other services, a Respite Care program, which provides funding for 140 hours of baby-sitting a year. They pay for most of the hourly cost, while the family pays a small percentage. Upon the advice of another family, we called them within the first few days and secured a spot on the list. The center sent us the necessary paperwork to fill out, which we did a few weeks later, but our place on the list was reserved according to the day we called. Even with that, we waited twenty-six months before receiving any services. This program has been such a blessing to our family, allowing Roger and me to spend time alone together more regularly. Once we were accepted on the waiting list, we were also eligible to apply for a one-time grant, which helped pay for materials to start the ABA program.

Since services will vary from city to city as well as state to state, you will need to research what is available in your area. Much of it is just legwork and could be done by a friend who would like to help out. If you have such help, give her your child's full name, address, and birth date, and have her do these things when she calls:

- Write down the name of the organization, its phone number, and with whom she talked.
- Ask them to send you information about, and applications for, their services.
- Put your child's name on any waiting lists they have.
- Find out the approximate waiting time for services.
- Ask them about any other services they know of in the area, along with the names and phone numbers.

Where to Start

If you know any families who have children with autism, start by asking them who to contact. They could save you a lot of time and energy, as well as point out the best services available.

Your next step is to find a central office that disseminates information, because each state is required by law to have one. There is no national number to call, so I've listed all the states' telephone numbers in Appendix B. Each state has a different name for its office—Wisconsin calls its office First Step—but they all should be able to help in the same way. They will inform you, at a state level, about services, financial aid, therapy providers, respite care and childcare, advocacy, and much more. They don't offer services, but they can give you valuable information on who does.

6. Apply for Funding

Within hours of the diagnosis I was asked, "Do you have an MA card?"

"I don't know," was my response. "What's an MA card?"

I found out that MA stands for Medical Assistance, which is basically a governmental insurance program. If you qualify for Medical Assistance and don't already have insurance, it will be your primary insurance. If you already have insurance, then it will pay the deductible and copayments from your primary insurance. Care providers who choose to take MA are willing to receive whatever payment they get from the combination of your insurance and MA. You won't be required to pay any of the bill. However, some providers choose not to take MA since it may not pay all their costs. If they don't take MA, then you are responsible for the charges.

Besides covering costs of medical treatments, MA may also be accepted by providers of supplemental services, including private speech, occupational, and physical therapy. Some states will even provide ABA in-home therapy through the MA benefits. Here again, other parents can guide you on what kinds of benefits they have received and what they had to do to get them.

The eligibility requirements for an MA card are different in each state, and there are two possible routes for obtaining one. The first way is through the Social Security Administration and is dependent upon income qualifications. If you have a disabled child and you earn and own less than the amount allowed in your state for your size family, you are eligible for Social Security Income (SSI). Once you're on this, you'll receive a monthly stipend to be used for your child and you become eligible for the MA card. In some states you automatically receive the MA card in the mail upon acceptance of SSI. Other states require that you fill out additional forms to receive your card. Either way, you are eligible for the card and its benefits. To find out if you qualify, call the Social Security office in your area or the national office at 800-772-1213. They will tell you the income limits based on your state and family size.

The other way to obtain the MA card is through a program not based upon income. Wisconsin calls this the Katie Beckett program; however, the name and the services vary from state to state. For example, Missouri's program is called the Sarah Jian Lopez Medicaid Waiver. Each state decides what disabilities it will cover and what benefits are offered. Unfortunately, some states do not include autism. To see what your state offers in this program, contact your local Department of Health and Human Services and ask about a program to obtain an MA card outside of SSI.

Again, time is of the essence. Although it often takes several months to get MA approval, some states will back pay claims for up to three months prior to the day you *call* to apply! For us, that meant all the doctor visits and all the testing required to get the diagnosis, including the EEG and blood and urine testing, was covered, which saved us hundreds of dollars in copayments!

Although getting MA approval usually takes several weeks or months, you can speed up the process by obtaining and keeping copies of every report from every doctor and specialist who examines your child. When MA representatives check the validity of your diagnosis, they send forms to each of your doctors, asking for information. It may take a few days for these papers to be prepared, sent, and delivered, and then the doctors must read them and respond to them, which may take awhile given their patient load. After they have filled out the paperwork and mailed it back, the MA receives it and finally begins to process your application. To save time, I brought in copies of each doctor's and therapist's report and presented them to the MA representative *in person.* I was able to collect them within a few days and cut out weeks of processing time. We had our MA card in less than four weeks!

7. Videotape Your Child

This may sound like common sense, but it can be very important and is often overlooked. Start today videotaping your child in his daily activities—eating, playing, talking. Tape him during good and bad situations to document what your child is like before treatment begins. Once treatment starts, videotape on a regular basis to record progress. We had lots of family videotapes of Ryan before treatment started, but I wish I had taken more and had captured more fully the autistic traits in his life then. We videotaped the initial evaluation and testing, as well as his workshop for his ABA therapy. The first week of ABA we taped all forty hours of treatment. After that, we taped a random two hours a week. Once a month is probably enough for documentation, but I felt the need to do more.

These videotapes help in three ways. First, they are wonderful for maintaining hope. Looking back at Ryan in the beginning, I can *see* the dramatic changes that have taken place. I could tell you about his progress all day long, but no words make the impression that watching him transform right before your eyes does. I've put together a fifteen-minute video of clips from pre-therapy to the present. Even though I've seen it dozens of times, I'm always amazed as I watch his progress. Without the videos, I might forget how far we have come.

Video documentation may also be necessary to obtain or maintain funding. Tapes can document progress, which may give you leverage in securing the support to continue therapy.

The third benefit of ongoing taping is for training. Our therapists used the tapes to watch themselves in action and to learn from their mistakes. They also provided me a tool for training teachers, friends, and family in ABA and demonstrating how they could incorporate it into their work with Ryan. When they saw what was happening at home, they were better able to accommodate Ryan's specific needs. It also helped us break down walls with teachers who resisted using ABA therapy because of outdated or inaccurate information.

8. Find Other Families

Although this is number eight, it is extremely important. It's easy to become isolated, wrapped up in finding help for your child. You may feel you're able to go it alone—perhaps even that doing so shows strength—but I encourage you to break free of that myth and seek support.

The Autism Society in your area will give you contacts for ongoing support groups. Go to one of them and find out what the group is like. Each group will have a different focus, so you may need to check out more than one. In our city we have many parental groups, including the Autism Society, a gluten-free and casein-free group, a group for those using ABA, and a prayer group of families with autism. I've been to all these groups, but I don't attend them all regularly. Try not to judge the benefit of the group by just one meeting, in case it wasn't typical. Attend two or more times before you decide if it will help.

When you go, remember that each person is at a different place in the autism journey. Some may be brand-new to this and need more support and information, while others may have older children with autism who have different needs. Within the group see if you can find one or two families you're comfortable with. Get their names and phone numbers, and take the initiative to contact them soon. More than likely they would love to help you and get to know you better.

You may argue that you don't have time to meet with other families, and I'd argue that you don't have time not to. Networking not only gives much-needed emotional support and strength, it provides essential information. Other families have walked farther down the path that you're just starting. They can help you avoid pitfalls they encountered; they can point you toward good doctors and therapists; they can save you from having to learn everything firsthand and perhaps the hard way.

9. Postpone Vaccinations

Before you jump to conclusions and assume that I oppose all vaccines, read what I have to say. Recent findings in the medical world have caused many parents and physicians to take a second look at vaccines. "Andrew Wakefield and colleagues generated intense controversy in the medical world this February [1998] when they reported evidence, in an article in the prestigious British journal *The Lancet,* that the measles-mumps-rubella (MMR) vaccine may cause gastrointestinal problems that in turn lead to autism."[3]

Since this is such an important and controversial topic, we'll look at it more thoroughly in chapter 8 on biomedical tests and treatments. What I stress here is that you consider postponing any vaccination for your child with autism *and* your other children until you have time to research more information and perform any relevant tests. I'm not suggesting you withhold vaccines forever, but I do urge you to wait until you're able to make an informed decision for each of your children.

10. Consider a Trial of B$_6$ and DMG Supplements

Chapter 8 on biomedical interventions outlines the use of supplements, including vitamin B$_6$ and a "food substance" supplement called DMG (dimethylglycine). Both of these supplements are safe and inexpensive, yet may cause dramatic changes in a short time. While you're waiting to start other therapy options, I urge you to read about these two supplements and try them one at a time so any results can be directly linked. I encourage you not to tell anyone except your physician of your plans; just give the supplements and watch for results. Then if people comment on your child's improvement, they are unbiased observers. You have nothing to lose and potentially much to gain.

Continue Learning

Autism information is not stagnant, and treatments are always changing. By contacting the organizations listed as well as networking with other parents, you are well on your way, but it is critically important for you to stay as well informed as possible. Unlike treating a broken arm, there is no consensus on the treatment of autism. There is no single person who can give you all the answers for your child. As a parent, you are responsible for finding the answers to give your child the best chance in life. In this information age, becoming educated in autism is easier than ever through books, newsletters, conferences, and the Internet. Explore these and *keep learning!*

Recommended Reading

Autism: From Tragedy to Triumph by Carol Johnson and Julia Crowder (Boston: Branden Publishing Company, 1994). Crowder is the mother of Drew, a boy who recovered from his autism through the therapy of Dr. O. Ivar Lovaas.

Emergence: Labeled Autistic by Temple Grandin and Margaret M. Scariano (Novato, Calif.: Arena Press, 1986) and *Thinking in Pictures and Other Reports from My Life with Autism* by Temple Grandin (New York: First Vintage Books, 1995). Grandin freely calls herself autistic, yet she has earned a Ph.D. in animal science. Her remarkable books explain many aspects of a world little understood.

Let Me Hear Your Voice: A Family's Triumph over Autism by Catherine Maurice (New York: Ballantine Books, 1993). I consider this a *must-read* book for every parent of a child with autism. Maurice beautifully chronicles the journey into and out of the autism that affected two of her three children and offers much-needed hope.

The Siege: The First Eight Years of an Autistic Child by Clara Claiborne Park (Boston: Back Bay Books and Little, Brown and Company, 1967, 1972, 1982). This book chronicles the first eight years of the life of the author's daughter.

There's a Boy in Here by Judy Barron and Sean Barron (New York: Simon & Schuster, 1992). Judy Barron's son Sean was diagnosed with autism and later emerged to tell his story. Written by both mother and son, this unique book describes autism from both perspectives, inside and out.

Chapter 6

Applied Behavior Analysis

*Whatever neurological processes had been reactivated in her brain, whatever
chemical imbalance had been corrected, we would probably never know.
Nor would we care, as she emerged into the light of human loving,
and lifted her blue-green eyes to ours.*

CATHERINE MAURICE

Since we started sending our "Operation Rescue Ryan" newsletter,
we've had the privilege of sharing each new discovery, each new
challenge and milestone in Ryan's life with literally hundreds of
people who have been praying for Ryan and his recovery. They, in
turn, have passed the newsletter on to others who have a child with
autism—a family member, a coworker, a neighbor, a teacher at
school. As a result, I get phone calls each week from parents around
the country, asking what's worked for us. Whether they want to
know about secretin infusions, the gluten-free and casein-free diet,
or auditory processing therapies, I always ask about their experience with Applied Behavior Analysis (ABA) because I credit ABA
for the majority of Ryan's dramatic improvement.

Now, four years into Ryan's therapy, if I had to do it all over
again, I would put my confidence in a well-run, professional ABA
program. We've benefited from other therapies and treatments, but
I consider our ABA program the foundation. A few, rare children

may recover purely from secretin or dietary intervention or Auditory Integration Therapy (AIT), but most will be like Ryan, needing a combination approach with ABA as the main staple.

Since the day Ryan was diagnosed, I've dreamed of a quick fix for his autism, thinking, *If I would only do such and such, then he would instantly recover.* The reality is, I have yet to meet a child who has experienced an immediate cure. ABA therapy is a long road marked by small steps, but those small steps can take you far if you persevere. Some parents shy away from the long-haul approach of ABA, opting instead for the minute chance their child will experience a miraculous recovery with some obscure treatment.

Even Dr. O. Ivar Lovaas, a pioneer of ABA therapy with autism, expected a major breakthrough.

> We were expecting a sudden step forward, that possibly somehow we would hit upon some central cognitive, emotional, or social event inside the child's mind that would help him make a sudden and major leap ahead. Traditional conceptions are filled with such promises. Such a leap would have been so gratifying and it would have made our work so much easier. It never happened. Instead, progress followed a slow, step-by-step upward progression, with only a few and minor spurts ahead. We learned to settle down for hard work.[1]

We all want miracles, and miracles can happen, but sometimes they come as a result of hard work. Victoria Beck is best known for discovering that autistic symptoms could be affected by a hormone called secretin, which did, in fact, produce "miracles" in her son's life. After Parker received an infusion of secretin to test the function of his pancreas, he improved dramatically. He started speaking and attending in therapy, and he became toilet trained in a matter of days. His progress over time was tremendous.

Although secretin was key to Parker's life, Victoria clearly points to ABA as vital to his success as well: "I also want to emphasize that we are deeply indebted to our team of home therapists and our school system who, together, provide Parker the other important part of the equation—thirty-five hours per week of excellent ABA therapy. We feel that the secretin 'allows' him to learn, and that his ABA program provides the tools he needs in order to advance. Without the ABA education, even the secretin would not allow him to be the spontaneous, joyful, and bright child that he is."[2]

We feel the same way about Ryan. He has been helped by secretin, vitamins, and other therapies, but ABA has given him the underlying ability to develop and overcome. While some children may not be good candidates for ABA and some families have used ABA without success, I believe it is the treatment of choice for the majority of children and their best hope for improvement or even recovery.

What Is Applied Behavior Analysis?

In simple terms, ABA teaches complex tasks by breaking them down into bite-size pieces that can be learned more easily, with each piece building upon the previous one. Rewards, called "reinforcers," are given for correct responses or behaviors while inappropriate responses are corrected, ignored, or redirected. Precise data on each learning trial is recorded, and adjustments in the educational program are made accordingly.

You may have heard the terms *discrete trial training* or *Lovaas therapy* used in reference to ABA, but they are not interchangeable. Discrete trial training, which breaks down a task and teaches it systematically, is merely a subset of the ABA program that is used extensively. The term Lovaas therapy comes from Dr. O. Ivar Lovaas, whose landmark research spurred the application of ABA techniques for teaching children with autism.[3] Dr. Lovaas isn't the only professional who uses ABA to target autism, though his name is perhaps the most recognized.

Behavioral therapy has been used in a wide variety of disorders for many years with notable success. B. F. Skinner in 1938 called this concept of changing behavior by the response of the teacher "operant conditioning."[4] If a reinforcer immediately followed a desired behavior, the chances of the behavior being repeated increased. If the reinforcer was taken away, the desired behavior would eventually decrease.[5] The same applies to negative behavior; it will increase if it's reinforced and decrease if it's properly ignored. For example, Ryan used to scream, loud and often. Using this approach, we ignored him when he screamed. We didn't give him what he wanted, nor did we make eye contact with him. But as soon as he stopped screaming, we quickly turned to him and reinforced the calm behavior. Within several days his screaming decreased, and over time it disappeared.

A reinforcer can be anything the child wants and likes—food, drinks, hugs, kisses, tickles, a favorite toy. At first Ryan responded best to small bites of his favorite treats, but later we replaced them with more natural rewards and praises. The therapists have to give reinforcement correctly, rotating a variety of rewards and varying degrees of rewards, depending on the accuracy of the response. For instance, hearing "good job" ten times in a row won't be much of a motivator. A good therapist will be creative and will prepare by testing the motivator outside the therapy session.

What Areas Does ABA Target?

The name Applied Behavior Analysis can be misleading since the therapy covers much more than behaviors. ABA targets development in many areas of skills, including attending, imitation, language, social, self-help, and academic.[6]

Attending skills include learning how to sit in a chair, decreasing tantrums, making eye contact, and listening. When Ryan began treatment, he was unable to sit in a chair and pay attention. In our first drill we called him over to his chair at the table by saying, "Come here." Ryan didn't respond at all, so we carried him over to his chair despite his tantrum. When we got him in the chair, we gave him a piece of cookie (a reinforcer) and told him how well he did. After a while, Ryan learned to come to the table when he was called. With each command, we gave him two opportunities to accomplish the task on his own before we physically prompted him to do it.

Imitation skills are both physical and verbal. At our first workshop, the therapist put Ryan through a few physical imitation drills. In one he was expected to put a red block on top of a blue block after he saw the therapist do it with a duplicate set of blocks. Our therapist, Michelle, said, "Do this," and modeled the action by putting one block on the other. She then took Ryan's hand and helped him do the same thing. Another drill asked Ryan to imitate a gross motor movement. The therapist put her hands on her head and said, "Do this." Then she helped Ryan imitate her action. When he did, even with help, she rewarded him. These skills eventually developed into complex imitations of actions, play, and language.

Verbal imitation skills start out simply. If a child is nonverbal, the goal is to get him to imitate a sound. The therapist says, "Say aah," and the child is supposed to say "aah." It took Ryan a couple of weeks to be able to imitate a sound when asked, but that led to teaching him to imitate whole words and eventually phrases. If the child is already verbal, he will start out with the more complex verbal imitation drills.

Language skills have two aspects, receptive and expressive. Before Ryan could speak, he understood language; he "received" it. The therapist would place a shoe on the table and tell Ryan, "Touch shoe." She then took his hand, physically helped him touch the shoe, and rewarded him. Over time he learned that objects had names (receptive), and when he began to speak, he called them by name (expressive).

Because of the complexity of language, we've continued language drills as a central part of Ryan's therapy. Dr. Lovaas says, "About 80 percent of intensive behavioral treatment with young children is focused on helping the children develop more meaningful language. The requirement of teaching language...requires that the provider of treatment knows how to teach a variety of skills, from helping mute children acquire verbal imitation, to teaching abstract language such as pronouns, prepositions, and time concepts. Finally, the therapist/teacher has to teach the child how to talk and play with normal peers."[7] Over time Ryan has learned more complex language, first through drills at the table and then through our modeling it in natural settings.

ABA can also help children who don't develop verbal language to express themselves through augmentative communication.

Social skills, which come naturally to most children, need to be specifically taught to children with autism. These skills include such basics as playing with toys appropriately and transitioning between them, initiating interaction, sharing toys and experiences, and developing friendships. Since Ryan had no play skills, we started by teaching him to play with toys. We took a small car, said, "Do this," and rolled it back and forth on the floor. Then we put the car in his hand and helped him do it. When he learned to speak, we added car sounds to our play. As Ryan progressed, we taught him how to share, take turns, pretend, and interact with his friends. A lot of our therapy time has been spent in interactive play with him.

Recently a boy from Ryan's kindergarten class invited him to his house. The mother didn't know Ryan's history or diagnosis. When we got there, Ryan rang the bell and greeted his friend. He asked if they could go upstairs and "check out his toys," and the two were off, laughing and playing. I went home. When the mother brought Ryan home, she said they had a lot of fun but the time was too short. All this from a boy who couldn't push a toy car when we began therapy.

Self-help skills include dressing and undressing, toilet habits, grooming, safety, cooking, and household chores. ABA targets each self-help task with small, attainable steps until the child can take care of his personal needs independently. At first Ryan couldn't undress himself, so we started by teaching him to take off his socks, since they are the simplest. For a long time we dressed him in sweatpants so he didn't have to struggle with snaps or zippers, but after a while he learned to handle those, too. Now he can pick out his clothes and dress himself, although that doesn't stop him from putting his underwear on his head like a helmet and pretending he's "Spaceman Ryan."

Academic skills begin with learning shapes, colors, letters, and numbers and then advance to reading, writing, spelling, and mathematics. Since many children with autism have scattered skills, some advanced and some lagging behind, a child as young as two or three may begin reading or spelling. When we realized Ryan had high visual skills and could learn to read, we used this strength to help him in a weaker area. Ryan struggled with differentiating between "he is running," "she is running," and "they are running." So we wrote out the words and let him read them as he looked at a picture of the action. Once he understood the difference, we removed the words and left just the picture for him to describe.

Beyond the skills that are taught to the child, Dr. Lovaas points out two fundamental goals of this therapy: "to make the child want to learn, and to make the child feel that he can learn."[8] Each time a child is called to the table for drills, the therapist tries to make him feel successful. If the child has trouble giving the right response, he is prompted after two attempts. The therapist may follow an easy drill with a harder one so the child can have success as well as be pushed to learn more, but a good therapist will ensure that each set of drills ends in success.

I loved watching Ryan's face when he learned something new. He was so proud of himself. When he learned what a circle was, he took me around the house and pointed out every circle he could find. And the first time he read a sentence, you could actually see the joy radiate from his whole body when he yelled out the last word in delight!

The ABA program doesn't take a cookie-cutter approach. Because each child learns differently and at his own pace, the program is tailored to the child's level. After your child's baseline is determined, between five and fifteen distinct program drills will be chosen. Each drill has a specific command, called an "SD" (Discriminative Stimulus), and an expected response. Every time an SD is given, a response is expected. If the child responds correctly without a prompt, he gets credit. Usually the therapist gives several SDs in a row and then records data for that set of drills on data collection sheets in the child's program book. This information forms a central part of ABA because it allows multiple therapists to continue or to build upon the previous session, and it gives accurate information about the child's speed of learning. When the data reflects that a skill has been mastered, the therapist replaces that drill with a new one.

Be assured, the child doesn't remain in his chair for the entire therapy session. He's called to the table for a few drills, which last from thirty seconds to ten minutes, depending on his age and ability. After a series of drills, the therapist tells the child to go play, and he's free to play with anything in the room. As soon as Ryan learned play skills, playtime became just as important as drill time. In fact playtime was treated like drill time in that specific activities were targeted and data was collected, but Ryan still considered it playing.

Besides teaching appropriate new skills, ABA addresses improper behaviors, such as aggression, tantrums, and self-stimulation like hand flapping, rocking, or spinning objects or themselves. These behaviors are analyzed to try to determine the catalyst, and a plan is implemented to stop them. Sometimes a child can be redirected to an alternate action; other times the problem behavior is ignored. This sounds strange but it works. For children with autism, even a negative response by the adult may act as a reinforcer since the child receives attention for his behavior.

At one point in his therapy, Ryan began hitting the therapists in the face during drills. Common sense says to correct the child with a harsh "no" or a time-out, and he'll stop. Actually, we did the opposite because that discipline would have caused Ryan to increase the hitting. Instead, we used "extinction," a process in which the negative behavior is ignored while the positive is reinforced. Although not easy, it worked. When Ryan hit the therapist, she didn't acknowledge it except to prevent him from hitting her again. Then with a benign expression she repeated the SD being targeted. At first this caused an "extinction burst," which means he increased the number of times he hit. But when he received no reinforcement, the behavior diminished and before long disappeared.

In the early stages of treatment, every detail is structured and carried out by a therapist in a one-to-one setting. All the therapists say the same words for the SD and use the same prompts, and the learning environment remains constant from day to day. However, as the treatment progresses and the child learns more, therapy becomes less structured. Sessions can move to other places, and SDs become more varied. The goal is to progress along the continuum until the child can learn in a natural setting like typically developing children.

What Does the Research Show?

Dr. Lovaas conducted research with three groups of children who had a diagnosis in the autism spectrum. The children in each group were similar in age, language ability, toy play, peer play, self-help skills, and self-stimulation. The experimental group consisted of nineteen children who received intensive behavioral therapy for an average of forty hours a week. One control group contained nineteen children who received behavioral therapy for ten or fewer hours a week, and a second control group had twenty-one children who received no behavioral therapy.

Before treatment the children from all three groups had similar mental ages and intelligence quotients (IQ). After treatment, however, the experimental group had changed significantly while both control groups remained closer to their initial evaluations. Nine of the nineteen children in the experimental group reached normal intellectual and educational functioning and attained average or above average IQ scores, with an average gain of thirty-seven points. "School personnel describe these children as indistinguishable from their normal friends."[9] Another eight were categorized in the aphasia group, meaning these children were moderately affected and needed classes for language delays. Only two of the nineteen children remained severely retarded and required special education classes specifically for retarded or autistic students.

In the first control group, which received no more than ten hours of ABA weekly, *no* children recovered. Eight advanced to the aphasia range, while the remaining eleven remained in the retarded or autistic range. One child in the second control group attained recovery, while ten children were placed in the aphasia group and ten remained in the retarded or autistic range.[10] Clearly, those children who received fewer hours of behavioral therapy didn't respond as well as those who had more.

"Applied Behavior Analysis has been proved, through extensive research over the past half-century, to be the most effective intervention we have for treating people with autism or pervasive developmental disorder," says Catherine Maurice, author and mother of two recovered children.[11] Other educational therapy choices offer high success rates, but to date, only ABA has published peer-reviewed data to confirm its claims. "Success" should be defined and documented with research, not merely testimonials and anecdotes. Research shows that children who receive intensive behavioral treatment, preferably starting between two and five years old, not only have a chance to learn and improve, but some may even completely overcome the effects of autism.[12]

How Much Therapy Is Needed Weekly?

Before Ryan started ABA therapy, he was receiving one hour a week of combined speech, occupational, and physical therapy from an early intervention program called Birth to Three, which we knew wasn't going to be enough. A typical child learns every waking moment, but a child with autism usually doesn't learn unless taught directly. When I cook dinner, my daughter watches me and then gets her play dishes and "cooks" too. Ryan couldn't do that. He wasn't learning from watching the world around him, but he needed to be.

ABA therapy takes that into account with the thirty-five- to forty-hour-a-week schedule and with the parents' follow-through. For this reason every person who consistently spends time around your child, including you, needs to be trained in ABA techniques so your child has the opportunity to learn as much as typical children and more.

Most practitioners recommend thirty-five to forty hours of therapy a week in the beginning. Based on Dr. Lovaas's research, Ryan's needs, and the limited therapy he was already receiving, we scheduled forty hours a week and attacked the autism full force.

Are the Benefits Long-Term?

Five years after Dr. Lovaas's initial research was released, a follow-up on the nine "recovered" children was published. These children, who were then between nine and nineteen years old, were examined to see if autistic symptoms remained after they completed the treatment and if they had retained their IQ gains. One child who functioned normally in first grade was later moved to a special education class, while another child who had previously been in special education in first grade was moved into a regular classroom. Therefore, the number of children in this group who attained normal functioning remained the same.[13]

Among other things, the researchers looked at the children's thought patterns, mannerisms, relationships, and interests, as well as affect, cognitive function, abstract reasoning, sense of humor, success in school, and use of leisure time.[14] To prevent bias, advanced graduate psychology students unrelated to the research tested the recovered children, along with typical children who had no history of behavioral problems. They found that the eight who were still in regular education continued to be indistinguishable from other children their age in both behavior and intelligence.

How Soon Should Treatment Begin?

Most agree that starting a child before age five is important, though Dr. Lovaas chose to treat children younger than four in his research. For the maximum benefit, the younger you start, the better. First of all, the older child has more catching up to do. By age three Ryan was already one to two years behind his peers in most areas of development. Had we waited longer, he would have fallen even further behind.

Our nephew, Carter, was diagnosed with autism just before his second birthday. Since Ryan was already receiving ABA therapy, his parents, Carol and Rob, were miles ahead of most parents in information. The day of Carter's diagnosis, Carol called to ask me to fax her information on which drills to start with. Within twenty-four hours they had begun therapy on their own! Once they found a consultant, they hired her to oversee their program. Carter is now four years old and attending a normal preschool with minimal assistance. Because of early intervention, his future looks bright.

The second reason for an early start is that the synapses, the connection between two neurons, in a young child's brain are still developing. As a synapse is used, the connection strengthens.

Conversely, when a synapse isn't used, it dies, which is called "pruning" or "elimination." For this reason, repetitive and intensive intervention may actually modify the patterns within the brain. But at some point in the first several years of life, the brain becomes less "plastic," and changes may be more difficult. Drs. Richard Perry, Ira Cohen, and Regina DeCarlo hypothesize that "in those autistic children whose condition is as yet modifiable, rigorous behavioral therapy modifies the neural circuitry before the condition becomes permanent."[15]

Can ABA Help Older Children?

Although very young children have the greatest chance for remarkable improvement, intensive ABA can facilitate improvement in a child of any age. The techniques used by ABA can teach appropriate social behaviors, work and recreational skills, and daily-life skills to a child battling autism, in the manner he needs to learn them. I've even heard of teenagers with autism starting ABA programs.

Is ABA Necessary If My Child Has PDD–NOS?

Although parents like to hear that their child may be on the milder end of the autistic spectrum, a diagnosis of Pervasive Developmental Disorder–Not Otherwise Specified (PDD–NOS) instead of autism may make decisions less obvious. In response to the question of whether intensive treatment is really necessary for PDD–NOS, let me ask, "What if your doctor diagnosed you as having a little bit of cancer? Would you treat it less seriously?" Even though children with PDD–NOS may not be as far behind their peers as a child labeled with autism, their struggles won't disappear by themselves. Their needs should be targeted aggressively so they can catch up as quickly as possible.

Where Does Therapy Take Place?

Most ABA programs begin in the home—the most familiar setting for the child—though some clinics offer treatment at a professional facility or an ABA school, which may allow for more normalcy in the home. If you can't be home during the day, you may need to conduct therapy in a day-care center or a relative's home. We converted Ryan's bedroom into his therapy room by adding a small table and chair, some shelves, and lots of toys. The therapists used the top of his dresser as their desk where they kept Ryan's data book and drill items, and Ryan "converted" his bed into a trampoline. At first this was the primary place for each session, but as Ryan progressed, we moved therapy into other rooms and even outside. During the summer we often put his table on the deck, so when he played between drills he could jump in the kiddy pool or swing.

After the second year as Ryan attended preschool two days a week, the in-home therapy hours decreased accordingly. "Home" therapy then frequently occurred in the community or with peers. Learning to play with kids at the park and to act appropriately at McDonald's were woven into his therapy goals.

Who Should Conduct Therapy?

Ideally, each child with special needs would have an experienced and well-trained ABA consultant working with him daily. If you live in a city that has an ABA clinic, you may have access to intensive guidance and training on a weekly basis, but many people have to hire a traveling consultant to train those who will work directly with their child. The consultant conducts workshops in the home every two to three months to provide additional training and update programming.

Once a consultant is hired, she normally travels to your home for an initial workshop. This workshop should be attended by both parents; your ABA therapists; your speech, occupational, and physical therapists; and others who will interact consistently with your child, such as grandparents, teachers, and day-care workers. It is important that *you* be trained thoroughly. Even though you won't perform drills throughout the day, you will play a major role in transferring those basic concepts and techniques into your child's everyday life in the "real world." If he's learning colors, you need to continue that teaching during his free time, which means knowing the SDs and how to reinforce appropriately. Being actively involved and trained will enable you to keep the team of therapists up to speed or even to fill in when people can't make their shift. Filling occasional shifts yourselves will also improve your skills and keep costs down.

What if long waiting lists or lack of funding prevents you from getting a consultant immediately? Start treatment yourself. Catherine Maurice, Gina Green, and Stephen C. Luce published a how-to book on ABA. In chapter 1 they use the following analogy to explain why they want to get ABA material into the hands of parents.

> A woman's time to give birth has arrived. She is far from any civilized place, where she could be hospitalized and receive all the latest in professional expertise and state-of-the-art delivery care. Two people are arguing over what to do for her.
>
> The first says, "I will help her delivery because I have this manual here that gives me a rough idea of how to do this."
>
> The second says, "You can't deliver babies. You don't have a medical degree! She should be in a hospital!"
>
> The first responds "Either someone helps her—now—or we will lose both mother and baby."[16]

While starting your own program may not be ideal, that is far better than waiting until you can have it done perfectly. Time is of the essence.

Does ABA Cure Children?

This question is difficult to answer because it depends on how you define *cure*. In the medical world, a cure is a treatment that alleviates illness in each person to whom it is administered. For example, the cure for strep throat is antibiotics; strep patients receive antibiotics, and they are typically cured. Since no treatment can be applied to every child with autism to alleviate the disorder, there is no cure for autism yet, nor does ABA claim to be a cure.

However, if you define *cure* as "a restoration or return to a sound or healthy condition,"[17] then *some* children can be considered cured. Typically professionals use the term *recovered* rather than *cured* to describe a child who has overcome the *effects* of autism, since we don't know the underlying causes of autism, nor do we know if physiological changes have occurred. Therefore, the better question is, can a child recover using ABA treatment? I say a resounding "yes!" In some people's eyes, Ryan has recovered.

Recently I met a woman whose son has autism, and I shared Ryan's story with her. Later, when she visited our church, she put her son in Sunday school and stayed with him during class. Being the same age, Ryan was in that class, but she didn't realize it until halfway into the period when she noticed Ryan's nametag. She watched him, trying to figure out if he was my son. When she realized he was, she was astonished! She said she never would have picked him out, and she knows autism.

Catherine Maurice has seen dramatic results from implementing ABA with two of her children. She chronicles the dramatic results in her book *Let Me Hear Your Voice: A Family's Triumph over Autism*, a must-read for anyone considering ABA. In fact, we require all our therapists to read her book prior to working with Ryan. Catherine and her husband, Marc, have three children, two of whom were diagnosed with autism. "In their desperate struggle to save their daughter, the Maurices plunged into a medical nightmare of false hopes, 'miracle cures,' and infuriating suggestions that Anne-Marie's autism was somehow their fault. Finally, Anne-Marie was saved by an intensive behavioral therapy."[18] Their story takes you through their struggle to find an accurate diagnosis for Anne-Marie, their pursuit of appropriate treatment, the regression of their third child into autism, and the recovery of both Anne-Marie and her brother Michel.

Besides Maurice's anecdotal information, Drs. Richard Perry, Ira Cohen, and Regina DeCarlo published their findings about the Maurice children in an article called "Case Study: Deterioration, Autism, and Recovery in Two Siblings" in the *Journal of the American Academy of Child and Adolescent Psychiatry*. These doctors validate Catherine Maurice's claim that her children did have autism, recovered from it, and live normally now.

According to Dr. Lovaas, even with early intervention, well-trained ABA therapists, and consistent therapy, slightly less than half of the children treated achieve recovery or normalcy.[19] However, his research shows that 90 percent of the children made marked gains. Most *will* learn and improve, but the majority will not overcome autism completely. Should this stop you from using ABA? I hope not. Considering that until recent years children had virtually no chance of significant improvement, much less recovery, the possibility that almost half will recover is phenomenal.

Although we are encouraged by Ryan's progress, Roger and I

know we still have some things to address in his life. Will he ever fully recover? We certainly hope so. One child in the initial Lovaas study had ongoing ABA therapy until he was in third grade before he was considered indistinguishable from his peers.[20] Ryan has come so far and improved so tremendously we believe that he is on that same path.

Arguments Against ABA

We've looked at the potential benefits, but what are the costs and the arguments against using ABA?

"ABA Costs Too Much"

There are several costs involved with pursuing ABA. One cost is your loss of freedom. At the start of Ryan's program, we scheduled therapy six hours a day for six days a week and four hours on Sunday afternoon. Our lives revolved around his therapy schedule. We set our alarm to wake us in time to get everything ready for therapy. We ate our meals, went to the park, and ran errands between sessions.

Along with that, we lost our privacy. The first therapist arrived at our house at 7:30 in the morning for a two-hour shift, and the last one left around 6:00 in the evening. We averaged having therapists in our home six to seven hours per day, so I felt like I never had time alone. Some mornings I was greeted by a therapist going into my son's room as I came out of the bathroom in my robe. Even though I'm an extrovert who loves being around people, many days I broke down in tears, wanting to scream and tell everyone to leave!

Obviously you won't necessarily follow the schedule we did. Since Ryan woke up around 5:30 in the morning, we found that his best hours were early in the day. As time went on, Ryan began sleeping later, so we changed to an 8:30 start. Your schedule will depend on your child's daily routine.

Undoubtedly the most significant cost for many families is the financial one. This therapy is expensive, and funding is generally hard to find. However, some states now cover it under Medical Assistance or another governmental program, and some school districts pay for home therapy out of the school budget. Securing funding takes a great deal of time and effort—and possibly a good lawyer—so there will be suggestions for funding later in this chapter.

"ABA Teaches Kids to Speak like Robots"

This popular argument is accurate to some extent. When Ryan was first learning to talk, he did sound like a robot. In order to teach him to converse, we had him read his response. When I said, "Hi, Ryan," he would look at the table and read, very robotically, "Hi, Mommy."

But the way he needed to learn language wasn't much different from the way I learned German in high school. The first weeks of class the teacher wrote words on the board, and we repeated them, much like robots. Did I understand all the words and say them with expression? No way! The process was rote for quite a while. Later, when I understood more and practiced what I'd learned, the words flowed more naturally. I could produce sentences and convey my thoughts, but this took time.

To Ryan, English was a foreign language, except he had no primary language to fall back on. At first his words were robotic and rote, but now they flow. Now he can say whatever he needs to and can express *his* thoughts with feeling.

"It Takes a Child Away from Inclusion"

Previously, children with special needs were generally separated from other children and placed in their own classroom. Now most public schools favor full inclusion of children with a disability. I applaud their change; however, we mustn't throw out the baby with the bathwater. At times a child needs additional help that can be better provided outside the inclusive classroom. Most educators agree with that, until it comes to in-home ABA treatment. Then you may hear, "How can you take a child out of an inclusive setting and teach him at home?"

I explain it this way. If I want to move to Russia, I can pack right now and be there in a matter of hours. When I arrive, I have to find transportation, housing, and food. There is a problem though. I don't speak Russian. But I'm a capable person, and I could probably survive. But what if I wait for a year before going to Russia and in that time I take Russian language courses, learn about the culture and how to fit in socially, and even meet some Russians while I'm still in America? By the time I move, I'll adapt more easily and probably enjoy myself more.

In a sense we prepared Ryan for living in a foreign country. He didn't speak the language the other kids did, he didn't understand the culture, and he didn't know the social rules. He could survive, but would he thrive? Instead of throwing him into a group setting from the beginning, we kept him at home and taught him to speak. He learned how to play and how to interact. At the right time, we brought children to *his* environment so he could test his new skills. And when he was ready, we sent him to "Russia," well prepared and eager to have fun.

Ryan now attends full-inclusion kindergarten without being pulled out for special education. Had we not spent time preparing him, he wouldn't be as successful as he is. Obviously, you and your consultant will have to decide when your child should start attending school, depending on the age of your child and his readiness.

"It's Too Hard on a Family"

When we first considered an ABA program for Ryan, many professionals opposed us, saying it's too hard on a family.

Jill, the four-year-old daughter of our friends Dan and Lisa, was diagnosed with leukemia. Did anyone tell them not to treat it because it would be too hard on the family? They had to put Jill through spinal taps and all sorts of tests. She had chemotherapy, which caused her to lose her hair, made her sick, and caused her body to swell. But they did it because they had a chance to help their daughter. Of course it stressed their family physically, emotionally, and financially, but because of her treatment Jill has had no sign of cancer since 1993.

Why is it accepted to put a child through these treatments for a physical ailment, while a noninvasive, nonpainful treatment is discouraged for a child with autism because it's a neurological ailment? Jill was offered a chance at life by enduring the traumas of chemotherapy. Ryan was offered a chance at life by "enduring" one-on-one teaching in our home. Ryan was *not* poked with needles. He was *not* harmed physically. *Yes,* it has been stressful on our whole family. *Yes,* our lifestyles changed, but so did Jill's family's. Both children were offered hope for recovery, yet only one was encouraged to seek it. Do you think anyone told Dan and Lisa just to accept Jill for who she was? Why then, with a chance of recovery, were we told we should just accept Ryan for who he is? We *do* accept and love him for who he is, but we won't accept the autism without a fight.

It frustrates me that children with autism are expected to endure their illness instead of working to overcome it or to excel within it. There's a book titled *Don't Accept Me As I Am: Helping "Retarded" People to Excel.* That's what we want for our son. We want him to excel, and we're willing to do whatever that takes. The stresses that came with raising our son before we started ABA were much worse than the stresses from doing ABA. Now that he has changed so dramatically, the stresses have been reduced even more. ABA is not too hard on a family, but untreated, or *undertreated,* autism is.

"I Don't Like Seeing My Child Unhappy"

A well-respected therapist in our city doesn't believe in doing anything that might make a child scream or be unhappy. That sounds nice, but I wouldn't follow that with my daughter, so why should I do so with my son? If my daughter screams because she doesn't want a shot at the doctor's office, should I stop? Not if the shot will help her. If she screams because she wants a toy another child has, should I get her the toy to stop her from screaming? No way.

I once heard a coach described as a person who makes you do what you don't want to do in order to be everything you want to be. There were days Ryan didn't want to "work" and he would scream, but other days he ran eagerly into the therapy room. Those short spans of "unhappiness" were nothing compared to the joy I see in my son's eyes now as he plays, learns, and grows—as he has become more of who he can be.

"They Use Aversives on the Children"

This argument almost kept us from pursuing ABA. Rumors came at me from many directions saying that the therapists hit, spank, spray water in the children's faces, and use electric shock. I was appalled. My child wasn't going to be treated like an animal. The truth is, Dr. Lovaas used aversives at one time, but that was many years ago. If people tell you this, they have outdated information. Not once has Ryan been punished in any of these ways. In fact, the clinic we work with states unequivocally in its policy handbook regarding therapist conduct: "Under no circumstances should you ever use contingent aversives."[21]

"Kids Don't Really Learn"

Charles Hart in his book *A Parent's Guide to Autism*, which I found disappointing, downplays the possibility of recovery. Hart says, "It's impressive to see how normal some of these graduates appear in a first contact, but this impression fades when conversation drifts into new and unfamiliar areas. Generally, there's no real habilitation behind these well-learned social gestures."[22] If that's true, then why were eight of the nine recovered children in Dr. Lovaas's study no different in intelligence and adaptive behavior from other children their age? If they had learned merely social gestures, why did they continue to advance and succeed in school long after treatment stopped? I counter Mr. Hart's opinion with these nine recovered children and my own son. Had we chosen to accept Mr. Hart's opinions, we would not have pursued ABA with our son, and I shudder to think where Ryan might be as a result.

His book, in fact, compares ABA to horse training. He says you can teach a horse to count, but it doesn't understand what it's doing. It has merely learned to behave on cue so it can be rewarded. He mentions that therapists "motivate the student with candy because the tasks themselves have no motivating or functional value to the learner."[23]

How many of us have never used external motivation with our typically developing kids? Have you ever said to your daughter something like, "Honey, if you're good while we're at Aunt Mary's house, I'll take you to McDonald's"? Do you think being good at her aunt's house has any motivating or functional value to her? What the child wants is the reward of going to McDonald's. How about grades? They're an external reward used to motivate children to learn. Do most third graders really want to learn to multiply? Does a nine-year-old see a functional value in multiplication?

It's no different for our children with autism, except the external motivators need to be more frequent and tangible in the beginning. When Ryan was locked in his autism, he had no internal motivation except to get his physical needs met. We used a lot of immediate reinforcers while he needed them, but as he began to be reinforced by his accomplishments, we didn't need to use tangible rewards.

Mr. Hart also states that "once the therapists get results from certain rewards and punishments, the parents must continue the same techniques forever."[24] That was definitely not true in our case; we quit using food and prizes long ago, and our son continues to learn every day. The teachers at his school use no reinforcers beyond those given to all the kids—praise and encouragement. The children from Lovaas's follow-up study don't have people rewarding them with handfuls of M&M's, yet they have remained indistinguishable from their peers.

"It Isn't Fair to Give Children with Autism Such Extensive Services"

As many families seek funding through their school district or state governmental program, others protest, "There's only so much money in the pot. These children shouldn't be allowed more than their share." In my opinion this is shortsighted. Ryan's therapy has been costly, but now he needs relatively few services. I hope that in the near future he won't require any. Had intensive behavioral therapy been withheld from him, he would still be requiring extensive support at home and in school. If he graduated from school, he would need support in a job, living arrangements, and ongoing treatment. At the rate Ryan's progressing, he may not need any of these services, eventually saving the schools and government perhaps more than two million dollars! If only a small percentage of children recover because of early treatment, that would more than make up the funding.

Shirley Cohen, a professor of special education, says this about services typically offered to children two to four years old:

> The cost of intensive (one-to-one) services for every two-, three-, and four-year-old diagnosed as having autism or another pervasive developmental disorder would undoubtedly be extremely high. But the current, often feeble, attempts at intervention for this population are unlikely to reduce the even greater cost of maintaining a very large proportion of autistic individuals as seriously disabled throughout their lifetimes. It is cost-effective to help as many young autistic children as possible become part of the mainstream of society early in their lives, and we need intensive efforts to accomplish this.[25]

I also question the idea of "fair." Is fair giving each person the same amount? Or is fair giving each person what he needs? Let's say two people walk into a hospital with potentially life-threatening illnesses; one has asthma, the other has cancer. The person with asthma is given ongoing treatment that controls its effects, as well as assistance in learning how to live with the illness. The person with cancer is told he *might* overcome it with extensive treatment. However, although it's his best chance, it costs more than the asthma treatment, so out of fairness it won't be offered. Who would stand for that?

"Some Professionals Advise Against ABA"

It's always wise to consider the advice of professionals; just don't stop there. I've run into professionals with outdated or erroneous information about ABA, and had we taken their opinions at face value, we might never have pursued this life-changing therapy with Ryan. I've also found that information from other parents who are intricately involved in a treatment may be more pertinent than the counsel of a professional who hasn't experienced it.

How Do I Get Started?

Hopefully, you've already done the first two things by putting your name on waiting lists for a professional consultant and videotaping your child. Appendix A lists providers I'm aware of. Please note that inclusion on the list doesn't mean I recommend them or their services. You will need to diligently check out the providers and decide for yourself.

Next I suggest you purchase some books, especially *Let Me Hear Your Voice* by Catherine Maurice and at least one how-to book on ABA treatment, which could include *Behavioral Intervention for Young Children with Autism: A Manual for Parents and Professionals,* edited by Catherine Maurice, Gina Green, and

Stephen C. Luce, or *A Work in Progress: Behavior Management Strategies and a Curriculum for Intensive Behavioral Treatment of Autism,* edited by John McEachin and Ron Leaf. These will get you started.

Two others you might consider are *Teaching Developmentally Disabled Children: The ME Book* and *Teach Me Language.* Dr. Lovaas wrote the first book, commonly known as "The ME Book," in 1981. Although some of the information is outdated— at the time he still promoted using aversives—it is helpful. *Teach Me Language,* written by Sabrina Freeman and Lorelei Dake, helps in language development and is designed for visual learners who are implementing ABA.[26] However, if your child doesn't speak yet, you can postpone buying this one.

While you're waiting for the books to come in, try to find other families in your area who are already running a program. Ask them what provider they use and if they're satisfied. See if they will allow you to observe one of their sessions or a video of their workshop. You can learn a lot from watching firsthand.

You can also extend your networking to other parents on the Internet. There are many support groups available at no cost. Just e-mail the list "owner" and ask to join. The ME-LIST is designed especially for parents and professionals implementing ABA. To learn more about the ME-LIST and how to join it, go to the ME-LIST home page at http://www2.addr.com/~me-list/.

Whenever a person writes a message with a question or comment, it's sent to everyone on that particular list. From your question you may receive insights from people around the world. What a tremendous resource!

There are many autism lists available, but be cautious about how many you join. Each list may send you thirty to fifty e-mails a day. I flip through the list daily, reading only the subject title. If I'm interested, I keep it. If not, I delete it without reading it. Otherwise, I could spend hours a day just keeping up on my mail. Much *can* be learned, but protect your time. There is much to do elsewhere.

While you're on the Internet, you may want to check out a site called The Recovery Zone at http://pages.prodigy.net/damianporcari/recovery.htm. This excellent site provides information about starting, running, and funding an ABA program.

A new Web site has been formed to collect information on running an ABA program. Parents and providers are asked to add to the database in the five areas of ABA—drills, resources, on-line support, geographical information, and ABA employment positions—so others can benefit. This site can be found at http://www.addr.com/~me-list/databases. Being a new list, the database is small, but with the large number of people who subscribe to the ME-LIST, it should grow quickly.

Also focus on finding two to five therapists. Be prepared with a written agreement and the pay rate before you seek applicants. Many families pay a flat hourly rate for therapy and half that rate for training or weekly meetings.

Remember to keep your receipts from everything you buy for therapy because you may be able to deduct the cost from your taxes if you don't find funding elsewhere. An accounting program can help keep track of these expenses as well as your therapists' payroll.

Most important, start the process right away. If you're fortunate enough to secure a consultant quickly, I suggest you don't begin therapy until you've had your workshop. This prevents you from doing drills inaccurately and having to take steps backward to correct them. However, if securing a consultant will require more than a few weeks, it's better to start targeting the autism with some of the beginning drills than to lose valuable time. One of the how-to books will give you numerous programs to begin with.

What Should I Look for in an ABA Consultant?

Since there is no standard certification around the country, you need to be careful who you hire. Unfortunately, some who call themselves consultants have received little or no training in ABA or their training is outdated.

Although we've employed male and female consultants, I've used feminine pronouns in the list of questions that I suggest as guidelines for your selection.

1. What is her definition of ABA?
2. How close is her therapy to that of Dr. Lovaas? In what ways is it different? (I would be wary of anyone who says she combines the best of all the therapies. Does she have data that proves her combination works?)
3. Where was she trained in ABA? How long and with whom? (Get names and numbers of those who trained her and call them.)
4. Did she have formal ABA training at a university? Which one? What degree did she receive?
5. How much experience has she had in ABA?
6. How many children has she worked with using the ABA program? (Get a list of family references.)
7. What age children has she worked with?
8. What were their behaviors like? What kinds of difficult behaviors has she had experience with? How does she deal with them?
9. What progress did the children in her care make?

APPLIED BEHAVIOR ANALYSIS

10. What is her average length of employment with one family?
11. Does she believe that some children can recover? Has she ever had a child recover through her program?
12. Has she had experience with children at different levels of progress? What levels?
13. How is she keeping up-to-date on treatment programs and techniques?

What Should I Look for in a Therapist?

These are the main things I look for when hiring a new therapist.

1. Why is she interested? (If she's doing this to make money, she won't last long.)
   Why does she want to do this type of therapy versus another job?
   Will she be satisfied with what you can pay?
   What is her career goal?
   Is she interested in children?
   Has she worked with children in the past?
   Has she worked with disabled children before?
2. Is she available?
   Can she fill the shifts you have open?
   Is she willing to work at least six to ten hours a week?
   Does she have plans for any long vacations or other commitments?
   Is she willing to commit for at least six months?
   Does she have reliable transportation to your home?
3. Is she a learner?
   Is she willing to learn new techniques that are unfamiliar to her?
   Can she follow precise instructions and do them repetitively?

Is she willing to read a book and go to training workshops?

4. Are there any reasons not to hire her?

Has she ever been fired from a job? Why?

Has she ever been convicted of a felony or serious crime?

When you decide on a therapist, have a contract ready for her to examine and sign. This makes everything clear between both parties and will save you future anxiety.

In your contract I recommend you cover these things.

1. A description of services
2. Procedure for missing a session
3. The number of hours per week she will be working
4. The length of time (months) to which she will commit
5. Where services will take place
6. The pay scale and the varying rates for therapy, meetings, and training, if applicable
7. Performance review periods and pay raises
8. Travel expenses—will they be covered and how much?
9. Taxes. It's best for therapists to be responsible for their own federal, state, and Social Security taxes. Since the therapist is working for your family as an independent contractor, you'll need to provide her with a 1099 each year covering all payments.
10. Confidentiality about therapy and your child

How *Do* I Pay for It?

The answer to this question alone could fill a book. Since I'm not a lawyer, I can't advise you on every aspect of getting your program funded. What I can offer are possible sources, basic strategies, and directions to go for help. I encourage you to actively seek funding even though it isn't easy to obtain.

As I've said regarding so many issues, first contact other parents in your area and ask them how they fund their programs. Each state has different policies and procedures, and even individual counties or school districts can vary greatly.

Whichever route you pursue, consider these tips.

1. Be well informed. You will need to have accurate information about ABA: what it is, how it works, and its success. Make copies of as many research articles as you can find to give to each person you're trying to influence. They may not know anything about ABA, and they first must be convinced that it is necessary and beneficial.

2. Show videos of your child before treatment began and after you started. A picture can speak more powerfully than words.

3. Analyze the cost for your child. How much will it cost them to fund your program, and how much might it save them in the long run? Know what you're asking for. Do your research ahead of time so you can present exactly how much money you will need and for how long.

4. Get a good lawyer who has experience in obtaining funding for ABA programs. You will need his expertise.

5. Be thorough and persistent!

Avenues to Pursue

Medical Assistance: The first place to look is Medical Assistance (MA). Some states will pay the wages of all the therapists and consultants through the MA card, but this is rare. Find out if your state has any programs like waivers or wraparound programs that will cover expenses. They are usually not publicized, so ask around.

Schools: Since schools are required to educate all children no matter how severe their disability, you probably have your best chance here. Sometimes schools are offered grants to try alternative programs, but most schools don't take advantage of them. Some schools have been forced to implement ABA programs for other families, but they probably won't tell you about it. You will need to initiate the discussion and be persistent in fighting for what your child needs. If schools say no to parents requesting ABA services, many parents, unfortunately, are willing to accept this answer without a fight. Don't give up! Challenge the school and actively fight for what your child needs. If you're persistent, "no" may not be the final word.

Insurance: Although unusual, funding from insurance companies can happen. Ours was rejected because our therapists were not certified medical practitioners.

Grants: Sometimes major companies will offer grants to help fund programs. Usually they give them only to organizations, not individuals. A few stores offer discounts or donations of materials if you take the time to ask.

College students: Traditionally, parents have hired college students and paid them for their work. Try placing fliers on bulletin boards around the school, especially in the education or psychology schools. The flier should include your child's picture and basic information about the job, its pay, and your phone number. The best times to get new people are at the start of each semester and right before summer.

However, another possibility is to ask professors at a local university if the students can receive college credit for performing therapy. When we started our program, we staffed entirely with volunteers who received credit in a psychology class for their hands-on experience. Because they were receiving credit, they weren't allowed compensation.

Volunteers: Family, friends, or church members can also be part of your therapy team. Although this sounds like a great solution, I would be cautious. Volunteers aren't always dependable or long-lasting therapists. You don't want to spend all your time training new people when volunteers change their minds. If you know someone will really commit to your team for several months, then pursue it, but make sure he or she realizes what the job entails before going into training.

Parent-administered therapy: Parents can perform therapy, but the hours necessary for your child make it difficult for one or two people to handle. You will probably need additional help along the way, especially if you have other children. Keep in mind that your child needs you to be a parent as well as a therapist, but only you can determine the proper balance of the two.

"Funding the Behavior Program: Legal Strategies for Parents": Mark Williamson wrote a chapter in *Behavioral Intervention for Young Children with Autism* that gives three outlines for obtaining funding, as well as a list of offices available to parents in each state.

The Internet: Two Web sites, http://www.feat.org/FEATorg/FeatLinks.htm and http://trainland.tripod.com/legal.htm, list links to other helpful sites and include several autism-related legal sites. These may be good places to start your research. One such link is found at http://www.mayerslaw.com/. Sponsored by lawyer Gary S. Mayerson, this site offers valuable information regarding statutes and court cases related to autism.

Tax Deductions

Document everything you spend. Keep receipts, and log your payments to your therapists. If you secure funding, you'll need this documentation for reimbursement. If you don't, you may be able to write it off your taxes. You will probably need verification of your child's autism as well as a prescription from a doctor for forty hours a week of ABA therapy. You will definitely need your 1099s for all your therapists and a signed contract from each, stating that they are responsible for their own taxes. If you are well prepared, you may be able to deduct your expenses for therapist wages, books, reinforcers, office supplies, and consultations but only the amount that exceeds 7.5 percent of your gross income. Because this gets complicated, I recommend you find a good accountant to work with you.

A Final Reminder

In the midst of all the logistics and research and potential lifestyle changes, it's easy to lose sight of the goal. *Every* child should have the opportunity to receive the treatment that has been proven to offer the best chance for combating this disorder: a professionally run, intensive ABA program. Our children have only so much time and we have limited resources, so we cannot afford to waste time or money. Every time I watch Ryan laugh and play; every time he looks me in the eye and tells me what is on his heart; every time I take him to school, knowing that he is learning just like the other kids, I am grateful for what ABA has done to rescue our son.

Chapter 7

Dietary Intervention

One thing that keeps coming back time after time...
is the central role of the gut in this disorder.

DR. ANDREW WAKEFIELD, GASTROENTEROLOGIST

Within a month of Ryan's diagnosis some friends of ours, Dave and Anne Frahm, sent us a stack of information on how diet and nutrition can play a major role in treating autism. *Yeah, right,* I thought. *Autism is a neurological disorder, so how could food make a difference?* I glanced at the list of foods Ryan should be eating—things like fruits, raw vegetables, fish, and brown rice—and compared it to the list of foods to avoid—wheat, corn, processed or fried foods, chocolate, and sugar, to name a few. Of course Ryan ate only foods on the "bad" list. "Even if I thought these foods would help," I told Roger, "Ryan wouldn't eat any of them! I'm sure Dave and Anne mean well, but they just don't understand."

Although I dismissed the idea, over the next couple of years I was bombarded by parents who had changed their children's diet and said it really helped. They were now shopping at health-food stores, making special breads without wheat, and using a variety of milk substitutes. To be honest, I thought these people were a little fanatical.

It wasn't until I read a book by Dr. William Shaw, titled

Biological Treatments for Autism and PDD, that I began to take the diet idea seriously. But I wasn't going to radically change our eating habits for something that *might* help. I needed to *know* it was necessary.

Why a Special Diet?

In a healthy body, the digestive tract takes complex foods and breaks them down into substances the body can absorb and utilize. As the food travels through the gastrointestinal system, the enzymes in the digestive juices convert the food into a simpler form. To put it simply, food starts out similar to a long chain of paper clips. Through digestion, they are unhooked and left as single paper clips, which is the form desired for the intestines to absorb and deliver nutrients to the body. During digestion, protein—which is made up of building blocks called amino acids—is broken down into the single amino acids.[1]

Many children with autism have trouble digesting certain proteins called gluten (which is found in wheat, barley, oats, and rye, to name a few) and casein (found in dairy products). Gluten and casein contain certain combinations of amino acids that are very difficult for the body's digestive system to digest or break down completely into single amino acids. Structures remain in the form of a chain of several amino acids called peptides. If proteins are like long chains of paper clips, then peptides are like shorter chains. Some digestion has taken place, but the chain has not completely broken down into amino acids.

A second problem then occurs. These peptides get out of the intestine and into the bloodstream, where they shouldn't be. The term *leaky gut* is used to describe this condition where the intestinal wall can't keep the contents of the intestine separate from the bloodstream.[2] Dr. P. D'Eufemia found that children with autism have a much higher rate of leaky gut. "An altered intestinal permeability [leaky gut] was found in 9 out of the 21 (43%) autistic patients, but in *none* of the 40 controls."[3] In a healthy gut, a few peptides may escape, but they are recognized as foreign and the body's immune system can deal with them. In a leaky gut, many peptides enter the bloodstream and cause harm.

What Kind of Harm?

The structures or peptides remaining after digestion of casein and gluten react at certain sites in the brain called opioid receptors, named so because these sites are where opiate drugs such as morphine act. The internal chemicals that react at the opioid receptors in the brain are called endorphins. These peptide structures from the diet have several names, one of which is *opioids*. Dr. Karl Reichelt, Paul Shattock, and others have found a relationship between gluten and casein peptides and an excess of opioids in the central nervous system.[4] In fact, the names of these peptides are *gluteomorphin* and *caseomorphin,* derived by combining the words *gluten* or *casein* and *morphin* (for morphine). If these peptides aren't breaking down into amino acids *and* they are getting out of the intestine, then when they reach the brain, they act like heroin and morphine![5] As we would expect, these opioids may radically affect behavior, cognitive abilities, emotions, pain thresholds, and even sound sensitivity. They also react "with areas of the brain such as the temporal lobes, which are involved in speech and auditory integration."[6]

In experimental studies, opiate drugs such as morphine have been found to bind to brain opioid receptors, and this binding leads to decreased glucose (sugar) utilization and decreased metabolic rate.[7] In other words, structures that bind to opioid receptors in the brain slow the brain down. One consistent factor in autistic children is that the brain is slowed down (metabolically less active, as shown by decreased blood flow, especially in speech areas).[8]

Second, when there is a leaky gut, proteins from dairy, wheat, or any number of other foods may be absorbed through the intestinal wall. When these peptides enter the bloodstream, the body's immune system may kick in. If there is an allergic reaction, it will occur within one minute to two hours with symptoms that include vomiting, diarrhea, skin rashes, headaches, or a runny nose. Serious allergies may be life-threatening if the reaction causes the airways to swell.[9]

Children with autism commonly have food sensitivities as well as true food allergies. Sometimes a sensitivity is referred to as a delayed-onset food allergy since the reactions can occur later. A sensitivity often occurs within the first twenty-four hours after the offending food is eaten, but it can occur up to seventy-two hours later. Gluten and casein foods are two of the most common offenders and the only ones that have an opiate effect, but children may have sensitivities to many different foods.

Food sensitivities have a variety of symptoms, including "physical and behavioral problems, such as headaches, stomachaches, feeling of nausea, bed-wetting, appearing 'spaced out,' stuttering, excessive whining and crying, sleeping problems, hyperactivity, aggression, sound sensitivity, temper tantrums, fatigue, depression, intestinal problems, muscle aches in the legs, ear infections and possibly seizures."[10]

Common physical signs of food sensitivities include pink or dark circles or puffiness under the eyes, red ears or cheeks after eating the offending food, excessive sweating, stomachaches, and headaches, although all of these may be caused by other things as well.

Can what our children eat really affect their brains? Dr. James Braly, a specialist in food allergies and sensitivities, says that the gut is now being called the second brain. The neurotransmitters in the brain have receptors in the digestive tract, and there are receptors in the brain for the hormones found in the gut. Not only can the gut affect the brain, but the two "communicate" with each other all the time![11]

Testing Ryan

Once we were convinced a special diet might be worthwhile, we needed to know if it was necessary for Ryan, so we proceeded with several tests.

First we tested Ryan for food sensitivities using the ELISA (Enzyme Linked Immunosorbent Assay) test. We weren't surprised to learn that Ryan reacted to fifteen foods, including wheat, barley, rye, oat, cheese, and milk. This showed he was having an immune reaction to these foods and they should be eliminated from his diet.

Shortly afterward we did a test for peptides in Ryan's urine to find out if he was affected by excess opioids, and we did a blood test for the levels of antibodies against gluten and casein. As we expected, Ryan's urinary peptides and his antibodies were abnormally elevated. With a normal range being 0–100 antibodies against gluten or casein, Ryan tested at 3710 against gluten and 3371 against casein. These tests proved to us that Ryan had excess opioids in his system as well as an immune reaction to gluten and casein. We were certain we needed to change his diet and were anxious to start, but our doctor recommended we first test for celiac disease.

With celiac disease the gluten can directly damage the intestinal lining, causing many symptoms, including gastrointestinal distress, weight loss, slow growth, seizures, and malabsorption.[12]

For years Ryan had sporadic diarrhea, but recently he had begun losing weight. Over six months he had lost about six pounds—quite a lot for a boy who weighed less than fifty pounds to begin with—and it was suspected that he might have a malabsorption problem as well. Because of this, we needed to check for celiac disease before we began taking away gluten, because once we started the diet, the celiac disease tests wouldn't be valid.

The first test for celiac disease is a blood test that checks certain IgA antibodies. Antibodies, also called immunoglobulins (Ig), are large molecules made by cells of the immune system that can then bind to anything foreign to the body. This binding makes it easier for other cells of the immune system to attack and kill foreign invaders. These antibodies come in five classes based on size and location in the body. IgA is a class of antibodies that is secreted across the intestinal wall.

Our doctor told us that if Ryan's blood test came back positive, he had an 85 percent chance of having celiac disease, but the only conclusive test would be a small biopsy on his intestine. For us the blood test would be inconclusive since we knew that Ryan had an IgA deficiency, which is common with autism. Therefore we had a gastroenterologist perform a biopsy, the results of which came out negative for celiac.

Medical Testing for Your Child

If you decide to test your child, you may want to begin with a urinary peptide test, a blood antibody test against gluten and casein, and possibly a celiac panel or biopsy if your doctor believes it's necessary. Some doctors recommend doing a food sensitivity profile at the same time so all offending foods can be removed. Others prefer to delay testing for food sensitivities because once you remove gluten and casein, the gut may begin to heal and no longer be as "leaky." As fewer foods escape from the intestine, the number of food sensitivities decreases.[13] On the other hand, many physicians don't encourage a food sensitivity test, believing either that delayed-onset allergies don't have any impact on a person's health or that they don't even exist.

Keep in mind, testing for food allergies or sensitivities isn't perfect. A negative test result doesn't guarantee those foods are acceptable to your child's body, nor does a positive result prove that the food is causing a reaction. Tests can be good indicators, but you can be certain only by removing offending foods and observing what happens.

To do this, eliminate any suspected foods for a minimum of two weeks, and if you notice positive results, add the foods back one at a time and watch for a reaction. I've read that if your child eats the suspect food on an empty stomach after having been off it for two weeks, you might see a reaction more quickly and clearly, perhaps as quickly as within fifteen minutes to an hour.[14] However, one ingestion of an offending food may not be enough to cause a reaction. For example, I may remove all grapes and grape products from Ryan's diet for at least two weeks. Then I feed him grapes with his breakfast, wait a few hours and give him some more for his snack or with his lunch. I may even continue to give him grapes throughout the day. If he doesn't react to the grapes after being exposed to them several times, he probably doesn't have a problem with them.

As documentation of the results, I suggest you make a chart of your child's behaviors before, during, and after the elimination test and rate him on each one daily. These behaviors may include self-stimulation (hand flapping, spinning, rocking), aggression, echolalia (repeating phrases directly), hyperactivity, seizures, or any other problem behavior for your child. Rate each behavior to see if changes occur after foods are eliminated or reintroduced.

This elimination test will *not* work as quickly for gluten and casein, since the body may take up to three weeks to rid itself of casein and up to nine months to remove all traces of gluten. Therefore, I recommend starting with just the gluten-free/casein-free (GF/CF) diet for several months to target the opioid problem and the sensitivity to gluten and casein. Then expand the diet to eliminate other possibly offensive foods. *It's extremely important to adhere to the diet strictly, or the results will be flawed.* In some children even minute amounts of these proteins can have dramatic negative effects.

This kind of testing is often difficult to do since a child may have *many* food sensitivities. If that is true for your child, then removing only one or two offending foods may show a little benefit, but you may not see the full benefit until you remove most of the problem foods. For example, let's say a child has possible reactions to peanuts, soy, and green beans. If I remove the peanuts, I may see only a little improvement. However, if I remove peanuts and soy, I might see even more benefit. Unfortunately, some people, seeing only a slight benefit from removing one food (peanuts), reintroduce that food before removing the next one (soy). That is why testing is beneficial. Ryan tested sensitive to fifteen foods. This knowledge allowed us to remove all the foods for a while and then add them back into his diet one by one to see if he had a reaction.

The Gluten-Free/Casein-Free Diet

Many different diets are recommended for children with autism, some of which overlap, but parents generally start with the gluten-free/casein-free diet. That is the diet we began with, although we later supplemented it with portions of other diets as well.

What Does the GF/CF Diet Involve?

How do you eliminate gluten and casein from your child's foods? To avoid casein, your child can eat *no* dairy products, including milk, cream, ice cream, cream cheese, sour cream, cottage cheese, yogurt, frozen yogurt, whey, and cheese. Whether butter has casein or not is debatable. Some sources say butter is all right since it's only the fat of the milk and therefore has no milk protein in it,[15] while other sources say only clarified butter, called ghee, should be used.

Foods that contain gluten include wheat, barley, barley malt, malt, rye, oats, oatmeal, bulgar, durum, spelt, triticale, semolina, and couscous.

Some products, like baking powder, soy sauce, bouillon cubes, vegetable or modified food starch, sauces, and sauce mixes, *may* have gluten in them, so it's best to read labels carefully or to buy products that state they are gluten-free or casein-free. As I began reading labels, I was surprised how often gluten and casein turn up on the ingredients list. Some canned tuna has "casein" listed as an ingredient, while one brand lists "vegetable broth," which may be made from wheat.

Even though it's not listed on the package, gluten is often used as filler in spices, vitamins, and medications. Products like raisins may come in canisters dusted with flour to keep them from sticking. The flour isn't listed as an ingredient, yet it could contaminate the food with gluten. To play it safe, I buy raisins in a bag. If you have any doubt, call or write the company to verify if a product is gluten-free.

What's Left to Eat?

At first it may seem no foods are acceptable, but you'll be surprised. Bread can be made from a variety of alternative flours, including rice, tapioca, potato starch, corn, and soy. *Most* sources say that quinoa, amaranth, and buckwheat are gluten-free and are therefore acceptable for a GF/CF diet, though some parents I've met have their doubts and avoid these items.

Fruits, vegetables, meat, and fish are all free of gluten and casein. However, you can't buy fish sticks or chicken nuggets because they're coated with wheat flour. Eggs, beans, lentils, and nuts are allowed on a GF/CF diet if your child isn't sensitive to them.

For snacks Ryan likes potato and tortilla chips, popcorn, and crackers called Rice Thins produced by Sesmark, which are made with rice flour, safflower oil, and salt. There are even gluten-free and casein-free cookies available in most health-food stores. Ryan likes the ones made by Pamela's, as well as the gluten-free variety of Frookies cookies.

What If My Child Eats *Only* Foods with Gluten and Casein?

This was true of Ryan, and to be honest, I was fearful. Since Ryan was already skinny and losing weight, I was afraid that if I took him off gluten and casein, he would starve. If the opioid theory is true, then it was logical Ryan was eating only gluten- and casein-filled foods because the opioids made Ryan crave them. Ryan ate no fruits or vegetables except peas and would drink no juice or milk. I was using milk in his morning pancakes so I knew he was getting some calcium, but if I took away that milk, he wouldn't have any. To my surprise, when I replaced the gluten- and casein-filled foods with alternatives, he didn't struggle as much as I had expected. In fact, he started eating new foods! I also came to real-ize that calcium is found in many foods besides dairy products, including green leafy vegetables, broccoli, beans, and tofu. However, if your child will not eat any calcium-rich foods, it is important to provide him with a calcium supplement.

Is Taking Away Only Gluten or Casein Enough?

It has been said that infants who show signs of autism probably react more to casein, while children who develop normally then regress around the eighteen-month mark tend to react more to gluten.[16] A book titled *Fighting for Tony* tells the story of a boy who was diagnosed with autism but, in actuality, had cerebral allergy to milk. When milk was removed from his diet, he began to respond, and eventually he recovered fully. However, this is not the norm. Most kids will need to eliminate both gluten and casein since their peptides are very similar.[17]

How Do You Start a GF/CF Diet?

Changing your child's diet may seem daunting, but once you're informed and prepared, the process isn't so overwhelming.

First, make a list of what your child likes to eat and drink, and try to find replacements. If your child drinks milk, you may want to start with this. To ease the transition, begin by diluting cow's milk with a bit of a milk substitute. Over a week, increase the sub-stitute until you have only the substitute. If your child can see the container, rinse out a milk carton and fill it with the alternative.

Many milk alternatives are available, including rice, soy, almond, and potato milk. Be aware that some milk substitutes contain gluten, so you need to read the ingredients carefully. We use a product called Vance's Darifree, which is a potato milk. It has only three grams of sugar compared to rice milk, which has fifteen, and it has as much calcium as cow's milk. I buy it in powdered form and use it to make bread, muffins, and pudding. At first you may want to purchase several kinds of milk alternatives to determine which you and your child prefer. If you can find at least two that you like, I suggest rotating them, since it's unwise to eat any food *every* day.

For main foods Ryan liked chicken nuggets, corn dogs, pizza, peanut butter and jelly sandwiches, spaghetti, breakfast cereals, pancakes, and waffles. Lisa Lewis's book *Special Diets for Special Kids* gave me replacements for most of these, with the first recipe in her book being gluten-free chicken nuggets. I tried making them and was thrilled when Ryan loved them. I now make about five pounds at a time and freeze them individually on a cookie sheet before storing them in a freezer container. This way I can pull out a portion to microwave for a quick lunch.

Though many hot dogs are GF/CF, to avoid the sugar, nitrates, and preservatives, we buy a natural hot dog made with only turkey or chicken, sea salt, mustard, and spices. Since they use no preservatives, they need to be frozen until you're ready to use them. I find they taste much better if they're boiled in water rather than cooked in a microwave. To create corn dogs, I begin with a bag of gluten-free pancake and baking mix by Arrowhead Mills. I follow the directions for pancakes, then put a hot dog on a stick, dip it in the batter, and fry it for a few minutes on each side. They look like triangles, but they taste good and Ryan will eat them.

Spaghetti can be easily replaced with rice or corn noodles. Spaghetti sauces are usually fine as they are, though most of the popular brands of sauce have sugar added.

Pizza can be acceptable if you make your own crust and use a cheese substitute. To my knowledge, only one cheese substitute,

Soymage, doesn't have casein. The rest add casein or caseinate to improve the texture. In my opinion, Soymage tastes noticeably different from cheese when eaten by itself, but on pizza or in a casserole it blends pretty well. The secret for pizza is to use a *lot* of toppings. The cheese makes the pizza look right, but the toppings make it taste right. We found a great recipe in Beth and Andy Crowell's book *Dietary Intervention As a Therapy in the Treatment of Autism and Related Developmental Disorders.* It doesn't use yeast, it's easy to make, and it can be frozen for a quick meal later on. If yeast isn't a problem, the Gluten-Free Pantry sells a pizza crust mix that tastes great and is easy to make. (See the end of the chapter for the phone number and address.)

As you find replacement foods or recipes that your child likes, introduce them one at a time. Start by replacing a food he likes—but not one of his favorites—and work your way from there. Save his favorite food until last so you've had time to find a new favorite before you have to take the old one away.

As you begin your transition, you'll need to check everything in your kitchen, reading every label for gluten or casein. You may be surprised at all the items that will no longer be acceptable. Take these out of your kitchen so you won't be tempted to use them.

Once you get a special cookbook, take time to glance through it. I started by choosing five recipes that sounded good, including one bread recipe, and wrote down all the ingredients. Then I took my list to the health-food store and asked them to help me find what I needed because I was clueless. What in the world was xanthan gum? I learned that gluten makes bread sticky so it doesn't fall apart. Without gluten, alternative flours become crumbly, so usually a teaspoon or two of xanthan gum is added to bind the flour. Now xanthan gum is a staple in our house.

In addition to new recipes, some of your current recipes may be adapted to avoid gluten and casein. Bette Hagman, author of three GF cookbooks, recommends a combination flour as a direct replacement for wheat flour. She combines two parts white-rice flour, two-thirds part potato-starch flour, and one-third part tapioca flour. This can then be used, cup for cup, as a substitution for regular wheat flour. She also has a recipe in her book *The Gluten-Free Gourmet Cooks Fast and Healthy* for creamed soups that can be used in your favorite, tried-and-true family recipes.

Once you've chosen some foods to try, plan a menu for the day or even a week. Because this diet requires more planning, especially initially, it's better to think about your menu ahead of time than to scramble at five o'clock, wondering what you'll serve.

What About Eating Out?
It's not easy, but it is possible. We still go to McDonald's, but we order the hamburger patty in a box without the bun, having brought our own bun from home. A company named Cybros makes a dinner roll out of rice, which is smaller than a hamburger bun but works nicely.

French fries are usually all right as long as the restaurants don't coat the potatoes in wheat flour or fry them in the same oil they use for breaded foods. For safety's sake, ask the manager of the restaurant.

Salads are okay, but leave off the croutons, cheese, and most salad dressings. Read the package closely to see if it's acceptable.

Most hot dogs are free of gluten and casein, but they're full of nitrates and other additives and may have fillers that contain gluten.

Broiled chicken and fish are good choices, but stay away from breaded or marinated entrées. Plain vegetables, baked potatoes, and rice provide good side dishes, but if you are removing all butter, you'll need to verify that the restaurant used no butter in preparing them. Be sure to stay away from pasta and sandwiches.

When we travel, we've learned where we can eat and what we can order. We also go prepared with additional food in our suitcases. If you're careful, you need not be trapped at home because of a special diet.

What About the Rest of the Family?

You have to decide if your whole family will follow this new diet or just your child with autism. To a large extent our whole family follows the diet, but we eat certain foods that Ryan doesn't like anyway. Since our daughter eats yogurt and Ryan doesn't, we still buy regular yogurt. Ryan loves ice cream, so we buy only a nondairy ice-cream replacement. Recently we got an ice-cream maker so we can make ice cream at home with our potato milk. Sorbet is also nice and easy to make, but Ryan refuses anything with fruit in it.

If your whole family doesn't follow the diet, be careful that your child doesn't get into the forbidden foods and isn't given any by a baby-sitter or relative. And don't overlook subtle things, like allowing crumbs of wheat bread to accidentally mix with his GF/CF bread if you share a cutting board.

What Are the Benefits?

With all that a GF/CF diet requires, you may be wondering if it's worth the effort. No one claims that a GF/CF diet will cure children of their autism, but most of us can expect to see positive results. Some children have even had their diagnosis of autism removed after going on this diet, but this dramatic response usually occurs in children younger than two or three.[18]

In her book *Special Diets for Special Kids,* Lisa Lewis shares how her son Sam improved greatly after removing gluten and casein from his diet. His aggressive behaviors decreased, and the school was sending home wonderful reports. Then one day Lisa accidentally fed him a piece of wheat toast, and within an hour he was "out of control."[19]

Franke, a seven-year-old boy with autism, has been on a GF/CF diet for three years. His parents directly attribute this diet for several improvements. During the first four years of his life, Franke developed an ear infection every six to eight weeks. Since he began the diet, he not only has stopped having chronic ear infections, but his response to colds and infections has improved as well. His seizures seem less frequent and less intense, although his parents often see signs of seizures during the night immediately following his eating any gluten or casein.

Franke's autistic symptoms seemed to have lessened as well. His eye contact, his ability to attend to tasks, and his receptive language have gone up, while his aggression and self-stimulatory behaviors have gone down. His sleeping patterns have improved, and his extreme energy levels have become more normal, as have his responses to pain and sound.

The diet has not cured Franke; he would still be classified in the moderate to severe range. But it has allowed him to be happier, calmer, and healthier and to integrate better at home and at school.

Dr. Sidney Baker poses this question about a special diet: "When you have lots of other things to think about, should you change the diet of a child who has decided to live on French fries, smooshed bagels, chocolate milk, pretzels, Twinkies, and diet Coke, rejecting all alternatives with an iron will? Yup! And when you get over the hump, you are likely to be rewarded with changes in sleep, behavior, attention, and 'sensitivity' that make the struggle worth it."[20]

When you start the diet, you may see positive results right away;[21] usually some improvements are noticeable within three months. However, since the kidneys can store these peptides for a long time, it may take as long as a year before you see the full benefits.[22] Be patient. It would be a shame to go to the trouble to start this diet and end it just shy of the benefits. If, on the other hand, you don't see results by the end of a year, your child may not need to be on the diet, and you can go back to your regular eating habits.

What Reactions May Occur?
When your child begins a GF/CF diet or is taken off other offending foods, his behavior may regress at first. Don't despair, because this could be a good sign. If the gluten and casein are affecting your child like opiates, then he may suffer withdrawal symptoms for one to three weeks.[23] In essence, children with excess opioids are addicted to the gluten and casein even though they react so negatively to it. Therefore, it may be wise to wean your child from gluten and casein gradually over several weeks. You may want to start by removing casein first, followed a week or two later by removing wheat, then oats, barley, and the remaining gluten items. Once you've removed *all* the gluten and casein from the diet, wait several additional weeks before expecting results.

Other Types of Diets

Besides the gluten-free/casein-free diet, you may want to consider other diets as well, which are not mutually exclusive.

Feingold's Diet

Dr. Ben Feingold is best known for his book *Why Your Child Is Hyperactive*, in which he suggests hyperactivity is caused by dyes, artificial colorings, preservatives, and other additives in our food. He recommends removing salicylates from your child's diet since they are peptidase inhibitors. Salicylates are found naturally in some fruits and vegetables, including tomatoes, cucumbers, apples, apricots, berries, cherries, grapes, oranges, plums, and tangerines, as well as in almonds.[24]

The Feingold Association advocates a two-stage approach. In stage one remove all the items with salicylates. Then after four to six weeks reintroduce, one at a time, each food containing salicylates to determine if there is a reaction. If there is no reaction, bring that food back into your child's diet. The dyes, additives, and preservatives should never be brought back into the diet, however.

We haven't followed this diet completely, but we have removed food colorings and preservatives from Ryan's diet. We recently discovered a strong connection between red food dye and Ryan's behavior. When Ryan began his anti-yeast treatment, he started taking a medication called nystatin in pill form to help kill the yeast. Since it's better to begin gradually, we started him on half a pill daily, then increased it slowly until he was taking eight a day. From the beginning we noticed more hyperactivity, aggression, and self-stimulation than we had seen in a year. After two months with the behaviors not improving, it finally dawned on me. The pills were coated in a red dye! I'd heard that red dye in particular can cause negative reactions in children, but I had forgotten. That day I began washing off the dye before I gave him the pills. Within a week of eliminating the dye, we saw a much calmer and more attentive child. Later, we switched to filling capsules with powdered nystatin. Based on Ryan's behavior, I'm convinced the red dye was the culprit.

Ketogenic Diet

The ketogenic diet is designed for individuals who suffer from seizures. This diet began seventy years ago when some doctors at Johns Hopkins Hospital gave patients high-fat, low-protein, and low-carbohydrate food in order to control their seizures.[25] In 1996 Dr. John M. Freeman, Millicent T. Kelly, and Jennifer B. Freeman published a book titled *The Epilepsy Diet Treatment: An Introduction to the Ketogenic Diet* that again brought this diet into the public eye.

Fat is the focus of this diet because when the body burns fat, it creates ketone bodies, which are suspected to inhibit seizures. Dr. Freeman points out that though this diet has not been studied in a scientifically controlled test, there have been "less rigorous studies done over many years that suggest that 30% of children treated with the ketogenic diet will have their seizures well controlled.... Half of those children will be seizure-free. An additional 30–40% will have their seizure frequency decreased by more than 50%."[26]

Although this sounds promising, the diet shouldn't be followed without the close supervision of a neurologist. The diet needs to be tailored precisely for each child, according to his or her age, height, and weight, and it must be carefully overseen by a knowledgeable professional.

Anti-Yeast Diet

Many children with autism struggle with yeast (Candida albicans) overgrowth in their system. We'll look more closely at understanding, testing, and treating this in the next chapter, but let's look at the diet now.

Dr. Bruce Semon is a child psychiatrist, nutritionist, father of a son with autism, and coauthor of the book *Feast Without Yeast*. Through treating his son and many others, he has come to believe that Candida overgrowth can be effectively treated. Along with antifungal medication, Dr. Semon recommends a four-stage diet.[27] The first stage eliminates barley malt (found in many cereals), vinegar (found in most condiments), chocolate, pickles and pickled food, alcohol, aged cheese, soy sauce, Worcestershire sauce, cottonseed oil, nuts, peanuts, apples and apple products, grapes and grape products, coffee, and any processed meats that contain nitrates or nitrites, like hot dogs or salami. He has found that by eliminating just the foods listed in this first stage, improvements may be seen within a few weeks.

According to Dr. Semon, the reason for eliminating the items in stage one is that these foods have the highest concentration of toxic yeast chemicals, which must be eliminated for two reasons. The first is that these foods contain chemicals that kill bacteria and act as constant, low-level antibiotics. Without the elimination of these foods, nystatin cannot be used at higher doses. Otherwise, the malt, vinegar, and other foods are bringing the yeast back as the nystatin is killing it. The second reason is that these foods contain chemicals that slow down the brain.[28]

During stage two, Dr. Semon suggests removing all baked products containing yeast, corn, rye, vanilla extract, dried fruits and raisins, concentrated fruit juice, monosodium glutamate (MSG), aspartame (NutraSweet), maple syrup, bananas, mushrooms, soda, brown sugar, white sugar, margarine, and buttermilk. He also recommends cutting back on meats and fish (except veal) and eliminating all cooking oils except safflower, soy, olive, and canola. Spices such as cinnamon, dried mustard, curry powder, chili powder, and cayenne pepper should be eliminated as well. Green herbs are acceptable.

His third stage eliminates all gluten and casein, and his fourth stage, which he says very few children ever require, eliminates melons, grapefruits, oranges, all meats, yellow onions, most fruits except very fresh ones that are in season, all canned goods, and fish.

We have followed some of this diet for Ryan, but we started with a combination of stage one and stage three since we were convinced Ryan needed to be free of gluten and casein. Fortunately, we never had to proceed to stage four since Ryan's yeast has remained under control without it.

If you decide to pursue this diet, Dr. Semon's book will give you a detailed description and understanding of each phase, along with more than two hundred and twenty-five recipes.

Rotation Diet

As the name suggests, foods that are not a problem for your child are rotated on a specific cycle, commonly every fourth day. Some people prefer to take days off from certain foods like rice or potatoes two or three times a week. Since a person on a GF/CF diet may consume a lot more rice or potato flours, the rotation can prevent a reaction to these from overuse. For example, if a child has a leaky gut and eats rice every day, his body may develop antibodies to rice. This can be reversed, but it requires removing the food for a while; therefore, it's easier to rotate the staples.

Additions to Dietary Intervention

After you've implemented a diet that fits your child's needs, you may want to take some other dietary precautions.

Enzymes

Since enzymes are required to properly break down proteins into amino acids, some suspect that an enzymatic deficiency may be a factor, although this hasn't yet been verified.

Dr. William Shaw, director of the Great Plains Laboratory, has received many positive reports from parents who have added digestive enzymes to their child's diet. He lists thirteen different enzymes in his book *Biological Treatments for Autism and PDD* that may help increase a child's digestive ability by breaking down the peptides.[29] Peptidases are one category of enzymes that may be deficient in our children. As of this writing, Klaire Laboratories is researching a peptidase supplement called SerenAid, which is designed for those who have difficulty breaking down gluten and casein. If the supplement is considered successful, it may be available by the time this book is released.

Digestive enzymes are found naturally in some fruits and plants, including avocados, bananas, mangoes, and sprouts. In addition, most health-food stores carry a wide variety of digestive enzymes in capsule form. Note that most enzyme capsules should *not* be opened and the contents sprinkled on food or in a drink. If the enzymes come in contact with the mouth, they can cause a burning sensation. Several prescription enzymes are also available on the market if you and your doctor decide to pursue this.

Besides adding enzymes to the system, we can remove those

things that hinder enzymes' effectiveness. As mentioned earlier, Dr.
Ben Feingold recommends removing foods that contain salicylates,
as well as substances with the additive benzoic acid listed in the
ingredients, since they are actually peptidase inhibitors.

For further information you can contact:

Klaire Laboratories
140 Marine View Avenue
Suite 110
Solana Beach, CA 92075
Phone: 800-859-8358 or 858-350-7880

Opiate and Opioid Blockers

Naltrexone is a drug that blocks opiates and opioids in the brain.
For best results many doctors use this drug in conjunction with a
GF/CF diet, though they disagree on the correct dosage. Our doctor recommends a minimum dose of twenty-five milligrams,
believing a lower dose would be ineffective. On the other end of
the spectrum, psychiatrist and nutritionist Dr. Bruce Semon recommends very low doses of three to six milligrams per day because
he believes the higher doses may have an opposite effect than
intended and actually increase children's headaches or pain.[30] Dr.
Karl Reichelt, a Norwegian scientist and researcher, states that no
set dose can be determined merely on factors like body weight.
Instead, he believes the proper dosage of Naltrexone depends on a
bell-shaped curve relating to the amount of peptides in the system.
Since this can change after each meal, the dosage needs to change.
Therefore, he recommends maintaining a strict diet so the level of
peptides remains more constant and an appropriate dose can be
determined.[31]

EPD Shots

"EPD (enzyme-potentiated desensitization) is a method of immunotherapy developed by Dr. Leonard McEwen, which involves desensitization with a combination of very low doses of mixed allergens with the enzyme beta-glucuronidase."[32] To put it simply, EPD attempts to adapt the body to the allergen by introducing small amounts of it. Over time a person may be able to handle foods that he or she couldn't before. Shots are given once every two to three months in the beginning and then reduced to two or three shots per year as the body adjusts. Dr. McEwen has found that half of his patients are able to stop the shots between eight and twenty doses, with some patients not needing additional treatments for years.[33] Eighty percent of those who complete the entire three-to-five-year program are cured of their allergies. Those who correct any gut problems first, like a yeast overgrowth, leaky gut, or parasites, have the best chance of benefiting from the EPD shots.[34]

If you decide to try this, you first need to find an experienced doctor. You can call the American EPD Society at 505-984-0004 for a list, or contact them on their Web site at http://epdallergy.com. You will also need to follow a strict diet for approximately a week before and after each treatment.

A Final Word

Once again, a prime source for help is families who are farther down this road than you. We network with other families who are on the same diet, exchanging recipes and sharing information on new products we find. A few months ago I learned that Rice Dream rice milk has very small amounts of gluten in it, so I passed this information on to my friends who were using it, assuming it was gluten-free. I recently heard that the Rice Dream company plans to make their product gluten-free, so you may want to call them and find out the status.

If there isn't a support group of parents in your city, consider starting one yourself. Two parents began the Autism Network for Dietary Intervention (ANDI) in order to help other parents "understand, implement and maintain a gluten- and casein-free diet for their autistic children."[35] Information on how to contact them follows.

No matter how you get started, I urge you to start soon. If you're going to do any testing, begin with that, but you don't have to wait for the results to begin the transition. If you find in retrospect that you didn't need to eliminate a food, you can always reintroduce it.

You don't have to have all the answers right away. The important thing is to begin. Everything you learn becomes a stepping-stone to help your child.

Peptide Testing
Great Plains Laboratory
9335 West 75th Street
Overland Park, KS 66204
Phone: 913-341-8949
Fax: 913-341-6207
E-mail: williamsha@aol.com
Web site: http://www.greatplainslaboratory.com

Autism Research Unit (ARU)
Paul Shattock and Paul Whiteley
School of Health Sciences
University of Sunderland
Sunderland SR2 7EE ENGLAND
Phone: 44-0-1915-108922 or 44-0-1915-152581
Fax: 44-0-1915-670420

Karl Reichelt, M.D.
Director, Clinical Chemistry Section
Department of Pediatric Research
Rikshospitalet—The National Hospital
Pilestredet 32
N 0027 Oslo, NORWAY
Phone: 47-22-86-91-10 or 47-22-86-91-11
Fax: 47-22-86-91-17
E-mail: K.L.Reichelt@rh.uio.no

Food Allergy/Sensitivity Testing
Great Plains Laboratory
9335 West 75th Street
Overland Park, KS 66204
Phone: 913-341-8949
Fax: 913-341-6207
E-mail: williamsha@aol.com
Web site: http://www.greatplainslaboratory.com

Immuno Laboratories
1620 West Oakland Park Boulevard
Fort Lauderdale, FL 33311
Phone: 954-486-4500 or 800-231-9197
Fax: 954-739-6563
E-mail: pcssales@inimmuno.com
Web site: http://www.immunolabs.com

Serammune Physicians Lab
14 Pigeon Hill Drive, Suite 300
Sterling, VA 20165
Phone: 703-450-2980 or 800-553-5472
Fax: 703-450-2981

Dietary Organizations

Autism Network for Dietary Intervention (ANDI)
P.O. Box 17711
Rochester, NY 14617-0711
Fax: 609-737-8453
E-mail: AutismNDI@aol.com
Web site: http://www.AutismNDI.com

The Feingold Association of the United States
127 East Main Street, Suite 106
Riverhead, NY 11901
Phone: 516-369-9340
Fax: 516-369-2988
E-mail: membership@feingold.org
Web site: http://www.feingold.org

The Food Allergy Network
10400 Eaton Place, Suite 107
Fairfax, VA 22030-2208
Phone: 800-929-4040 or 703-691-3179
Fax: 703-691-2713
E-mail: fan@worldweb.net
Web site: http://www.foodallergy.org.

Red Star
433 E. Michigan Street
Milwaukee, WI 53202-5106
Phone: 800-4-CELIAC (800-423-5422)
E-mail: carol.stevens@ufoods.com
Web site: http://www.redstaryeast.com

Gluten-Free/Casein-Free Retailers
Abersold Foods
P.O. Box 3927
Citrus Heights, CA 95611
Phone: 800-275-1437
Web site: http://www.amazingfoods.com
They sell Vance's Darifree milk substitute.

Allergy Resources
557 Burbank Street, Suite K
Broomfield, CO 80020
Phone: 303-438-0600
E-mail: allergyre@aol.com

Dietary Specialties Inc.
865 Centennial Avenue
Piscataway, NY 08854
Phone: 888-636-8123
Web site: http://www.dietspec.com

Ener-G Foods
5960 First Avenue South
Seattle, WA 98124-5784
Phone: 800-331-5222
Fax: 206-764-3393
E-mail: heidi@ener-g.com
Web site: http://www.ener-g.com/index.html

The Gluten-Free Pantry
P.O. Box 840
Glastonbury, CT 06033
Phone: 800-291-8386 (inquiries and orders) or
    860-633-3826 (customer service)
Fax: 860-633-6853
E-mail: pantry@glutenfree.com
Web site: http://www.glutenfree.com

Glutafin
Nutricia Dietary Care
Newmarket Avenue, White Horse Business Park
Trowbridge, Wiltshire BA14 0XQ ENGLAND
Phone: 44-0-1225-711801
Fax: 44-0-1225-711567
E-mail: acook@nutricia.co.uk
Web site: http://www.glutafin.co.uk

Recommended Reading

Allergy Cooking with Ease by Nicolette M. Dumke (Lancaster, Pa.: Starburst Publishers, 1992). This cookbook eliminates wheat, milk, eggs, corn, soy, yeast, sugar, grain, and gluten from its recipes.

The Allergy Self-Help Cookbook by Marjorie Hurt Jones, R.N. (Emmaus, Pa.: Rodale Press, 1984). This book provides more than 325 recipes that are free from wheat, milk, eggs, corn, yeast, sugar, and other allergens.

Dietary Intervention As a Therapy in the Treatment of Autism and Related Developmental Disorders by Beth and Andy Crowell (1992). This small booklet contains good information about starting a GF/CF diet and has about fifty recipes. Before I ordered a copy, I borrowed a friend's book to check out some of the recipes. Judging by the splattered food all over the pages, it was obvious she used it often. You can order this booklet by sending $14.95 plus $2.00 for shipping and handling to the Crowells at 208 South Street, P.O. Box 801, Housatonic, MA 02136-0801.

Feast Without Yeast by Bruce Semon, M.D., Ph.D., and Lori Kornblum (Milwaukee: Wisconsin Institute of Nutrition, 1999). Along with its four-stage method of combating yeast, this book includes over 225 original recipes that are all yeast-free and sugar-free. Most recipes are also gluten- and casein-free. This book can be ordered through the Wisconsin Institute of Nutrition at 877-332-7899 (toll-free) or 414-351-1194. They also maintain a Web site at http://www. nutritioninstitute.com.

The Gluten-Free Gourmet, More from the Gluten-Free Gourmet, and *The Gluten-Free Gourmet Cooks Fast and Healthy*—all by Bette Hagman (New York: Henry Holt and Co., 1990, 1993, and 1996, respectively). Each of her books is fantastic, but I've used the last one the most since it explains how to prepare foods in bulk so they can be ready for later use. For instance, I make a big batch of basic cake mix and store it in an airtight container. Then when I want a cake, I pull out two cups of my mix and add a few ingredients, and I have a cake.

Special Diets for Special Kids by Lisa Lewis, Ph.D. (Arlington, Tex.: Future Horizons, Inc., 1998). This excellent book will help you understand in detail why and how to implement a GF/CF diet. She includes over 150 recipes aimed at children, such as GF chicken nuggets. Order through Future Horizons at 800-489-0727.

Sweet and Sugarfree by Karen E. Barkie (New York: St. Martin's Press, 1982). This book gives all-natural recipes for desserts that are sweetened by fruit instead of refined sugar.

The Yeast Connection Cookbook by William G. Crook, M.D., and Marjorie Hurt Jones, R.N. (Jackson, Tenn.: Professional Books, 1989). This book helps with the anti-yeast diet, but not all the recipes are GF or CF.

Chapter 8

Biomedical Intervention

Be mindful not to overlook the break in the forearm
when you've found the break in the wrist.

ROBERT D. SCHMIDT, M.D.

Imagine that a patient has three tacks stuck in his foot and he goes to his doctor complaining of pain. His doctor looks at his foot and sees a red tack, a blue tack, and a yellow tack. After careful investigation he decides that the red tack is causing the pain, so he removes it and sends the patient home. A few days later the patient returns, complaining of the same foot pain. The doctor then decides that the blue tack rather than the red tack must be causing the problem, so he puts the red tack back in and pulls out the blue one, gives the patient some medication for the pain, and sends him on his way.[1]

Like the three tacks, autism seems to be a multifaceted disorder that includes many dysfunctions, which may need to be addressed simultaneously. It isn't enough to find and remove merely one tack. However, once many parents have their child diagnosed with autism, they have an explanation for their child's behavior so they quit looking for the underlying causes. I understand; I was one of those parents. Within two months of Ryan's diagnosis we were targeting his autism through intensive Applied

Behavior Analysis (ABA) and were seeing results. We were addressing the effects of the autism and helping correct the damage that had been done, but we weren't motivated to seek out the underlying biomedical causes. We had pulled out the red tack, but we hadn't yet given thought to the others.

In the four years since Ryan's diagnosis we've learned that he has many different issues within his body. He is intolerant of gluten and casein, and removing them from his diet has helped, but we also know that he has elevated yeast in his system, an immune deficiency, a mineral imbalance, and more. How can a parent address all the underlying issues at once?

The tricky part of pursuing biomedical intervention is that there are so many options and combinations of options. The best combination of tests and treatments for your child may be very different from the ones we chose for Ryan. I'll present a few of *many* possible options you can investigate further, but since these can be costly, you need to weigh each one carefully.

Secretin

Dr. Bernard Rimland, director of the Autism Research Institute, says that secretin "is possibly the most important discovery in the history of autism."[2] According to the textbooks, secretin, a hormone produced by the small intestine, stimulates the pancreas to release sodium bicarbonate, as well as enzymes that help with digestion. The bicarbonate neutralizes the stomach acids, which allows the enzymes to break down the food properly.[3] However, there now seems to be much more to the secretin story than the textbook writers knew.

Although porcine secretin has been used for years for testing pancreatic function, only recently has it been used to treat autism. The serendipitous discovery came in April of 1996 when Gary and Victoria Beck's son, Parker, received an endoscopy where a secretin challenge test was performed. Prior to this procedure, Parker was "completely nonverbal, had constant and chronic diarrhea, and was 'zoned out' most of the time."[4] Although the results of the endoscopy were rather unremarkable, within days of this procedure Parker began to change dramatically. His bowel movements normalized, his eye contact improved, he began sleeping through the night, his facial tics disappeared, and he spoke for the first time in over two years!

Unfortunately, Parker's doctors refused to believe that secretin had anything to do with his changes. It took Gary and Victoria months to find a doctor who believed what they had witnessed and who would explore the possibility that secretin might work for other children.[5]

In January of 1998, stimulated by the Becks' discovery, Karoly Horvath and his associates published a paper presenting the results of three children with Autism Spectrum Disorders (ASD) who had received secretin infusions. With secretin, their bodies produced between 7.5 and 10 milliliters of pancreatic solution versus the normal response of 1 to 2 milliliters. Also, within five weeks of the infusion the children's gastrointestinal symptoms improved, and they showed dramatic changes in behavior, including eye contact, alertness, and language ability.[6]

We've given Ryan several secretin treatments and have seen significant results. Before secretin, our son had already progressed greatly through the use of ABA and other interventions. However, his language was still about three years behind that of his peers.

To determine secretin's effectiveness, we wanted unbiased opinions from those who had contact with Ryan, so we didn't tell his therapists or teachers about the treatment. The day Ryan received his first infusion we saw results; he interacted more with his sister and the number of his words increased greatly. We might have thought we were reading our expectations into the results had it not been for Marge Blanc, Ryan's speech therapist. Unaware of the secretin treatment, Marge performed a language test on Ryan, called the Developmental Sentence Scoring (DSS), in order to train a new pathologist. This test was done by videotaping Ryan and transcribing fifty consecutive spontaneous utterances regardless of what was said, with each utterance receiving points on several criteria.

Marge tested Ryan the first time four days before the secretin infusion. The second time was ten days after the infusion. The first test scored Ryan as having language abilities equivalent to a three-year-ten-month-old child, which was consistent with Ryan's baseline test five months earlier that had placed him at three years two months. According to the test, Ryan had increased his language skills by eight months in a five-month period, which would typically be quite good.

However, it was the second test, done just two weeks later, that got Marge's attention. Ryan scored at the level of a five-year-four-month-old child! That's eighteen months of language growth in ten days.

Unaware of the secretin, Marge was very concerned because she couldn't explain the results. She checked and rechecked them to verify their accuracy. While Roger and I knew our son was speaking more, we couldn't have quantified how much more. But with Marge's perfect timing, she proved the progress.

Not every child will have the extremely positive results Ryan did, but Dr. Rimland reports that more than 70 percent of patients are showing improvement to varying levels. However, data are still coming in that need to be analyzed.[7]

What Are the Possible Side Effects?

As with all medications, side effects are possible. However, Dr. Sidney Baker has given over 400 infusions and has seen only a handful of short-term negative responses, ranging from red lips or a pinkish rash on the chest, which disappears after a few minutes, to hyperactivity, diarrhea, or constipation, which may last several days. However, these children have then returned to where they began (their baseline) or have improved beyond the baseline.[8] Dr. Paul Hardy has given over 200 secretin treatments. He reports that approximately 10 percent of these patients become hyperactive for a week or two after receiving secretin and approximately 5 percent develop loose stools within the first twelve hours, though in these cases, a positive response to the secretin usually follows.[9]

Some physicians are cautious about giving secretin to individuals who have a history of seizures or who are on medication for seizures. According to Dr. Rimland, "One youngster had a seizure while the secretin was administered but, after investigation, it was concluded that the secretin was probably not the cause of the seizure. The child's family has a history of seizures, the child had an abnormal EEG to begin with, and the child had struggled against the infusion, so the stress of the situation might have led to the seizure."[10]

Dr. Karl Reichelt has commented on a possible danger of secretin infusions. He points out that the structures of the naturally occurring secretin within our bodies, which is made up of twenty-seven amino acids, and the porcine secretin used for treatment differ by two amino acids, which might be enough to cause the body to produce antibodies to the porcine secretin. His concern stems from the fact that when porcine insulin was developed, some people developed antibodies to it. If this should occur, the antibodies would affect not only the porcine secretin but possibly any natural secretin as well.[11]

In response, Dr. Baker stresses that the reaction from porcine insulin was merely a localized reaction to the injection site.[12] Research is being done on synthetic human secretin, which would not differ in amino acids from natural human secretin. If synthetic human secretin is found to be beneficial, then this concern would no longer be an issue.

As with any treatment for your child, you should discuss with your doctor, in detail, the possible risks and benefits before making a decision.

How Does Secretin Work?

No one knows for sure. We know there are secretin receptors in the brain, as well as in many areas of the central nervous system, so it may affect the brain directly. Dr. Rimland points out that "secretin is intimately involved in many activities of the brain, including stimulating the production and utilization of the neurotransmitter serotonin."[13] Or it may affect the brain indirectly by causing the pancreas to function.[14] Dr. Baker says, "My guess is that a pulse of secretin through the bloodstream unlocks some stuck biochemical or immune mechanism that is involved in the difficulty some people have with processing material that enters the body."[15]

Victoria Beck in her book *Unlocking the Potential of Secretin* lists many physiological changes that have been documented in children after secretin infusions. These include the normalization of serotonin levels, a drop in blood ammonia levels, normalization of fungal and bacteria levels, decreased antibody levels to certain proteins, as well as reduction of rubella or mumps antibodies.[16] Based on before and after SPECT scans, one child even showed improved blood flow to the right temporal lobes after being given secretin.[17]

Several studies are currently being conducted to explore the validity of secretin treatments for autism and to examine the changes that occur in the body.

How Is It Given?

Secretin is generally administered through an IV (intravenous) infusion. The entire procedure takes less than five minutes and can be performed by any willing doctor, including a pediatrician or family-practice physician. Some doctors believe that an individual should receive secretin on an empty stomach after he has fasted four to six hours. If a child has a gut problem, Dr. Hardy recommends preparing the gut first by following a gluten-free and casein-free diet and/or treating any yeast overgrowth for at least one month before an infusion.

To make the IV less painful, our doctor prescribes EMLA, a thick lotion applied an hour in advance to numb the skin. This has really helped us keep Ryan calmer during the procedure. Some children benefit from mild sedation to keep anxieties to a minimum.

Many other methods of giving secretin are being explored, including intramuscular injection (a shot in the muscle), transdermal application (through the skin), sublingual drops (under the tongue)—a homeopathic use of secretin—and oral ingestion.[18] Of these alternatives, the most common is the transdermal method, which uses an agent—often a solution called DMSO—to allow the secretin to be absorbed through the skin into the bloodstream.

With DMSO, only a small portion of the secretin vial is used each day. Giving secretin transdermally stems from the idea that the body may best utilize a small portion of secretin daily, much as a diabetic may require insulin daily rather than a large amount every few weeks.

If you choose the transdermal method, first apply the agent by itself for one to two weeks to make sure your child doesn't react to it. If not, then add the secretin to the agent. Your doctor can guide you on which transdermal agent may be best for your child and how to use it properly.

Currently there's no verification of the proper dose of secretin or its safety when given in any of these alternative ways, so the IV infusion may be safest until further data is collected.

Note that secretin is given for autism "off-label," which means it's not being used for the purpose approved by the FDA. In 1999 RepliGen Corporation, a biotechnology firm, purchased the patent for using secretin to treat autism. Until they have completed the necessary research and testing and receive FDA approval, doctors have the right to use this drug off-label if they believe it will help their patients. As RepliGen researchers investigate the effectiveness of secretin in treating autism, they are seeking ways to administer it conveniently and painlessly as well.

What Is the Recommended Dosage?

Ferring Pharmaceuticals, the previous producer of secretin, recommends 1 to 2 CU (Clinical Units) per kilogram of body weight. Following this scale, Ryan received 50 CU of secretin in his first infusion. Since his second infusion, we've given Ryan the entire 75 CU vial, which is a second option. Dr. Baker gives his patients a full vial regardless of their age or weight because he feels that not only is the increased dose safe but that a large amount of secretin in the bloodstream may cause the benefit.[19]

From the data that Dr. Rimland has been collecting through the Autism Research Institute, he has found that many children respond well to a dose of 1.5 to 2 CU per kilogram of body weight, with those who receive more than 3.5 CU per kilogram having a slightly higher chance of experiencing hyperactivity.[20]

How Frequently Should Secretin Be Given?

Since there is no protocol to follow, you and your doctor will need to decide on appropriate intervals if you pursue multiple infusions. The average interval ranges from two to six weeks, though some children go months without needing another infusion. Dr. Baker sees a number of patients who return after six to eight weeks when some symptom relapses have begun.[21] Some children have done so well with just one infusion that they haven't needed more, and others have seen no benefit until after their second or third infusion.

After Secretin

If you pursue secretin treatments, I urge you to document your results and after three weeks to send the information to the Autism Research Institute for compilation and analysis. Be sure to include the dose and brand of secretin used. Your experience may help many others.

Since research regarding the use of secretin with autism just began to appear in 1998, information changes daily. As research is released, information will be available through articles, newsletters, Web sites, and Internet news groups. Because of the newness of the information and the benefits some parents are seeing, I believe it's particularly important to continue learning, reading, and researching information on secretin.

Candida Albicans

Candida albicans is the medical name for one type of yeast. Most of us have heard of thrush, a yeast overgrowth in a child's mouth, and vaginal yeast infections that women often get after taking antibiotics. However, we may not realize that individuals can have a yeast overgrowth in their gastrointestinal tracts. In a healthy gut, bacteria, yeast, and other fungi exist together and aid the digestion process. However, when a person takes antibiotics to fight an infection, the balance of these is disturbed. Good and bad bacteria are killed off with the antibiotic, while yeast organisms are not. With the good bacteria diminished, yeast organisms become more abundant and in turn release more toxins in the body that can damage the central nervous and immune systems.[22]

Dr. William Crook, author of *The Yeast Connection,* believes that a yeast overgrowth produces a vicious cycle in children. First antibiotics are taken for upper respiratory or ear infections, which in turn weaken the immune system. A weakened immune system, combined with other irritants, can lead to more infections and more antibiotics. Not surprisingly, the use of antibiotics has increased greatly over the last half of the century—from eighty tons in 1949 to over twenty thousand tons in the 1990s.[23] This cycle of using antibiotics allows for extensive yeast overgrowth.

Dr. William Shaw is the director of the Great Plains Laboratory and author/editor of the book *Biological Treatments for Autism and PDD,* which describes the yeast problem and many other biological issues in great detail. He points out that the yeast in the gut produces enzymes that actually break down the lining of the intestinal wall, which can lead to a leaky gut. We already discussed in the last chapter how leaky gut can lead to digestive problems. In addition, the damage to the intestinal wall may hinder the production of the hormone secretin and, because foods are escaping from the gut into the bloodstream, may play a major role in the body having allergic reactions.[24]

Dr. Stephen M. Edelson, director of the Center for the Study of Autism, attributes many behavioral problems to yeast over-growth, including "confusion, hyperactivity, short attention span, lethargy, irritability, and aggression."[25] Dr. Bernard Rimland states that "yeast infections, usually brought on by antibiotic overuse, can cause or exacerbate autism."[26]

Physical symptoms of a yeast overgrowth include an assort-ment of gastrointestinal distresses—diarrhea, gas, constipation, or stomach pains—as well as headaches, muscle aches, or skin irrita-tions including rashes, hives, eczema, and psoriasis. However, a yeast overgrowth can manifest itself purely with behavioral signs. Dr. Shaw has reported, based on parental observation, that chil-dren who have been treated with antifungal medications have had a decrease in behavioral symptoms such as hyperactivity, self-stimulatory behavior, and aggression, along with improvement in eye contact, language, concentration, sleep, and academic perfor-mance.[27] Dr. Bruce Semon has treated many children and adults with antifungal medication and concurrent diet and has observed clinically all of these same responses.[28]

Testing for a Yeast Overgrowth

The most comprehensive and reliable test for a yeast overgrowth is done by Dr. Shaw through the Great Plains Laboratory. His com-prehensive urine test for organic acids checks for almost seventy bio-chemical compounds and will show if there is a yeast overgrowth, additional fungi and bacteria, and inborn errors of metabolism.

Along with the test readout, Dr. Shaw provides an individual interpretation of his findings to help your doctor direct you to the best treatment options. When we had Ryan tested, he showed signs of elevated yeast levels in his urine.

The Great Smokies Diagnostic Laboratory or Great Plains Laboratory can test for yeast with their Comprehensive Digestive Stool Analysis (CDSA). In addition, this test checks an individual's digestive function, metabolic function, microbiology, mycology, and parasitology. Because Ryan has had chronic but sporadic diarrhea, I expected them to find parasites in his system. Instead, he had elevated yeast levels, which surprised me since we had been treating it with medications. One of the tests included with the CDSA checks which antifungal agents, prescription or natural, best combat a particular strain of Candida. From this we learned the medication Ryan was taking fell only in the midrange of effectiveness for him.

You need to take into account that even if a child tests negative, there is still a possibility that he has a yeast overgrowth, and an anti-yeast diet and nystatin should be considered.[29]

Treating a Yeast Overgrowth

If you find your child has a yeast problem, you may choose from a variety of treatments, but you may want to begin with the anti-yeast diet outlined in the previous chapter. That alone might bring improvements. Dr. Bruce Semon has found that the diet plays such an important part in the treatment plan that antifungal medications have little benefit without it.[30]

Probiotics

The first line of attack for getting rid of the overgrowth of yeast is to replenish the good bacteria. Products that contain these can be purchased from almost any health-food store. Though there are many types of good bacteria, termed *probiotics*, two common ones are Lactobacillus acidophilus and Bifidobacterium bifidum. Lactobacillus acidophilus is found in yogurt, which is why doctors recommend eating yogurt when taking antibiotics; it replaces the good bacteria being lost and in turn prevents a yeast infection.

Probiotics come in many forms, including chewable tablets, capsules, powders, and a suspension formula. Before Ryan could swallow pills, we put the powder in his water without his even noticing. In choosing a probiotic product, first make sure it is dairy-free. Most have dairy in them unless they specify dairy-free. Also, the best brands are refrigerated and have a short shelf life, around six months, to ensure that the bacteria remain alive and useful. Ryan takes twenty billion good bacteria (two capsules) per day in a product that combines Lactobacillus acidophilus and Bifidobacterium bifidum. Some products contain FOS (fructooligosaccharides), which "feeds" the good bacteria and helps them grow. As with the diet, it's good to have multiple types of probiotics and rotate them to prevent the gut from becoming dependent on a single kind.

Dr. Shaw recommends that a probiotic be taken at the same time any antifungal product is used, whether it is prescribed or over-the-counter.[31] We found this out the first time Ryan took nystatin. Within the first few days, Ryan developed a serious raised rash on his bottom and had severe diarrhea. After a few days, our doctor recommended we stop the antifungals because of the die-off reaction.

Die-off refers to the side effects that can occur as the yeast begin to die and large amounts of toxins are released into the system. Yeast can be compared to water balloons that release toxins when they pop. When antifungals are used, a significant number of yeast are dying off at the same time, and the amount of toxins released and absorbed into the system can be extremely high for three or four days. As the die-off decreases, the toxins should also decrease and benefits should become noticeable.[32] The next time we gave Ryan nystatin, we prepared his gut for two weeks in advance with probiotics, and he had no die-off reaction. Beginning an anti-yeast diet several days before the use of nystatin may also help decrease or eliminate die-off.

However, there are varying opinions about probiotics. Dr. Semon generally does not recommend their use, stating, "It is true that if one puts a little Candida into a culture full of acidophilus, the Candida will not grow. However, when they are at more equal quantities, Candida and lactobacillus actually grow quite well together." Dr. Semon finds that acidophilus usually works for a few weeks, then stops working or possibly even makes things worse. He found that some children, including his son, got better when they removed the probiotic.[33]

Antifungal Treatments
Antifungals come as prescription medications or over-the-counter "natural" remedies. The most common antifungal prescription is nystatin, considered a very safe medication that has passed the test of time. Doctors usually try nystatin first because it stays in the intestinal tract and almost 100 percent of it is eliminated through the feces instead of being absorbed into the bloodstream. Dr. Shaw states that he has never heard of a documented serious side effect from using nystatin, which is critical since some children need to be on antifungals for a long time to keep the yeast in control. Dr. Semon has had his son on nystatin for more than eight years with

no side effects,[34] and Ryan was on it for several months without adverse reactions.

Nystatin comes in pill and powder form. When we first started, we hid the powder in Ryan's food, which was hard to do since it has a bitter taste. For a while I put it in his sandwich, hoping the peanut butter and jelly would cover the taste, but they didn't.

After that, I tried different methods—hiding it in honey, mixing it in suspension syrup. One form of nystatin comes mixed in a syrup, but we knew Ryan wouldn't take anything with a fruity or syrupy taste. Be creative. One of my friends mixes up a nystatin solution and puts it in the well of a raspberry. Her son eats ten of these a day to get his complete dose. Dr. Semon urges using any food necessary to get the nystatin ingested so that when the child begins to feel better, he may be more open to taking the medicine.[35] When Ryan began to swallow pills, he would take the nystatin without any hassles. However, to avoid the red food dye that coats the pill, we made our own pills by putting the powder into empty capsules. I have since learned that the Apothecary pharmacy (301-530-0800) will fill a nystatin prescription in capsules. The pharmacies in our area were unable to offer that. Some practitioners recommend using the Lederle brand of nystatin since it is free of chemical contaminants.

You'll need to determine the dosage with your doctor. Dr. Shaw states a "typical dose" as 400,000 units of nystatin divided into four doses a day, while Dr. Semon recommends building up to one million units four times a day for a total of four million a day.[36]

According to Dr. Semon, the dose level depends on whether the individual is following an anti-yeast diet. He explains that when nystatin is given without the special diet, clostridia increases —clostridia being another bacteria that produces its own bad chemicals. Therefore, to avoid this, Dr. Shaw recommends doses no higher than those just mentioned. However, Dr. Semon states that when a person follows his stage-one diet, especially eliminating products that contain vinegar and malt, clostridia does not grow when nystatin is taken, even in very high doses.[37]

Most people start with nystatin, but other prescriptions are available if the nystatin doesn't work. Your doctor can direct you on which treatment may be best suited for your child.

Nonprescription products can also be used to kill the yeast and can be very effective. These include garlic, Pau D'arco, cranberry, black walnut, caprylic acid, sustained release oregano oil, MCT oil, grapefruit seed extract, goldenseal, lactoferrin, and Tanalbit. These products can be purchased individually or in a combination form from most health-food or nutrition stores.

Laboratories

Great Plains Laboratory
9335 West 75th Street
Overland Park, KS 66204
Phone: 913-341-8949
Fax: 913-341-6207
E-mail: williamsha@aol.com
Web site: http://www.greatplainslaboratory.com

Great Smokies Diagnostic Laboratory
63 Zillicoa Street
Asheville, NC 28801
Phone: 800-522-4762
Fax: 828-285-9293
E-mail: cs@gsdl.com
Web site: http://www.greatsmokies-lab.com

Metametrix Laboratory
5000 Peach Tree Industrial Boulevard, Suite 110
Norcross, GA 30071
Phone: 800-221-4640 or 770-446-5483

Nutritional Supplements

Nutritional supplements can be used for a variety of reasons. Most obvious, our children often have a very limited diet, so supplements can provide them the vitamins, minerals, and fatty acids they may lack. Supplements can also target imbalances in the body to promote healing. Dr. Rimland, after years of gathering data from scientific literature and parental reports, has found that certain nutrients have benefited many children with autism.

Ryan takes a wide variety of supplements daily, which have changed as professionals have worked with us to find the best combination. There are *many* more vitamins, minerals, herbs, and other supplements than I am able to cover here. The best thing is to work with a nutritionist who can design a supplement plan for your child. If you want to learn more about supplements, I recommend you get *Prescription for Nutritional Healing* by James F. Balch and Phyllis A. Balch, an excellent book with recommendations for designing a supplement regimen for your child.

B₆ and Magnesium

Vitamin B_6 has a long history as a treatment for autism with the evidence for its benefits growing. Since the first studies in the 1960s, eighteen studies have been published to date.[38] Each study has shown benefits of vitamin B_6, often combined with magnesium, while none have shown harm.[39] The benefits have ranged from improved language, eye contact, and behaviors, "improved brain electrical activity, improved conditionability, and improved immune system function" to a decrease in the "excretion of abnormal metabolites in the urine."[40] Across the eighteen studies, an average of 46 percent of those tested showed improvements from high doses of B_6.[41]

Magnesium is needed with high doses of B_6 because, as Dr. Rimland points out, high doses of B_6 taken alone may cause a deficiency in magnesium and other B vitamins. Taking magnesium with B_6 will minimize side effects, such as irritability, bedwetting, and sensitivity to sound.[42] Kirkman Laboratories has designed a multivitamin specifically for people with autism called Super Nu-Thera, which contains high doses of B_6, magnesium, and many other nutrients and comes in pill, powder, or liquid form.

We tried the powder first, but we had difficulty hiding the strong taste, and Ryan refused it. The liquid has a pleasant taste, like weak Kool-Aid, but Ryan refused it also since he only likes water. When he began to swallow pills, we tried again, this time with success.

Even though I didn't see any results, I was thrilled he was getting some vitamins. After several months we decided to have Ryan's body chemistry tested so we could develop a nutritional supplement specifically for him. As we waited for the pills to be made, we ran low on the Super Nu-Thera. About three weeks before they were completely gone, we began to wean him from them, and eventually we stopped giving them. For two or three weeks Ryan wasn't on any vitamins. In that time his behaviors deteriorated as he became aggressive and more hyperactive. When our therapists asked if I knew why Ryan was behaving this way, I looked at the chart of the supplements he takes. The therapists mentioned that Ryan's behaviors had begun to change about two weeks prior, which correlated with the time we withdrew the Super Nu-Thera. That really caught me by surprise, because I didn't think the vitamins were having an impact. But within two days of resuming the Super Nu-Thera, Ryan's behaviors returned to normal.

Holly is a mother in our city who has seen a dramatic difference in her daughter after high doses of vitamin B_6. Within days of starting the B_6, her daughter began playing imaginatively for the first time in her life. To verify the connection, Holly stopped and started the vitamins a couple of times. Each time she stopped giving the vitamins, her daughter's play disappeared, only to reappear when the B_6 was reintroduced. However, Holly's daughter became hyperactive due to the B_6. When she tried the Super Nu-Thera formula, the hyperactivity decreased greatly.

Dr. Rimland recommends B_6 by saying, "In view of the consistent finding showing the safety and efficacy of the nutrients B_6 and magnesium in treating autistic individuals, and in view of the inevitability of short- and/or long-term side effects of drug use, it certainly seems that this safe and rational approach should be tried before drugs are employed."[43]

How much B_6 and magnesium should you give your child? The general recommendation is eight milligrams (mg) of vitamin B_6 and three mg of magnesium per pound of body weight, daily, though only experimenting will determine the correct amount for your child.[44]

Sometimes results from vitamin B_6 therapy can be seen in just days; however, it may take a few weeks. If you don't see any results after a month or so, your child may not need the extra B_6.

Dimethylglycine (DMG)

Dimethylglycine, commonly known as DMG, is classified as a food substance rather than a vitamin. The benefits from taking DMG range from behavioral changes, reduction of seizures,[45] and decreased obsessive-compulsive behaviors[46] to improved language —even a child's first words. *Autism Research Review International* gives these two accounts.

> A Los Angeles mother was driving on the freeway, three-year-old Kathy in the backseat, five-year-old mute autistic son Sammy in the front. DMG had been started the day before. Kathy began to cry. Sammy turned and spoke his first words: "Don't cry, Kathy." The mother, stunned, almost crashed the car.
>
> A Texas mother secured her six-year-old mute autistic daughter in the front seat, then before driving off, turned to tell her husband, "I'll drop Mary at the babysitter's house first." Mary, on DMG for two days, startled her parents with her first words: "No! No babysitter!"[47]

DMG comes in capsules or tiny tablets that can be chewed. We use the 125-mg foil-wrapped tablets. In this form, the tablet is sweet and easily taken by most children. Ryan takes two in the morning and two at noon, but I know people who give their children nine or more tablets a day. Dr. Rimland suggests that preschool children start with half a tablet and older children with a whole tablet, then gradually increase the dose until the child takes one to four tablets a day. Adults usually take four to eight per day.[48] Dr. Rimland points out that some children have taken up to twenty tablets per day, and adults up to thirty a day, without adverse effects, though most won't need this high dose.

Some children become more hyperactive when taking DMG. If this happens, try adding 1600 mcg (micrograms) of folic acid for each DMG pill in your child's supplements.[49]

DMG has been tested many times in humans and animals and found to be safe even when given in high doses.

Folic Acid

Folic acid is a nontoxic B vitamin, which has been reported as helpful in combating autism. French researcher Jerome Lejeune found that giving autistic children 250 mcg of folic acid per pound of body weight brought considerable improvement.[50] Dr. Sidney Baker states that folic acid "has the franchise for distributing single carbon units needed for synthesis and repair of nucleic acids, which are the building blocks of RNA and DNA."[51] It also aids in treating depression and anxiety and can prevent some birth defects if taken before and during pregnancy. It is most effective when taken with vitamins B_{12} and C.[52]

Vitamin A

For years high doses of this vitamin have been used successfully to treat the measles virus. But because vitamin A is found naturally in items we don't often eat—liver, kidney, milk fat, and cod liver oil—most people are not getting enough of this important vitamin. One form of vitamin A, palminate, which often is added to milk, infant formulas, and breakfast cereals, doesn't offer the same benefits as the natural form of vitamin A found in the foods mentioned above.

Using cod liver oil, Dr. Mary N. Megson began vitamin A therapy with some of her autistic patients and produced exciting results. Some patients began speaking more frequently and clearly than ever before. Others made tremendous gains in eye contact; it seems the increase in vitamin A may have improved the rod function in the eye.[53] During her presentation at the 1999 Defeat Autism Now! Conference, Dr. Megson mentioned other benefits of the natural form of vitamin A, including cell growth and differentiation, repair of epithelial cells found in the gut wall, immune system function, and gene expression and transcription. Vitamin A, along with G proteins, may affect retinoid receptors in the hippocampus portion of the brain. These receptors, which act like "switches for learning and memory," may become disconnected after a DPT (diptheria-pertussis-tetanus) or MMR (measles-mumps-rubella) vaccination.[54]

In 1999 Dr. Megson began a double-blind, placebo-controlled, crossover clinical trial with sixty autistic children, using natural vitamin A found in cod liver oil, to see if "the receptors in the brain that may have been disconnected can indeed by reconnected." The results of that trial should be available in early 2000.

She identifies three important pieces of information to know before beginning vitamin A therapy:

1. Please work with your child's doctor. It is important that your doctor order a vitamin A level lab test. Too much vitamin A or D (also found in cod liver oil) can be toxic.

2. I am using only US RDA amounts in my trial. For example, children 10 and older are using 5000 IU. They get 2500 IU in the morning and 2500 IU in the evening, both times with meals. Children ages 2-9 get 3500 IU total. Theirs is divided into 1750 IU two times a day. Infants get less than one-fifth a teaspoon once a day.

3. Some children have undiagnosed food sensitivities, intolerances, or allergies that may contribute to symptoms. Please discuss with your child's doctor the need to avoid wheat and/or dairy products or other foods that may trigger symptoms.[55]

When I heard about vitamin A therapy, I thought, *I don't know if I want to do this. Too much vitamin A can be toxic.* While that is true, Dr. Megson is recommending only the US RDA (United States Recommended Daily Allowance) of natural vitamin A, which normally shouldn't cause a threat of toxicity. Dr. Donald R. Davis, in his article "Using Vitamin A Safely," warns that "doses of 10 to 20 times the usual recommended allowances if prolonged more than a few months placed sensitive infants and young children in danger of serious toxicity."[56] Since we won't be using an amount close to those levels, we have decided to try this therapy.

Vitamin C
Everywhere I turn I see articles on the benefits of vitamin C, and, yes, it can benefit a child with autism. We know that vitamin C is an antioxidant that helps the brain utilize oxygen.[57] Beyond that we can only theorize its role with the brain, although we know it's crucial for brain function. Without this vitamin, confusion and depression can set in. With it, cognition can actually increase.[58] Vitamin C can also help support the immune system, aid in detoxification, and fight viruses and bacteria, which is why many people take it to minimize the effects of colds.

Vitamin C is nontoxic, even in very high doses. If you take too much, your body will react with diarrhea, but typically no other harmful side effects occur.

Zinc

I once heard a doctor say that if he could recommend only one supplement for children with autism, it would be zinc. Zinc promotes brain development, improved immune function, and overall health and can help reduce other out-of-balance minerals. When Ryan had extremely high levels of lead and copper in his system, giving him zinc allowed his body to lower these levels.

The interesting thing about zinc is that your body can tell you if you need it, merely by taste. We give Ryan prescription liquid mineral drops from Women's International Pharmacy. The liquid mineral sent from the pharmacy includes potassium phosphate, zinc sulfate, magnesium chloride, copper sulfate, potassium chromate, and potassium permanganate. We didn't order the copper because we already knew Ryan had high levels in his system that needed to be lowered.

When the five minerals arrived, we were told to try a "taste test" to see which of the five Ryan needed. We were instructed to put a certain number of drops of zinc in a glass of distilled water and give it to Ryan. He drank the water without dispute; he couldn't taste the zinc at all. This showed that his body needed zinc. We then proceeded with the other minerals. In each case if Ryan didn't taste it, we added it to his daily regimen. Out of the five minerals prescribed for him, he needed four. With the last one, Ryan drank the water and made a horrible face and told me it was gross. That meant he didn't need it, so we put that bottle aside. Each month we test the minerals again to see if he still needs them.

Fatty Acids

For years we've been told to cut down on fats, and for the most part that's true. Some fats we *should* cut back on, but many of us should actually increase our intake of other fats. We need more of certain fatty acids: cis-linolenic acid (cLA), alpha linolenic acid (ALA), gamma linolenic acid (GLA), eicosapentaenoic acid (EPA), docosahexaenoic acid (DHA), and arachidonic acid (AA). Because Ryan, like most of us, doesn't get enough of these naturally in his diet, we give Ryan fatty acid supplements each day.

Dr. James Braly, director of Immuno Laboratories, notes these reasons for the importance of fatty acids:

> One is that they are a major source of energy (calories). Secondly, they are a crucial ingredient of the membranes in all body tissues and thus an important factor in determining the biological properties of those tissues. A deficiency of essential fatty acids, therefore, can cause serious problems. *One of these may well be an increase in the permeability of the mucosal membrane of the digestive tract [leaky gut], leading to the increased ability of incompletely digested food and other toxins to enter the bloodstream, eventually as immune complexes causing inflammatory reactions anywhere in the body.*[59] (emphasis mine)

We've already looked at the possible connection between diet and autism, with one factor being a leaky gut. Could a fatty acid deficiency be linked to the problem? Based on Ryan, it seems likely. Ryan has several of the illnesses and symptoms that Dr. Braly lists as resulting from fatty-acid deficiency, including hyperactivity, eczema, migraines, immune deficiency, and excessive thirst. Does this mean fatty acids are responsible for Ryan's autism? I doubt it, but I believe they may be connected to some of his symptoms. Consequently, we have begun a supplement plan that includes a variety of fatty acids.

Before you buy supplements, I suggest you test your child for fatty acids to see what he or she needs. Two options for testing are the Kennedy Krieger Institute and the Great Plains Laboratory. If you are unable to test, you may want to begin supplementation with flaxseeds or flaxseed oil, evening primrose oil, borage oil, or fish oil. These are categorized as omega-3 fatty acids, which are the ones most of us are deficient in. It is also important to avoid margarine, shortening, artificial colors and flavors, and the preservatives BHA and BHT, because they can hinder the conversion process of fatty acids.[60] Gay Langham-McNally, certified clinical nutritionist, recommends checking for pancreatic function before beginning fatty acid supplementation to see if the individual is able to digest and utilize the fatty acids. If the pancreas is not functioning properly, she recommends getting the pancreas in order, then beginning fatty acid treatment.

Melatonin

Many children with autism have difficulty sleeping. Some sleep only a few hours a night, while others wake up several times throughout the night. Melatonin, which is actually a hormone and not a vitamin, can be purchased over the counter at most health-food stores and helps regulate sleep. Our bodies produce melatonin in response to the diminished light at the end of the day until sunlight triggers its cessation. It should be taken within two hours of bedtime so it can work in conjunction with the body's natural melatonin.[61] Ryan was able to overcome his sleeping problem without any help, but many children with autism need melatonin nightly.

One word of caution: Dr. Rimland points out that "while

melatonin can benefit sleep and behavior, its long-term hormonal effects on puberty are unknown."[62]

Working with Professionals

As with other treatments, it's best to work with a professional whenever possible. While supplements like vitamin B_6 and DMG are safe even in large doses, others can be harmful if taken when they aren't needed. Vitamins and supplements are not as regulated as medications are, so quality and potency may vary. Even "natural" substances can have devastating effects if misused, but they can have tremendous benefits when used properly. A well-trained nutritionist or physician or a clinic like HRI Pfeiffer Treatment Center can test your child's blood, urine, and hair to determine what supplements he may need and structure a supplement plan specifically for him.

Resources

HRI Pfeiffer Treatment Center
1804 Centre Point Circle, Suite 102
Naperville, IL 60563
Phone: 630-505-0300
Fax: 630-505-1907
E-mail: info@hriptc.org
Web site: http://www.hriptc.org

Gay Langham-McNally, CCN
P.O. Box 1686
Issaquah, WA 98027
Phone: 425-837-8161
Fax: 425-837-8162
Web site: http://www.healthyrecovery.com

Provides lab test interpretation and correlation, as well as individual supplemental formulation according to lab results.

Mary N. Megson, M.D., F.A.A.P.
Pediatric and Adolescent Ability Center
Highland II Building
7229 Forest Avenue, Suite 211
Richmond, VA 23226
Phone: 804-673-9128
Fax: 804-673-9195

Supplement Suppliers

Kirkman Laboratories, Inc.
P.O. Box 1009
Wilsonville, OR 97070
Phone: 800-245-8282 or 503-694-1600
Fax: 503-682-0838
E-mail: dave@kirkmanlabs.com or jim@kirkmanlabs.com
Web site: http://www.kirkmanlabs.com
Supplier of Super Nu-Thera, DMG, cranberry extract, folic acid, B_{12}, probiotics, FOS, and other products for individuals with autism.

Women's International Pharmacy
5708 Monona Drive
Madison, WI 53716-3152
Phone: 800-279-5708 or 608-221-7800
Fax: 608-221-7819
E-mail: info@wipws.com
Web site: http://www.wipws.com

Medications

Some people consider medications before any other treatment, while others use them only as a last resort. Whichever approach you take, medications are available to help with attention span, panic attacks, hyperactivity, self-injurious behaviors, aggression, obsessive-compulsive disorders, sleeping disorders, and seizures.

Temple Grandin struggled with panic attacks from a hyper-aroused nervous system. For twenty years she tried to find answers through psychology, but by the time she turned thirty her panic attacks had begun causing other stress-related health problems. In her midthirties she sought biochemical intervention and began using Tofranil. At the writing of her book *Thinking in Pictures,* Grandin had been on medication for thirteen years.

> Taking the medication is like adjusting the idle adjustment screw on an old-fashioned automobile engine. Before I took Tofranil, my "engine" was racing all the time, doing so many revolutions per minute that it was tearing itself up. Now my nervous system is running at 55 MPH instead of 200 MPH, as it used to. I still have nerve cycles, but they seem to go between 55 and 90 MPH instead of 150 and 200 MPH.[63]

We've used two medications with Ryan. For about a year, Ryan was on Ritalin. Although it greatly improved his hyperactivity and attention, we became concerned about its long-term effect on the brain. I know of children who've been on Ritalin for many years with no apparent side effects, but we were concerned and took Ryan off it.

For about two years Ryan was also on Zoloft for his obsessive-compulsive behaviors. Besides his lining of toys and ritualistic behaviors with objects, he was overwhelmed with certain decision making. At night he would become terrified and yell, "Turn on the light!" When we turned it on, he would get hysterical and tell us to turn it off. As soon as we did, he would demand it be on. Or he would cry out, "Mommy, come here," but as soon as I got by his side, he would yell at me to go away. As soon as I left, he would cry for me to return. When he went on Zoloft, these behaviors stopped.

Since most drugs are researched for use in adults, I urge you to work with a doctor who has experience helping children with autism through the use of medications. He can explain the benefits and side effects of each one and advise you on which may be best for your child. Also, the Autism Research Institute has developed a chart that shows how parents rate the effectiveness of many drugs and nutrients, and that chart is provided at the end of this chapter.

Vaccinations

From the time we were children, we've accepted vaccinations as a part of growing up, as automatic as buying school supplies. Their benefits have long been documented. Donna Shalala, secretary of the Department of Health and Human Services under President Clinton, said, "Over many years, vaccines have protected millions of people from serious diseases and death. They are among the most cost-effective of all preventive public health practices."[64]

But there's another side to the issue, which Ms. Shalala hints at as she continues: "Like other medications, vaccines will never be

100 percent safe, but they save thousands of our children's lives every year. For those very few cases where a vaccine may cause an injury, we need to provide fair compensation. We also need to work vigorously to develop the safest possible vaccines. But most of all, we must not forget the great benefit we are gaining from widespread vaccination. We need to continue to protect our children from the diseases that have threatened them throughout time."[65]

Intellectually, we understand that vaccines will never be 100 percent safe, but what if our children are among the few injured by the vaccine? And how many are a "few"? Just how safe are the vaccines? Do clinical studies prove their safety? Do the benefits outweigh the risks? What are the risks of not vaccinating a child? Could autism be connected to vaccines? Am I risking my child's health by vaccinating or not vaccinating? I've asked myself these questions repeatedly since Ryan was diagnosed.

Dr. Bernard Rimland, in his article "Vaccinations: The Overlooked Factors," states that the benefits of vaccinations have been exaggerated while the risks have been minimized. "The fact is, vaccines are not nearly as safe, nor anywhere near as effective, as vaccination proponents claim." He points out that the death rate from measles decreased by 95 percent and the death rate from polio dropped 60 percent from its highest point *before* the respective vaccines were introduced.[66]

Aware of damages caused by vaccines, Congress passed the National Childhood Vaccine Injury Act of 1986 (PL 99-660) and directed the United States Department of Health and Human Services to administer the Vaccine Injury Compensation Program (VICP), which financially compensates vaccine-injured people after cases are heard in the U.S. Court of Claims in Washington,

D.C. The list of reactions includes death, anaphylactic shock (severe allergic reaction), seizures and convulsions, encephalopathy (brain inflammation), chronic arthritis, brachial neuritis, and vaccine-strain measles or polio viral infections.[67]

In her statement Ms. Shalala mentions that there are very few cases of vaccine injury, though I wonder if the numbers are accurate. Dr. Rimland states that, though physicians in the United States and the United Kingdom are *supposed* to report any adverse vaccine reaction that parents recount to them, the vast majority of these reactions go unreported. "A telephone survey by the National Vaccine Information Center (a parent advocacy group) reported that 94% of New York State doctors said they would not turn in official reports when parents notified them of significant vaccine side effects."[68] I can only guess why. Do they believe parents are overreacting to what they *think* is a reaction? Is it because there are no penalties for not reporting reactions? Or is it just too much paperwork? Whatever the reason, if adverse reactions are not being reported, then the statistics regarding vaccine safety are unreliable.

When you have to decide whether to vaccinate your child, you need to make an informed choice. Since there's much more than I can cover in one chapter, I hope you'll research this issue further in the books and associations noted in the chapter. It's not an easy decision.

The DPT Shot

Each vaccine can cause a variety of reactions, but two immunizations have drawn the most attention for children with autism: the DPT (diphtheria-pertussis-tetanus) and the MMR (measles-mumps-rubella). Harris Coulter and Barbara Loe Fisher, authors of *DPT: A Shot in the Dark*, point out that the pertussis portion of the DPT vaccine may cause what is known as "minimal brain damage," as well as encephalitis (brain inflammation) that can lead to autism. They also note that we vaccinate our children at younger ages than other countries,[69] perhaps before their immature immune systems are ready for these toxins.[70] In 1979 Japan changed its policy for DPT shots, postponing them until after the age of two. When it did, sudden infant death syndrome (SIDS) almost disappeared in Japan.[71]

The MMR Shot

In recent years studies have suggested a link between exposure to the measles vaccine and inflammatory bowel disease, including Crohn's disease and ulcerative colitis.[72] However, in February 1998 Dr. Andrew Wakefield and associates published the most controversial research in which autistic symptoms are linked with the MMR vaccine.[73]

Dr. Wakefield and his colleagues studied twelve children, ranging in age from three to ten, who had developed normally but then lost skills, including language. All of the children had intestinal abnormalities. The parents of eight of the children noted the onset of their behavioral difficulties corresponded to their MMR vaccination. Dr. Wakefield "identified associated gastrointestinal disease and developmental regression in a group of previously normal children, which was generally associated in time with possible environmental triggers."[74] He goes on to say that "in most cases, onset of symptoms was after the measles, mumps, and rubella immunisation," though he realizes that further studies are necessary to determine a definitive link.[75] Since their study was published in the *Lancet* in early 1998, they have observed an additional forty-eight children who experienced significant behavioral changes following the MMR vaccine. Forty-six of those children had gastrointestinal problems similar to those found in their study.[76]

Dr. Vijendra Singh and his associates have also found a link between the measles virus and a negative response in autism. His research looked at exposure to two viruses—measles and human herpesvirus-6 (HHV-6)—and an autoimmune response, in which the body attacks itself. "It is believed that early exposure to these viruses forces the body into mounting an immune response gone wrong."[77] Though it is not certain that the exposure to the measles virus was through the MMR vaccination, "virtually all subjects in the study had their MMR immunizations and none had any history of wild-type measles virus infection."[78]

What can be done? Dr. Singh says that "immunotherapy with intravenous immunoglobulin [IVIG] and transfer factor produces significant improvement of autistic characteristics."[79] Both of these types of immunotherapy will be looked at later in this chapter.

What about giving future vaccines? Dr. Wakefield says, "In all conscience I cannot support the idea of using all three vaccines together" and calls for the cessation of the MMR combination vaccine.[80] Some people who choose to continue vaccines separate the MMR into three vaccinations given several months or even a year apart.

Since Ryan is at the age for an MMR booster, we tested him for antibody levels to measles, mumps, and rubella. He tested immune to measles and rubella but not mumps. However, immunity levels can change over time, so without an MMR booster, Ryan's immunity to measles and rubella may diminish. We've chosen not to give him the booster unless we're convinced otherwise in the future.

The National Vaccine Information Center suggests eight questions to ask *before* you vaccinate your child:

1. Is my child sick right now?
2. Has my child had a bad reaction to a vaccination before?

3. Does my child have a personal or family history of:
   Vaccine reactions
   Convulsions or neurological disorders
   Severe allergies
   Immune system disorders
4. Do I know if my child is at high risk of reacting?
5. Do I have full information on the vaccine's side effects?
6. Do I know how to identify a vaccine reaction?
7. Do I know how to report a vaccine reaction?
8. Do I know the vaccine manufacturer's name and lot number?[81]

Before deciding about any vaccination, ask your physician for the consent form that is required for each vaccine, as well as the vaccine manufacturer's product information insert, which accompanies the vials of vaccine. This insert is an excellent source of information regarding reactions and contraindications, since the makers of vaccines are required by law to list all known risks. Take both the insert and the consent form home, and read them carefully. Another important resource for information is the *Physician's Desk Reference* (PDR), which should be available in your doctor's office or a local library.

Since most physicians believe that vaccinations are extremely important, you may feel pressured to get your child "caught up" that day. Don't be intimidated. This is your child and your decision. Take the time to choose wisely. You may feel obligated to follow the "schedule" for vaccinations, but this schedule is based on regular doctor visits, not necessarily on medical and scientific evidence that these are the best times for the shots.

If you suspect your child may have had a reaction to a previous vaccine, review family videos taken before and after the immunizations. If you find that he showed signs of a reaction, do your own research and talk with several trusted health professionals about whether or not to continue vaccinations.

If you decide to proceed with the vaccines, some physicians suggest using monovalent vaccines instead of combination shots and spreading out the vaccinations over time to avoid overloading the child's immune system. Make sure your child is well at the time of vaccination, since an illness could complicate his reaction to the vaccine.

If you choose not to vaccinate your child or to limit vaccinations, you need to be aware of your state laws regarding exemption forms for your child to attend school. These waivers allow for exemptions from immunizations due to medical or religious reasons.

Roger and I have wrestled with this issue extensively, for both of our children. As a parent, you will need to weigh the risks and benefits carefully so you'll be able to stand firm in your decision.

For More Information
National Vaccine Information Center (NVIC)
512 W. Maple Avenue, #206
Vienna, VA 22180
Phone: 703-938-DPT3 or 800-909-SHOT
Fax: 703-938-5768
E-mail: info@909shot.com
Web site: http://www.909shot.com

The Centers for Disease Control and Prevention
National Immunization Program Information Hotline
Phone: 800-232-2522
Web site: http://www.cdc.gov/nip/vacsafe/

Thinktwice Global Vaccine Institute
P.O. Box 9638-A
Santa Fe, NM 87504
Phone and fax: 505-983-1856
E-mail: global@thinktwice.com
Web site: http://www.thinktwice.com

Autism Autoimmunity Project
45 Iroquois Avenue
Lake Hiawatha, NJ 07034
Phone: 973-299-9162
Fax: 973-299-2668
E-mail: truegrit@gti.net

Enhancing the Immune System

In the quest to discover why some children become autistic while others do not, a growing body of evidence suggests that a poorly functioning immune system may often be an underlying cause of autism.[82] So strengthening the immune system may benefit the child with autism. Like every other system in the body, the immune system depends on an adequate supply of vitamins, minerals, fatty acids, and other nutrients to develop properly. When the immune system becomes compromised, it can be enhanced through a good diet and dietary supplements. Several other non-prescription supplements, as well, are likely to improve immune function. Two in particular have attracted the attention of autism researchers: colostrum and antigen-specific transfer factors.

Colostrum

Colostrum is the mother's "first milk" produced by all mammals, including humans, just before giving birth. For a couple of days after birth, the colostrum is secreted into the mother's milk to be passed on to the baby while nursing.

Colostrum contains a mix of components that are highly beneficial to the immune system, including "transfer factors." Simply put, transfer factors are molecules that can be taken from immune-sufficient donors and given to those with an immune deficiency in order to strengthen their immune systems. These transfer factors are credited with many aspects of health and have been used successfully in treating viral, fungal, bacterial, and parasitic diseases.[83] This means colostrum might benefit some children with autism since many have high yeast (fungus) in their gut and some have parasites or viral or bacterial infections in their systems.

Colostrum also contains high levels of "growth factors," which aid in healing cells of the intestinal mucosal lining of a leaky gut.[84] This also is good news for children with autism. As noted in chapter 7 on dietary intervention, one study showed that 43 percent of the autistic children studied had a leaky gut.

And the benefits don't stop there. Since colostrum contains both transfer factors and PRP (Proline-Rich Polypeptide), which can calm an overactive immune system, colostrum may even help autoimmune disorders, a possible factor in some cases of autism. In addition, colostrum may "stimulate the release of serotonin and dopamine and prolong their re-uptake,"[85] thereby allowing these important neurotransmitters to stay in the system longer.

Although several companies sell colostrum taken from animals, particularly cows, Kirkman Laboratories is one company that sells *casein-free* colostrum, which is important for many children. However, the possibility remains that some children may have an immune reaction.

Is colostrum a miracle product? I doubt it. But it may benefit our children, and there seem to be no side effects, even when it is taken in high doses. However, much like the die-off effect that can occur with initial antifungal treatments for Candida, the use of colostrum may have an initial die-off effect also. Because of this, you may want to start your child at a low dose and increase it over time. On the other hand, some practitioners suggest just the opposite—starting at high doses to get the immune system functioning better and after one to three months, when you can see the benefits, lowering the dose to a maintenance level. Each company's product differs in strength and content, so no set dosage can be recommended. Whatever the dosage level, it is important for the child to take it on an empty stomach with plenty of water. You may want to give it before three or four o'clock in the afternoon so it doesn't interfere with the child's sleep.

Antigen-Specific Transfer Factors

Another method of enhancing the immune system is through antigen-specific transfer factors or dialysable lymphocyte extract (DLyE). Unlike colostrum, which contains polyvalent (multiple specificities) transfer factors, this form of therapy collects *specific* transfer factors from appropriate donors and gives them to the beneficiaries. For example, if an individual needs to combat measles, then anti-measles transfer factors are collected and given to him so his body will have help in "learning" to fight the measles virus. Though this treatment seems promising, relatively little is currently known about its use with autism.

In a study published in 1980, E. G. Stubbs and associates found that transfer factors produced noteworthy improvement in the motoric (muscle movement) and social behavior of a severely autistic child with a congenital viral infection. The social improvement plateaued when the transfer factor was stopped.[86]

A study reported in 1996 described using DLyE with forty autistic patients, ranging in age from six to fifteen. Twenty-two of these children were considered "classically autistic," while the other eighteen did not meet all the criteria for infantile autism. Of the twenty-two children with classic autism, twenty-one responded to the treatment. Ten of those "became normal in that they were main-streamed into school and clinical characteristics were fully normalized."[87] Of the eighteen who were not classically autistic, only four responded to this therapy.

Formerly this type of immunotherapy could be administered only through intramuscular injection, which carried inherent risks and wasn't terribly accessible. However, Kirkman Laboratories is investigating several antigen-specific transfer-factor products developed to enhance immune function that would be taken orally and may particularly benefit those with autism and related disorders. Just a note of caution here. Some transfer-factor products are already on the market, but these *may* not include the antigen-specific transfer factors.

Remember, our children may be dealing with numerous microbes within their systems, much like an army battling multiple enemies at the same time. Our bodies have the ability to fight some germs, but if the body's "armies" are unarmed or are busy fighting various small battles, they won't have the strength to combat a larger, stronger enemy. So it's important to develop a "battle strategy."

With Ryan, we first had to deal with an underlying strep virus he carries in his body. We know this because he gets numerous strep infections each year. Once that virus is under control, we will move on to the next set of viruses. Finally, we plan to address any "childhood illness" viruses he may have received from his vaccinations.

To determine which viruses to begin with, we are working with a qualified professional and performing a variety of blood tests, then planning our attack strategy based on the test results. Unfortunately, some insurance companies will not cover the necessary blood tests, so parents and practitioners may have to determine where to begin without the benefit of testing. In either case some physicians recommend proceeding cautiously so the child's body is not trying to combat too much at any given time. One professional warns that if nutritional deficiencies aren't initially corrected or if this type of immunotherapy is not used at the right time for the child, some symptoms may actually be amplified rather than alleviated.[88] To find a qualified professional who has experience using this form of immunotherapy, contact Kirkman Laboratories at the number that follows.

Over the years many studies have been conducted on colostrum and other immune-enhancing factors, but now studies are underway to determine specifically how helpful they are for people with autism. I look forward to those findings.

For Further Information
Kirkman Laboratories, Inc.
P.O. Box 1009
Wilsonville, OR 97070
Phone: 888-KIRKMAN or 503-694-1600
Fax: 503-682-0838

E-mail: dave@kirkmanlabs.com or jim@kirkmanlabs.com

Web site: http://www.kirkmanlabs.com

This Web site provides a wealth of information on many products that may be useful in autism.

Intravenous Immunoglobulin (IVIG) Therapy

Garrett, son of Cindy and David Goldenberg, was developing like a typical child until he received his MMR vaccination when he was thirteen months old. Within two weeks he lost his eye contact and language skills and began to exhibit autistic behaviors. After his Hib (Haemophilus influenzae type b) vaccination at eighteen months, Garret regressed even further.

At that point Cindy took him to numerous doctors, searching for an answer. As she read medical information, she concluded that the MMR vaccine caused Garrett's autism, since the rubella virus can lead to brain inflammation, which in turn can disrupt the development of the myelination (the fatty myelin sheath surrounding the nerve cell). But it wasn't until she met with her fifty-fifth physician, Dr. Sudhir Gupta, that she found what she was looking for. He confirmed through an immunological panel that Garrett's rubella titers were very high and his IgA and IgG subclass levels were low. Because of Garrett's low IgG and history of upper respiratory infections, Dr. Gupta recommended Intravenous Immunoglobulin (IVIG) treatment.

The Goldenbergs began this treatment with Garrett, along with vitamin and nutrient therapy. Garrett, at nearly three years old, began to show tremendous improvement. Before IVIG therapy "Garrett had been distant and noncompliant. Afterward, he suddenly became focused and started to respond to our requests. The autistic behavior began to diminish and never came back. All of the speech, sensory integrative and behavior therapies began to work, because now, Garrett had the 'desire' to interact and learn." The Goldenbergs continued to give Garrett IVIG treatments for several months, and now he is considered recovered from autism.[89] Cindy has put together an information packet, available through the National Vaccine Information Center.

What Is IVIG Therapy?

IVIG therapy is a blood product that is extensively tested for several viruses and purified by physical and chemical processing of the blood. It is used as a replacement therapy for immune deficiency syndromes and as an immunomodulatory therapy for autoimmune and immunoinflammatory disorders. How IVIG works in children with autism isn't certain. It may have an anti-inflammatory effect on the brain, or it may suppress the manufacture of antibodies that attack the CNS myelin.[90] There just isn't enough information yet to know.

When Dr. Gupta gave IVIG therapy to ten children every four weeks for at least six months, each child showed improvement, ranging from mild to striking. He reported, "A consistent (although variable) change was observed in calmer and improved social behavior, better eye contact, loss of echolalia, and response to commands. The speech was improved in terms of better articulation and improved vocabulary; however, little effect was observed on spontaneous meaningful speech in most patients. One of the patients almost completely recovered speech and another had marked improvement in speech. These two patients are attending regular school."[91] Dr. Gupta found that younger children seemed to respond positively to the treatment earlier than older children.

We considered this treatment for Ryan, but since he has absent IgAs and normal IgGs, his chances of having a serious allergic reaction to it were increased. Also, the use of blood products always carries a risk of transmitting diseases even though the World Health Organization has established testing criteria for its production, which includes testing for the HIV virus and hepatitis B and C.[92] We didn't feel that the possible benefits *for us* outweighed the risks.

IVIG therapy is also very expensive, since there is a low supply of the product, and most insurance companies deny payment for it.

As with any treatment for autism, this therapy will not help every child. Dr. Rimland states that a study "concluded that the treatment may benefit only a small subset of autistic individuals—although that subset may improve dramatically."[93]

Detoxification

Every day our bodies obtain unwanted substances (toxins) that can be harmful. These can be internal, which include the "leftovers" of our own metabolic processes and by-products of our gut flora. Or the toxins may be external, like heavy metals, pesticides, or other contaminants, as well as the residuals of good things like medications or foods that are taken from our environment through our food, air, or water. Whether the toxins are made internally or brought in from the outside, our bodies still need to get rid of them. Detoxification rids the body of toxins.

Dr. Sidney Baker describes detoxification this way.

Getting rid of toxins is a two step operation. The way I deal with my household trash is a reasonable analogy.

After separating the recyclables I do step one, which is the placing of the trash in containers and leaving it out in the driveway. Periodically Harry comes with his truck to take care of step two, which is removal of the stuff from the premises. The process depends not only on the completion of both steps, but a degree of balance between the two.[94]

Two organs, the liver and the kidneys, help with detoxification, with the liver primarily in charge. It removes toxins from the blood and converts them into harmless substances that can be eliminated from the body. This is done in two phases. In phase one the toxins are activated, or "made sticky," so that carrier molecules will attach to them better.

Phase two occurs when carrier molecules attach to the toxins and remove them from the body. Sulfation occurs when the active form of the toxin is connected to sulfates for removal. If a person is deficient in sulfates, then the toxins have no way of leaving and can build up. If there is phase-one activation, without proper phase two, the now-sticky toxins can attach themselves to normal proteins instead of the carrier molecules, which should have removed the toxins from the system.

Sulfate Deficiency

According to Dr. Rosemary Waring, most children with autism show a deficiency of sulfates in their plasma. Ninety-two percent of the children with autism she has tested show sulfate levels that are approximately one-eighth the level of her healthy controls.[95] Low sulfates can lead to a leaky gut, often found in children with autism, and increased colonization of viruses in tissues and a weakness in the phenolsulfotransferase (PST) system.

Dr. Waring mentions several symptoms of a PST weakness or abnormality, including "migraine or migraine in a family member, red face, red ears, dark circles under eyes, bloated stomach, colic as a baby, runny nose, eczema, asthma, thirsty, sweating at night, unexplained high temperatures with or without vomiting."[96]

Testing for a PST abnormality can be done in two ways. The first, which can be conducted through Great Smokies Diagnostic Laboratory, adds safe amounts of probes (aspirin, caffeine, and acetaminophen) into the child's system to see how well the body detoxifies them.[97] The second is through an MHPG test, which looks at a twenty-four-hour urine sample to evaluate how the body detoxifies both external and internal toxins. Your physician can perform this test using the Mayo Medical Lab.

To my knowledge, there is no recommended treatment for a weakness in the PST system, except trying to raise the levels of sulfates. Some limit the amount of phenols ingested to keep the PST system from being overburdened, but this is difficult to control since phenols are found in any food with color. The Feingold diet, which removes all artificial flavors and colors, can be a good step toward unburdening the detoxification system.

Sulfates aren't easily absorbed through the gut, so adding sulfates to the diet may not help. An organic sulfur called MSM (methylsulphonylmethane) may be a "pre-cursor" for the lacking sulfate. That means oxidation should make MSM become sulfate, but whether it does is not yet known.[98] MSM is available as a nutritional supplement from Kirkman Laboratories and some health-food stores. Another possibility is adding a supplement called molybdenum. Dr. Waring notes that adding molybdenum raises sulfate levels in some children but not all.[99]

Some parents have tried adding magnesium sulfate (Epsom

salts) to their children's bathwater with varying degrees of results. Since magnesium sulfate can be absorbed through the skin, it *may* increase the amount of sulfates in the system, and it's simple to do. We dissolve two cups of Epsom salts in hot bathwater. After the water is a comfortable temperature, Ryan plays in the tub, for a half-hour or more if possible. The water is fine for washing the hair or body, just not for drinking.

Amino Acid Abnormalities

Amino acid abnormalities—either deficient or elevated levels—can also hinder detoxification since an "important task of amino acid metabolism is to provide carrier molecules to rid the body of unwanted substances."[100] People can be tested for imbalances, and amino acids can be given to try to bring the system into balance.

Learning More About Biomedical Treatments

Since there are *many more options* for testing and treating the biomedical aspects of autism, I strongly recommend two excellent books that will give further details, as well as additional treatments to pursue.

Biological Treatments for Autism and PDD by William Shaw (Overland Park, Kans.: self-published, 1998). This book has been so helpful to me that the pages are falling out from overuse. Dr. Shaw explains in great detail and with medical accuracy many aspects of biomedical treatments that should be considered. I found it helpful to read his book after we had Ryan tested with Dr. Shaw's organic acid test so I could compare what I was reading to

Ryan's results and put into action what pertained to him. This book can be ordered directly through Dr. Shaw's laboratory.

Biomedical Assessment Options for Children with Autism and Related Problems by S. M. Baker, M.D., and Jon Pangborn (San Diego: Autism Research Institute, 1997). This book, also known as the "DAN! protocol," reports the findings of leading specialists from around the world who gathered at the first Defeat Autism Now! (DAN!) Conference in 1995, though it has been periodically updated with new information. It provides information and guidance on a number of tests available, including bowel permeability studies, secretory IgA, mineral studies, amino acid analysis, and autoimmunity evaluations. This book can be purchased from the Autism Research Institute.

ARI Publ. 34/July 1999

Autism Research Institute • 4182 Adams Avenue • San Diego, CA 92116

PARENT RATINGS OF BEHAVIORAL EFFECTS OF DRUGS AND NUTRIENTS

The parents of autistic children represent a vast and important reservoir of information on the benefits—and adverse effects—of the large variety of drugs and other interventions that have been tried with their children. Starting in 1967 the Autism Research Institute has been collecting parent ratings of the usefulness of the many interventions tried on their autistic children.

The following data have been collected from the more than 16,000 parents who have completed our questionnaires designed to collect such information. For the purposes of the present table, the parent responses on a six-point scale have been combined into three categories: "made worse" (ratings 5 and 6), "no effect" (ratings 1 and 2), and "made better" (ratings 3 and 4).

% WORSE[A]	% NO EFFECT	% BETTER
■	□	▨

Note: Several seizure drugs are listed twice. The first listing (behav) shows their behavioral effects, and the second listing (seiz) shows their effects on seizures.

DRUGS — I. DRUGS

DRUGS	% WORSE	% NO EFFECT	% BETTER	NO. OF CASES[B]	BETTER/ WORSE[A]
Aderall	33	18	48	33	1.5:1
Amphetamine	48	28	24	990	0.5:1
Anafranil	34	34	32	261	0.9:1
Antibiotics	28	63	9	1357	0.3:1
Antifungals[C]					
Diflucan	7	21	71	28	10.0:1[D]
Nystatin	4	48	47	384	10.6:1
Atarax	24	53	22	360	0.9:1
Benadryl	23	50	26	2038	1.1:1
Beta Blocker	18	43	39	214	2.2:1
Buspar	23	43	33	145	1.4:1
Chloral Hydrate	42	32	26	257	0.6:1
Clonapin	21	27	52	67	2.5:1
Clonidine	22	31	47	641	2.2:1
Clozapine	38	41	22	37	0.6:1
Cogentin	19	54	27	106	1.5:1
Cylert	47	32	21	492	0.5:1
Deanol	15	55	30	183	2.0:1
Depakene (behav)	24	45	32	601	1.3:1
Depakene (seiz)	11	28	61	419	5.4:1
Desipramine	34	14	51	35	1.5:1
Dilantin (behav)	28	49	24	975	0.8:1
Dilantin (seiz)	13	34	53	317	4.0:1
Felbatol	27	36	36	22	1.3:1[D]
Fenfluramine	20	51	29	426	1.4:1

DRUGS

Drug	Bar values	NO. OF CASES[B]	BETTER/ WORSE[A]
Halcion	39 / 21 / 39	33	1.0:1
Haldol	38 / 27 / 35	992	0.9:1
Lithium	26 / 42 / 31	299	1.2:1
Luvox	17 / 39 / 43	23	2.5:1[D]
Mellaril	27 / 38 / 34	1863	1.3:1
Mysoline (behav)	47 / 39 / 14	113	0.3:1
Mysoline (seiz)	14 / 60 / 26	42	1.8:1
Naltrexone	24 / 41 / 35	157	1.5:1
Paxil	18 / 41 / 41	34	2.3:1
Phenergan	35 / 40 / 26	168	0.7:1
Phenobarbital (behav)	47 / 37 / 16	956	0.3:1
Phenobarbital (seiz)	14 / 44 / 42	376	3.0:1
Prolixin	31 / 27 / 42	62	1.4:1
Prozac	33 / 30 / 37	552	1.1:1
Risperdal	16 / 21 / 64	58	4.1:1
Ritalin	45 / 27 / 29	2788	0.6:1
Stelazine	28 / 44 / 28	393	1.0:1
Tegretol (behav)	23 / 45 / 32	1081	1.4:1
Tegretol (seiz)	10 / 32 / 58	572	5.9:1
Thorazine	36 / 40 / 25	836	0.7:1
Tofranil	31 / 36 / 32	535	1.0:1
Valium	35 / 42 / 23	695	0.7:1
Zarontin (behav)	32 / 45 / 23	97	0.7:1
Zarontin (seiz)	16 / 51 / 33	61	2.0:1
Zoloft	38 / 29 / 33	69	0.9:1

NUTRIENT — II. SUPPLEMENTS

Nutrient	Bar values	NO. OF CASES[B]	BETTER/ WORSE[A]
Calcium[E]	2 / 56 / 41	417	19.2:1
Dimethylglycine (DMG)	7 / 51 / 43	3217	6.5:1
Folic Acid	3 / 54 / 43	579	13.9:1
Magnesium alone	6 / 64 / 30	187	4.7:1
Melatonin	34 / 66	38	-F
Vitamin B3 (niacin/niacinamide)	5 / 51 / 44	255	8.5:1
Vitamin B6 alone	7 / 62 / 31	431	4.5:1
Vitamin B6 and magnesium	4 / 49 / 45	3582	11.5:1
Vitamin C	3 / 57 / 41	637	14.3:1
Zinc	4 / 52 / 44	349	11.9:1

A. "Worse" refers only to behavior. Drugs, but not nutrients, typically also cause physical problems if used long-term.
B. No. of cases is cumulative over several decades, so does not reflect current usage levels (e.g., Haldol is now seldom used).
C. Antifungal drugs are used only if autism is yeast-related.
D. Better/worse ratios marked "D" are unstable due to the small number of cases rated "worse." A small change in "worse" changes the ratio greatly.
E. Calcium effects not due to dairy-free diet; statistics similar for milk drinkers and non-milk drinkers.
F. Caution: While melatonin can benefit sleep and behavior, its long-term hormonal effects on puberty are unknown.

Chapter 9

The Parent-Doctor Balance

What I am intrigued by is how this is a parent led phenomenon.
[Almost] everything I've learned about this disease has come from parents.

DR. ANDREW WAKEFIELD

A few months after our daughter was born, I ruptured my appendix. I didn't *know* that it was ruptured; I just knew that I couldn't bear the pain, so Roger took me to the emergency room. After several examinations, an x-ray, and some blood tests, the doctor informed me of the diagnosis and the surgery he would perform. I didn't know anything about treating a ruptured appendix, but that didn't matter. My doctor did.

Unlike a ruptured appendix, autism—a disorder with no known cause or cure—calls for a different kind of relationship between doctor and patient. I often urge parents to stop seeing the doctor as the ultimate authority and to start viewing him or her as a member of their board of advisors. And our doctors need to see us for who we are, the CEOs of the partnership, the ones who have insight and knowledge and the ability to make decisions for appropriate treatment. Ultimately, we are the ones who make the final decisions on what is best for our children.

We've had the good fortune of working with some excellent doctors who are extremely dedicated to our son's progress.

However, at times when I pursued a new treatment or test for Ryan, I've almost engaged in a hostile takeover to convince a doctor to help. If he agreed, I came out feeling like the victor. This shouldn't be the case. Parents and doctors have the same goals in facing autism: to find answers and make the best decisions for the children affected by this disorder. To reach those goals, the parents and the doctors each have a role, well described by Victoria Beck, mother of a child with autism: "[The] parents' determination, information and education [should] meet the consideration, investigation and facilitation of doctors. When this equation is out of balance, what you get is polarization. [It is important] to never compromise doing whatever is needed to put this equation back in balance."[1]

The Parents' Side of the Equation

Determination

One of the greatest things parents bring to the partnership is determination. We are motivated to do what may seem impossible to others. I like the way this story describes it.

There were two warring tribes in the Andes, one that lived in the lowlands and the other high in the mountains. The mountain people invaded the lowlanders one day, and as part of their plundering of the people, they kidnapped a baby of one of the lowlander families and took the infant with them back up into the mountains. The lowlanders didn't know how to climb the mountain. They didn't know any of the trails that the mountain people used, and they didn't know where to find the mountain people or how to track them in the steep terrain. Even so, they sent out their best party of fighting men to climb the mountain and bring the baby home.

The men tried first one method of climbing and then another. They tried one trail and then another. After several days of effort, however, they had climbed only several hundred feet. Feeling hopeless and helpless, the lowlander men decided that the cause was lost, and they prepared to return to their village below.

As they were packing their gear for the descent, they saw the baby's mother walking toward them. They realized that she was coming down the mountain that they hadn't figured out how to climb. And then they saw that she had her baby strapped to her back. *How could that be?* One man greeted her and said, "We couldn't climb this mountain. How did you do this when we, the strongest and most able men in the village, couldn't do it?"

She shrugged her shoulders and said, "It wasn't your baby."[2]

As a parent, I understand the determination that would drive a mother to find and reclaim her baby. We are just as truly fighting for our babies, and we would climb any mountain in our way to rescue them. Some people tried to discourage us from pursuing ABA therapy, but we were determined, and Ryan's life was changed. When Victoria Beck tried to show the benefits of using secretin to treat autism, she was scoffed at, but her determination ultimately led to a possible breakthrough.

Then when the news of secretin was first reported in 1998,

there was great excitement, but with that excitement came a secretin shortage. Two other families and I teamed up to find the secretin we needed. We spent hours calling every hospital and pharmacy we could find in our part of the state, and when we located a precious vial, we drove to neighboring cities to pick it up. But it was worth it. Because of our determination, our children began secretin therapy, and Ryan's language skyrocketed. And it will be *your* determination that will drive you to seek answers and help for what your child needs most.

Information

As parents, we watch our children day in and day out, and we know them best. We may not know all the medical terminology and labels, but we know their condition. Only we are aware of their complete history. It's imperative that we accurately document our children's ongoing medical treatments and reactions, recording anything that may affect treatment decisions. Does your child have bowel problems? Does he wake up during the night? Does he have headaches or stomach pains? Document it. How often does it occur? How severe is it? Keep track daily to see if changes occur as a result of different events, diets, or medications.

Because Ryan takes many supplements and medications, I've posted a chart in our kitchen, and every day I check off what he takes and how many of each. This chart not only helps Roger and me monitor what we give him, it enables us to look back when we see changes in Ryan—positive or negative—to determine if there's a connection. As I mentioned earlier, this is how we discovered the benefits of his vitamins and the problem with the red dye on the nystatin capsules.

Obviously you can't document *everything* your child does, nor is that necessary. Just keep track of what seems important. If you're trying a new treatment, keep detailed records of the results. Not only will this help you determine its effectiveness, but it may also be needed to convince your doctor or insurance company of its necessity.

The information we possess is invaluable in our children's treatment, but it doesn't do much good if it remains merely with us. We need to accurately relay that information to the doctors we've put on our "board of advisors." I do this, in part, through a notebook I've created about our son.

Develop a Notebook About Your Child

I made two identical binders on Ryan, one that I gave our primary doctor and one that I keep at home. The books contain three main sections clearly separated with dividers. The first is a brief, written "snapshot" or profile of Ryan. The second section follows it up with a more thorough history. The last section contains medical records—copies of test results and pertinent information from doctors and laboratories.

This notebook helps our primary doctor keep all of Ryan's tests and treatments straight, and it allows me to quickly bring a new doctor up to speed on Ryan's medical background.

The Profile

The first section summarizes in one or two pages your child's history, treatments, and test results without conveying all the details. Keep this short and succinct so that it serves as a quick reminder for the doctor on where you stand in the therapy process. We keep Ryan's profile on the computer so we can update it periodically, allowing our doctor to be current with the total picture.

A Thorough History

After the snapshot pages, include a more thorough history, covering everything from your child's history that may be helpful, even if it seems minor or insignificant to you.

Before you start, I recommend you get a copy of your child's medical records from any doctors you've seen. At our clinic I had to sign a release form and pay a nominal fee to cover the copying costs, but it was well worth it because the documentation either verified what I remembered or reminded me of things I'd forgotten. The documents also revealed patterns in his illnesses and treatments. Three years ago I wouldn't have considered the frequency of Ryan's use of antibiotics important, but I do now. Although I knew he'd had several doses of antibiotics, I was shocked to see how often he was put on them. When I learned that antibiotics can change the gut flora and allow yeast to grow more rapidly, I decided to test Ryan for yeast. The testing confirmed my suspicion of an overgrowth, and we were able to treat it. The time you invest in writing out your child's medical history may lead you to treatments you otherwise would have overlooked.

In this section I would include:

- Pregnancy and childbirth information (Note any complications or medications.)
- Vaccines (Give the dates and any response to each vaccine.)
- Antibiotic use (Note the frequency, type of antibiotic, and any known reactions.)
- Allergies (Does your child or any family member have a history of allergies?)
- Travel (Has your child traveled outside the United States?)
- Eating habits (Is he a picky eater? What kinds of food does he eat?)

- Food sensitivities (Does your child behave differently after eating certain foods?)
- Sleeping habits (Does he sleep through the night? How many hours at a time?)
- Changes in diet or appetite (When did this occur? Did it normalize after time?)
- Constipation or diarrhea (Note the frequency and severity of these occurrences.)
- Surgeries (List pertinent information about each procedure.)
- Injuries (List injury and outcome of injury.)
- Family history (Does any other family member have autism or a related disorder?)
- General health (Is he sick often? What have others said about his appearance?)
- How your child spends a typical day (Log twenty-four hours to see if there are clues to an underlying problem. Your doctor might recognize a connection you've missed.)

Although your primary doctor will know much of this information, he may still learn from it. You may also need it for any specialists, since they won't know your child as well as your pediatrician. Systematically reviewing and analyzing your child's medical history and behavioral patterns will also increase your observations and awareness, which in turn will make you better informed as the CEO of this project to rescue your child. The preparation will not be wasted effort.

Test Results

This last section includes several subsections, also separated by dividers and clearly marked to allow the doctors easy access to the information. Each subsection should contain one doctor your child has seen or a lab where he has undergone testing. I include any specialists we've taken Ryan to, such as neurologists, developmental specialists, allergists, immunologists, or gastroenterologists. I also include any tests done by independent labs like the Great Plains Laboratory. Be sure to include a photocopy of test results, doctors' letters, and other pertinent information.

Having Ryan's history organized this way allows me to make better use of our visits to the doctor. For example, when I asked our primary doctor about the need for a particular test, he quickly turned to the neurologist's section and found that the test had already been done as part of a group of tests in Ryan's preliminary evaluations for autism.

Education

Recently I had a phone call from a man who was angry that his doctor hadn't told him about a certain treatment for autism. I reminded him that autism is a multifaceted disorder generally requiring more than one approach for each child. If a doctor is familiar with autism, he or she probably specializes in one area of treatment. He may be an expert in that arena, but with the amount of information readily available these days, he can't be an expert in all fields and have all the answers. As parents, we have to take the initiative to educate ourselves on the options. We need to take responsibility for finding answers and researching leads.

So how do we educate ourselves?

Newsletters

As I mentioned earlier, I subscribe to several newsletters to stay current. My favorite is the *Autism Research Review International*, edited by Dr. Bernard Rimland, which is a "quarterly publication…

reviewing biomedical and educational research in the field of autism and related disorders."[3] Although the publication is only eight pages long, it summarizes a wealth of information. As such, it becomes a springboard for me. If an article piques my interest, I get the original material it condensed, as well as related articles that may help me understand more fully. Other publications you may want to consider are located in Appendix C.

Other Parents

Mary Alice, who has a child with autism, reads everything she can get her hands on. She first was my mentor, then my partner in the fight against autism, and now is my dear friend. However, our initial conversation overwhelmed me.

As we spoke on the phone that first time, she asked me so many questions. "Have you had Ryan tested for yeast?"

"No," I replied, "why would I?" She explained why I should.

"Have you started Ryan on the gluten-free and casein-free diet yet?" she asked next.

"No. It just sounds too hard, and I don't think Ryan would be a candidate for it anyway." I didn't know enough about the diet to say that, but I was already feeling defensive.

In a matter of forty-five minutes, Mary Alice had explained many tests and treatments she had pursued that I hadn't given a second thought. When I finally excused myself and hung up the phone, I broke into tears. Ryan was doing so well with the ABA treatment that I hadn't taken time to explore the biomedical needs he might have. I felt so guilty. I went upstairs and found my husband. I needed him to hold me and tell me that it was okay, that I hadn't messed up Ryan's life by not pursuing these things yet.

Even though I was overwhelmed that night, Mary Alice

became a catalyst in my education. Since then I've learned to talk more with other parents and find out what they're doing. Several of us have become close, so when one learns something new, she is quick to inform the rest. By doing this we save each other a lot of time and research.

DAN! Conferences

When it comes to educating yourself in biomedical advances in testing and treating autism, no experience compares with attending the Defeat Autism Now! (DAN!) Conference. Not only will you hear leading autism specialists and researchers from around the world, but you'll be able to interact with them throughout the weekend. For people who are unable to go or for those who attend and want to review the conference, tapes are available afterward. Tapes from previous conferences can be ordered through the Autism Research Institute or Insta-Tapes (800-NOW-TAPE).

Passing on Your Education to Your Doctors

Dr. Andrew Wakefield, leading gastroenterologist and researcher, has stated that "parents of autistic children are amongst the most well-informed that I have ever come across in my practice."[4] The better educated we are in autism, the stronger our hope for our children. But our education doesn't end with ourselves. Whatever we learn from our research needs to be relayed to the professionals who can help process and facilitate the information.

Give Them Information

When I read a new article that I feel may be important in Ryan's recovery, I copy it and deliver it to several of our doctors, not just our primary physician. One of the most important things you can give your doctor is the DAN! protocol, since it is written for physicians to guide them in testing and treating patients with autism.

Have you recently been to an autism conference that stirred your interest in a new treatment? Get a tape of the speaker, along with the handout, and give them to your doctor. My doctor appreciates my highlighting some of the key points so he doesn't have to wade through the entire article if it isn't necessary. Don't expect him to run home that day and tackle it, but ask if he will do so before your next visit, and give him the date for it. Also, allow him the chance to discuss the information with other doctors who may have already performed the treatment. Do your homework, and give him the phone numbers of these doctors. Giant walls can be broken down when doctors talk with doctors.

Send Them to a Conference

A great way to educate your doctors is to help send them to a conference, especially a DAN! Conference. There they will hear firsthand the top specialists in the world, and they can interact with them and other doctors. Questions can be answered by those who know the answers best. Not only will they come back with more information than you could pass on through articles or tapes, but they will likely be even more motivated and open to working closely with you.

Since going to the DAN! Conference is expensive, consider contacting other parents who see the same doctor and pooling your money to cover his plane fare, registration, or hotel costs. He may not accept the funding you offer, but on the other hand, your commitment and financing may be what it takes to get him to attend. If you've found a good doctor, invest in him. The better educated your doctor is, the more rewards you'll reap in treatment options and cooperation.

Be Prepared

Before you meet with your doctor, prepare so you make the best use of the time. Write out your questions in order of priority. Try to learn as much as you can ahead of time so your questions are more specific and focused. Rather than saying, "What can you tell me about a gluten-free, casein-free diet?" you might ask, "We're thinking about changing our son's diet to be gluten and casein free. Do you think that's a good idea for him? Are there reasons why we shouldn't do it? Should we perform any tests before or after we start?" By being prepared and educated before your visit, you'll get specific answers for your child, and you'll make the most of everyone's time.

Adopt a Positive Approach

Being in sales for several years, I learned that a positive presentation is half the battle. The same is true here. If I'm well informed and well prepared, patient, yet persistent, I have the best chance of swaying my doctor to explore new tests or treatments.

When I'm interested in a new idea, I first give the doctor written or taped material on it. Then I make an appointment to discuss it with him face to face. I go in, well educated, ready to explain my reasons for wanting to try this, yet open to hearing his thoughts. If he's negative, I ask why he thinks it wouldn't be a good idea. Are there harmful side effects? Is the risk too high? If the risk is minimal, I ask him to explain what would be the harm in trying.

As well as being a person of action, I'm very emotional. So when I learn something that might help my son, I get emotionally charged. But if I communicate that my desire to pursue a treatment is based not on desperation but on a well-thought-out, logical plan, then I have a better chance for success. I keep my emotions in check, using them to motivate me but not to control me.

Respect Your Doctor's Opinion

Just as you want your doctor to consider your ideas, so you must consider his. Don't immediately decide whether to follow or reject his advice. Take time to go over his opinions with your spouse or a friend and weigh the pros and cons. This allows you to make a rational decision rather than an emotional one.

If the doctor has closed the door on a treatment you want to pursue, think about his reasons, but don't let that be your deciding factor. Trust yourself. If you believe there's a treatment that will help your child and you've thought it through, fight for it. You're the CEO! And if this doctor isn't doing the job you need, seek out another.

On the other end of the spectrum, if your doctor is supportive, thank him. Has your doctor gone out of his way to learn more about autism for you? Has he taken the time to read or research a new form of treatment? Take time to write a note of appreciation.

Be Selective About Your Board of Advisors

As the CEO of this operation, analyze what you're looking for in each doctor and choose carefully. You'll be working closely with these doctors to guide your child's treatment plan. Over the last four years we've seen numerous doctors of varying specialties, and from them we've chosen a few that we consider our board. Two criteria stand out as critical.

First, how much experience does the doctor have with autism? Does he have other patients with autism? Is he up-to-date on treatment options? Is he open to new ideas, or is he stuck in outdated methods?

Second, is the doctor willing to partner with you? Will he consider what you say? Will he take the time to investigate your research? Will he be open to facilitating appropriate treatments? I would much rather have a doctor who is not as experienced but willing to learn than one who has worked extensively with autism yet sees only his point of view.

Although there are many things we can do as parents, one thing we can't do is facilitate medical treatments for our children. If we don't have a medical doctor on our board to put them into practice, the answers do us no good. When you ask your doctor to facilitate tests or treatments that are outside his expertise, he may be concerned that unscrupulous doctors or researchers are preying on you as desperate parents. That's a valid concern, but if you show yourself to be well informed and capable of making educated decisions, he will be more open to your wishes. We've learned much about our son from unconventional tests that some doctors shunned. Often we had to pay for these tests out of our own pocket, but we're grateful to our doctor who was willing to order these tests to help us find more pieces to our son's puzzle.

If you have difficulty finding a doctor who will partner with you, contact the Autism Research Institute. They keep a list of doctors who have attended one or more DAN! Conferences and, therefore, may be more open to exploring new avenues.

Remember, you're not locked into a contract with any doctor. Your goal is to find the best care for your child. Be faithful to finding the right doctors, and once you do, strive to keep the relationship in balance.

Partner with your doctors for your child's sake.

Chapter 10

Sensory Issues

Without your senses...your brain...would be an eternal prisoner
in the solitary confinement of your skull.

SENSATION AND PERCEPTION

Each of us brings meaning to our surroundings through our senses.

Yesterday I baked brownies but forgot to take them out of the oven at the right time. I had gone outside for a while, and when I came in, my house smelled wretched. I quickly remembered my brownies and put two and two together. I didn't need to look at them, touch them, or taste them to know they were burned. My nose gave me a clue, and my experiences filled in the missing pieces: The brownies would be black and hard as rock. When I took them out of the oven, my sight and touch confirmed my assumption.

Sometimes, however, our senses can be wrong. One year, as a practical joke, I made a special sponge cake for a friend. I took two large, rectangular sponges, placed one on top of the other in the shape of a pound cake, and then completely covered the sponges with delicious frosting. I topped it off with candles and gave it to my unsuspecting friend.

My friend's senses told him he was one lucky guy. The cake looked delicious, and when he snitched a bit of the frosting, it tasted great. Then he tried to cut it. He graciously *continued* trying to cut it—without hurting my feelings—but to no avail. As a smile crept across my face, he figured out the joke.

Our senses are designed to help us decipher life experiences. Sight, smell, touch, hearing, and taste act as our guides. But what if our guides aren't accurate? Individuals with sensory disorders have inaccurate guides sending them faulty or exaggerated messages. Some people have hyposensitivity (underactive), which prevents them from picking up cues from their senses, and some have hypersensitivity (overactive), which causes them to overreact to stimulation. A child with hypersensitive hearing will hear sounds you and I don't hear or choose not to hear. Temple Grandin struggled with sensory issues, which she described in her book *Thinking in Pictures.*

> When I was little, loud noises were also a problem, often feeling like a dentist's drill hitting a nerve. They actually caused pain. I was scared to death of balloons popping, because the sound was like an explosion in my ear. Minor noises that most people can tune out drove me to distraction.[1]

Another aspect of sensory malfunction is the inability to understand and organize sensory information once it's received. With her books *Sensory Integration and Learning Disorders* and *Sensory Integration and the Child,* Dr. A. Jean Ayres, an occupational therapist, pioneered what is now commonly called sensory integration. She describes the importance of the senses properly integrating.

> Sensory integration is the neurological process that organizes sensation from one's own body and from the environment and makes it possible to use the body effectively

within the environment.... Sensory integration is information processing.... The brain must select, enhance, inhibit, compare, and associate the sensory information in a flexible, constantly changing pattern; in other words, the brain must integrate it.[2]

When we first began treating Ryan's autism, two occupational therapists mentioned Ryan's sensory problems, talking about his "proprioceptive needs" and "vestibular system." I had never heard these terms before, and I was skeptical. Were they reading that into our situation? Watching them work with him, I saw that he enjoyed all the sensory input, but was this really a need or more of a bonus therapy for Ryan?

Jude Teicher, an autism specialist in a public school, believes sensory problems are so common within autism that if she meets a child without sensory issues, she questions the autism diagnosis. Certainly there will be varying issues and degrees of severity, but the majority of children with autism have at least one sensory issue. As we investigated Ryan's sensory responses, we were amazed at what we learned.

Symptoms of Sensory Disorders

Let's look at the most common indicators that a child may have faulty sensory guides. Then we'll examine ways to deal with these issues.

Tactile
If you suspect your child is sensitive to touch, compare his behavior to the following list:

- Doesn't like being touched
- Rubs skin after being touched
- Doesn't feel a touch immediately (delayed sense of touch)
- Has high tolerance for pain
- Doesn't like certain clothing or tags on clothing
- Has difficulty wearing new clothes
- Wears clothes for the wrong season
- Often removes clothes
- Has trouble wearing shoes or socks
- Doesn't like having his hair or teeth brushed
- Doesn't like having his nails cut or cleaned
- Doesn't chew his food
- Avoids certain textures of food
- Avoids certain textures of sensory materials (play clay, mud, shaving cream)
- Has a hard time sitting still
- Is uncoordinated
- Washes hands often; doesn't like dirty hands
- Uses fingertips instead of entire hand
- Walks on toes
- Is a heavy walker

Ryan had several tactile issues that developed so gradually we didn't recognize them. The first ones related to his head. As an infant, Ryan had loved having his hair washed, but as he grew, he became increasingly agitated by someone washing or brushing his hair. Although he didn't mind washing his body, he would scream and cry each time we put water on his head. Trying to get his hair cut took three adults and some interesting contortions. The stylist usually took us in the back room so we wouldn't scare the other children.

Ryan also hated having his teeth brushed. Before we knew

about his hypersensitive mouth, one of us would hold him still while the other brushed his teeth. When we learned that brushing his teeth might actually be painful to him, we felt guilty about forcing him. Later we discovered that an electric toothbrush helped desensitize his mouth.

We believe Ryan's picky eating resulted from both taste and tactile sensitivities. Ryan refused to eat foods with certain textures. He liked crunchy or soft foods but couldn't stand anything slimy, like spaghetti, or mushy, like applesauce, in his mouth. Even a speck touching his tongue sent him into hysteria. One day our occupational therapist put a tiny bit of applesauce into a big cup of water and let Ryan drink the water from a spoon. Ryan did great as long as the spoon contained only water. But when a *very* small bit of applesauce touched his tongue, he arched his back, screamed, and almost vomited.

Today, Ryan no longer deals with these tactile issues. Although he's still a picky eater, probably due to his oversensitive taste buds, he now eats foods with various textures, spaghetti being one of his favorites.

Auditory

As with Ryan, your child's reaction to auditory stimuli may be a concern. Symptoms of auditory sensitivities include the following:

- Overreacts to loud noises
- Overreacts to common noises in public places
- Covers his ears at times
- Turns to listen to sounds most people ignore
- Turns up the volume on the television or stereo fairly high
- Tunes others out
- Is distracted or disturbed by background noises

- Is noisy or loud
- Doesn't like being in a group
- Throws a tantrum when he hears certain noises
- Is delayed in his language
- Bangs items together
- Crinkles or tears paper
- Has no tolerance for noisy household appliances (vacuums, blenders)
- Hums or sings to himself frequently

Ryan didn't have many auditory problems, but he was extremely sensitive to the sounds in a public bathroom. The sounds created by tiled floors and walls overwhelmed him; flushing the toilet or turning on the hand dryer terrified him. Overcoming his reactions to these sounds took months, but now he actually uses the hand dryer like a toy, blowing his hair around while he watches in the mirror.

Because a magnesium deficiency can cause sound sensitivity, you might try supplementing your child's diet with magnesium if he overreacts to sounds. Twenty milligrams per ten pounds of body weight is the recommended dose. If a magnesium deficiency is the culprit, you should see a noticeable decrease in sensitivity within a few days.[3]

Visual

Spinning objects is commonly associated with autism, but there are many other signs of visual issues.

- Holds objects (toys, hands) close to his eyes
- Walks near a wall while watching it
- Rolls head (often side to side)
- Prefers dark places or is very sensitive to light

- Stares at lights
- Is fascinated with shiny objects
- Stares at objects with moving parts (clocks, cars, CDs playing)
- Watches small objects like dust or string
- Is distracted by movement around him
- Pokes or presses his eyes with his fingers
- Spins self or objects
- Turns lights on and off
- Stares through people
- Moves cautiously between different floor surfaces
- Likes order (lines up objects)
- Opens and closes drawers or doors

In retrospect I can see that Ryan had some visual issues, like lining up objects and staring through people, but at the time we didn't know they were sensory issues. When we did realize it, we targeted his lining through behavioral methods, which dramatically decreased the problem. Although he will occasionally revert to lining when he becomes stressed or overwhelmed, now we can easily redirect him.

Taste

Symptoms of exaggerated sensitivity to taste include the following:

- Is a picky eater
- Eats only spicy food
- Eats only bland food
- Mouths objects (when it is not age-appropriate)
- Chews on clothes, pencils, hair, toys
- Gags when brushing his teeth

We'll probably deal with Ryan's taste issues for a long time. Even though he now tries new foods and is learning to enjoy some of them, he still gags and vomits with certain tastes. We've imposed a "one bite rule" in our house, which forces him to try new things, but his sensitive gag reflex often gives him instant veto power.

Olfactory

Some children have such a hypersensitive sense of smell that odors undetectable to us may nauseate them. Indicators of sensitivity to smells include the following:

- Smells common objects
- Avoids groups of people
- Avoids the kitchen
- Smells his food before eating it
- Gags at certain smells (especially food)
- Smears feces
- Comments or complains about the smells of food, soap, perfumes, animals, or people

We are so bombarded by smells that we "tune out" most of them; we may not even realize how many things have a distinctive smell. Each person has a unique smell, though you and I may not detect it. For children who are hypersensitive to smells, covering a "bad" smell with a "good" smell may not help either, since good and bad are subjective. If smell is an issue for your child, opening windows and allowing plenty of fresh air may be an easy way to help.

Vestibular (Movement and Gravity)

If a child is hypersensitive to movement and gravity, he may exhibit the following patterns:

- Fears being upside down or tipped sideways
- Is anxious when his feet aren't touching the ground
- Is anxious about walking up or down hills

- Is anxious about stairs
- Is anxious in water
- Seeks out gross motor movement
- Can't sit still
- May appear uncoordinated
- Needs to be moving but it interferes with listening and interacting
- Needs to be moving in order to listen or be attentive
- Gets motion sickness easily
- Needs to jump or spin

Ryan definitely had these sensitivities. If he was turned upside down, he screamed uncontrollably. As an infant and toddler, he would scream most of the time we were in the car, regardless of the length of the trip, probably because of motion sickness. His motion sickness and fear of being upside down have disappeared, but his need for jumping and moving continues to be strong.

Proprioceptive (Joint, Muscle, and Body Awareness)
While proprioceptive sensitivities may not be as observable as other sensory issues, there are indicators.

- Has difficulty planning and executing a motor task
- Has a high need for jumping
- Enjoys hanging by his arms
- Enjoys falling down
- Assumes odd body positions
- Tends to lean on or hang on people or furniture
- Grips a pencil too loosely or too tightly
- Has difficulty with fine motor skills (coloring, picking up small objects)
- Has messy handwriting

- Has sloppy eating habits
- Is clumsy
- Plays roughly
- Breaks toys often
- Didn't crawl much when young

I know Ryan has proprioceptive sensitivities because he becomes calmer and more organized with therapy. Eileen Hamele, our sensory integration therapist, noticed that allowing Ryan to jump on the trampoline or crawl through a pillow tunnel helps him organize his body. When he is more organized, he calms down, makes clearer decisions, and is more creative.

Effects of a Sensory Disorder

Whether a child has a single faulty sense or several, his sensory issues will affect multiple functions. For example, if he can't tune out background noises, his attentiveness may be hindered. He may avoid groups if the smell of other people bothers him, the noise is too high, or others touch him. If his senses tell him something is dangerous—even though most people would feel perfectly safe—he may run from the situation or even become aggressive to avoid it.

In particular, a child's ability to learn depends greatly on his level of stimulation. If a child has hyposensitivities, his body may be understimulated, making him inattentive to his surroundings. On the other hand, if a child's senses get overstimulated, he may become overactive, or he may go to the other extreme and actually "shut down" to protect himself. All of these hinder learning.

The best learning occurs in the middle ground—where a child has a proper balance between over- and understimulation. So how do teachers find the right alertness level or "range of arousal" for the child? A popular approach, called the "engines" program, teaches children to know when their internal engines are too fast, too slow, or just right. When a child is too young to understand this program, or his sensory needs are too great, the therapist or teacher may give him a "diet" of sensory activities either to speed up or to slow down his engine. Activities that involve the proprioceptive system, which include heavy work like lifting, pushing, climbing, or being "squished" in an oversized pillow, work well since they promote alertness or calm behavior.

Mary Sue Williams and Sherry Shellenberger have a booklet called "An Introduction to 'How Does Your Engine Run?' The Alert Program for Self-Regulation" if you want to learn more about the engines program.[4] This can be purchased through Therapy Works at 505-897-3479.

Therapy Options

If your child appears to have sensory problems, an experienced sensory integration therapist can conduct a complete evaluation and advise you on therapy options. Appropriate therapy can help a child deal with, or possibly even overcome, his sensory problems, thereby improving other areas of his life as well. Here are some of the possibilities.

Sensory Integration (SI)

Sensory integration focuses on the tactile, vestibular, and proprioceptive systems, though others may be included. A good sensory integration program can make a huge difference in a child's functioning, not only during therapy but also at home and in school.

SI therapists are often occupational therapists, though physical and speech therapists are sometimes trained in the techniques as well.

Therapy rooms may be equipped with swings, trampolines, scooters, water mattresses, large therapy balls, body pillows, and slides, as well as toys, clay, and bubbles. Through "play," the therapist helps a child understand what he's sensing and organize his senses. Sometimes the therapist also carefully exposes him to negative sensations to lessen his sensitivity to them.

"Brushing," more properly called the Wilbarger Protocol, is a technique many parents use to calm a child or to desensitize his nervous system. Brushing should be initiated only by a trained SI therapist and the exact technique taught to parents. Patricia Wilbarger conducts workshops on the dramatic results possible through a carefully applied brushing program.[5] More information can be found in her booklet "Sensory Defensiveness in Children," which can be obtained through the Ayres Clinic.

Integrating sensory therapy with ABA or speech therapy can have good results. Several families I know work on sensory techniques with their child before an ABA session. Others use them between drills, as the child needs to process or organize what he's learning. We placed a hammock in our basement and a trampoline, swing, slide, and other climbing structures in our backyard so Ryan can use them whenever he needs to. A large therapy ball and body pillows are good for in-home use.

We also take Ryan to a sensory integration clinic an hour a week to address some of his larger needs and to get further direction. Our SI therapist happens to be a speech and language pathologist, which allows her to probe Ryan's language and take advantage of learning opportunities during SI sessions.

For Further Information

Sensory Integration International (SII) / The Ayres Clinic
1514 Cabrillo Avenue
Torrance, CA 90501-2817
Phone: 310-320-2335
Fax: 310-320-9982
E-mail: sensoryint@earthlink.net
Web site: http://www.home.earthlink.net/~sensoryint/

The Association for the Neurologically Disabled of Canada
59 Clement Road
Toronto, Ontario M9R 1Y5 CANADA
Phone: 800-561-1497 or 416-244-1992
Fax: 416-244-4099
E-mail: info@and.ca
Web site: http://www.and.ca

Targeting Auditory Issues

Listening therapy began in the 1960s with an ear, nose, and throat physician named Dr. Alfred Tomatis. Using the Tomatis Method, clinicians treat patients with "filtered" sounds of music, Gregorian chants, and voices, through an electronic device, in hopes of retraining the ear.

Dr. Guy Berard, also a physician, trained under Dr. Tomatis in France but decided that the Tomatis Method was too lengthy and expensive, since it sometimes lasted 100-150 hours or more, extending over weeks, months, or years. So Dr. Berard developed his own electronic device where patients could listen to filtered music for a total of ten hours over a ten-day period. His method, commonly called Auditory Integration Training (AIT), has become known since the release of the book *The Sound of a Miracle: A Child's Triumph over Autism*. The author, Annabel Stehli, has a daughter with autism who struggled with hypersensitive hearing. Georgie received AIT from Dr. Berard, and after twenty sessions her autistic symptoms were alleviated. Although I haven't heard of any other child recovering from autism through AIT, I understand many children have benefited.

Auditory Integration Training consists of twenty half-hour listening sessions, usually two sessions a day over ten days. Before treatment begins, the therapist tests and charts the child's hearing on an audiogram to determine if any frequencies are uncomfortable or painful for the child. If so, those frequencies are filtered out through the AIT device.

The AIT device not only filters out disturbing frequencies, it randomly modulates the music, dampening either high or low frequencies. During the listening sessions, the child is free to play, jump, or move about as he chooses. Ryan enjoyed swinging and jumping on a trampoline as he listened to the music.

Listening therapy is used to combat many disorders, including hyperacusis (acute auditory sensitivity), auditory processing difficulties, dyslexia, and autism. Benefits attributed to AIT range from language acquisition and understanding, improved attention and focus, better balance, more organizational skills, decreased self-stimulatory behaviors, increased affect and socialization with others, and increased motor planning abilities.

Drs. Bernard Rimland and Stephen M. Edelson have conducted four studies on AIT, the first being a blind, placebo-controlled pilot study of AIT, using seventeen children. Eight in the experimental group received AIT, and nine in the control group listened to the same music but without the electronic modification. The children were tested before treatment, after the ten days of listening, and regularly for three months afterward. They discovered the experimental group tested significantly better on the Fisher's Auditory Problems checklist as well as the Aberrand Behavior Checklist.[6]

Some individuals show improvement during the treatment period or immediately afterward. Others report changes days, weeks, or even months later. We couldn't see any differences in Ryan after his AIT treatment. Perhaps there wasn't any effect, or perhaps changes weren't noticeable because Ryan underwent the treatment near the beginning of his ABA program when we were already seeing excellent results. Or perhaps it boosted Ryan's ability to learn language in ABA.

One child in our city, named David, received AIT when he was four years old. Although he had been in speech therapy for six months, he was nonverbal. The speech therapist confided in Cathy, David's mother, that he would probably never communicate through verbal language. David also had many sensory issues, including such poor balance he couldn't walk up or down stairs independently. Consequently, Cathy and her husband, Doug, installed railings on both sides of the staircase in their home in hopes they could enable David to one day climb the stairs independently.

When David received AIT, the changes were indisputable. Five days into treatment, David wanted to go outside and literally ran down the stairs, unassisted, and out the front door! Cathy screamed with excitement as her son ran by her. Seven days into AIT, David went from being nonverbal to echoing language. At dinner that night, David said, "Eat more, David." Even friends who were unaware of the listening therapy noticed differences in David and commented on his new "awareness."

David then had two more AIT treatments of ten days each,

bringing more benefits. Before AIT, David couldn't tolerate the sound of people singing in unison. After AIT, he not only tolerated it but tried to join in. Before AIT, David became overly stressed by noises like airplanes or even wind. After AIT, he tolerated the noise and returned to what he was doing. One day he said, "I hear the wind. It's really windy." Then after pausing, he added, "It's okay," and went back to work. Following the second and third AIT treatments, David also quit banging on his ears and grinding his teeth.

Cathy believes AIT made it possible for David to learn from Applied Behavior Analysis therapy. Before his AIT treatment, his senses were so skewed that he couldn't have tolerated the learning atmosphere of ABA. After his first AIT, Cathy and Doug realized he was now ready to learn through the behavioral program. Cathy also sees how AIT and ABA work side by side. As the music adjusts her child's sensory processing, the ABA allows him to learn new responses to his changing senses.

Since David's three AIT treatments, his therapy has now moved from the clinic to his home where he can receive ongoing, *daily* therapeutic listening. To the delight of Cathy and Doug, the benefits of AIT for their child have been obvious.

At-Home Listening Therapy

Though AIT may benefit some children with autism, the cost of treatment or lack of available practitioners can make it inaccessible. So in recent years several compact discs have been produced to allow listening therapy to take place in the home or school with the use of high quality headphones and an ordinary CD player. This reduces the cost considerably and allows for ongoing treatment. Programs include EASe (Electronic Auditory Stimulation effect), Sonas, and Samonas, which can be purchased, along with the headphones, through clinicians trained in listening therapy. If possible, it's better to have a therapist guide your program since your child may need a combination of CDs based on his issues.

For Further Information

The Georgiana Institute
P.O. Box 10
Roxbury, CT 06783
Phone: 860-355-1545
Fax: 860-355-2443
E-mail: georgianainstitute@snet.net
Web site: http://www.georgianainstitute.org/index.htm

Society for Auditory Intervention Techniques
P.O. Box 4538
Salem, OR 97302
E-mail: sait@teleport.com
Web site: http://www.teleport.com/~sait/table.html

Vision Audio Inc.
611 Anchor Drive
Joppa, MD 21085
Phone: 888-213-7858 or 410-679-1605
E-mail: visionaud@earthlink.net
Web site: http://www.vision-audio.com/visiondocs/ease.htm
This company produces and sells the EASe home audio disc.

Fast Forword
Fast Forword and the follow-up program, Fast Forword Two, are CD-ROM and Internet-based training programs designed to

enhance language skills in children ages four to fourteen. An SLP (speech and language pathologist) or other professional who has been trained to offer Fast Forword can perform an initial assessment to determine if your child could benefit from the program. Children who have trouble understanding and using oral language or who have reading difficulties are most likely to benefit from the program.

Using gamelike exercises, Fast Forword employs four training principles—frequency, intensity, adaptivity, and motivation—to help children improve their language skills. These principles are applied in a cross-training format that allows children to work on multiple complementary language skills. In all, the exercises provide training on over forty different language structures to help the child gain higher-level language skills. Fast Forword exercises use enhanced sounds and provide more time between certain sounds to help children improve oral language comprehension. As the child progresses in the program, the sounds adapt to the child's skill level by becoming increasingly like normal speech.

The seven interactive exercises in Fast Forword are rotated so that five are played each day. Each game requires twenty minutes, for a total of one hundred minutes a day, five days per week. Most children complete the entire program in four to eight weeks, although some take longer.

After the child completes the five games for the day, his progress data are sent via the Internet to Scientific Learning Corporation, the creators of the program. Periodically, often at the end of each week, the professional supervising the program can download interpretive summaries provided by Scientific Learning, which can be used to review the child's performance and make recommendations.

Scientific Learning claims that the average growth in receptive and expressive language skills after four to eight weeks of training is one to two years. The company lists over two dozen other benefits from their program, including improved auditory processing, working memory, verbal retention, phonological awareness, sequencing, expressive language, and word recognition.[7]

If you own an appropriate computer and have access to the Internet, you can use Fast Forword at home. As an alternative, many clinicians have a computer at their office that can be used by families who don't own a computer or who prefer to conduct the sessions outside the home. We enjoyed doing ours at home so Ryan could play the games whenever he wished. Since Ryan was an early riser at that time, we often played one or two games at six o'clock in the morning.

If you decide to use your home computer, it will be easier if it is a newer model, preferably not more than one or two years old. Besides having a computer with the proper technical requirements, you'll need a quality set of headphones. We found it necessary to listen along with Ryan, so we bought a special Y-splitter cord to allow two sets of headphones to be plugged into our computer. Of course Ryan wore the good headset while we used ordinary ones.

If you want to pursue Fast Forword, you'll need to find a certified provider. By contacting Scientific Learning Corporation through their Web site or their toll-free phone number, you can get a list of professionals in your area. If there is no provider in your region, Scientific Learning can provide an on-line professional.

At this time the Fast Forword program license fee is $850. In addition, you have the expense of hiring a qualified provider and purchasing acceptable headphones. If you add the expense of the SLP, the cost may reach $2,000–2,500, since SLPs often try to provide intensified speech and language therapy along with Fast

Forword, noting the greater accessibility some children have to language during the program. Using an on-line professional reduces the overall cost, currently $1,200 including licensing fee, but this doesn't allow the hands-on supervision and therapy that a clinician in your area can provide.

For Further Information
Scientific Learning Corporation
1995 University Avenue, Suite 400
Berkeley, CA 94704-1074
Phone: 888-665-9707
Fax: 510-665-1717
E-mail: info@scilearn.com
Web site: http://www.ScientificLearning.com

Earobics
The Earobics Auditory Development and Phonics Program is designed for children with a developmental age of four to seven years, and Earobics Step 2 is designed for children who are developmentally between seven and ten years of age. The Earobics brochure states that it teaches "the listening skills necessary for your child's speech and language development and academic success." It's less intense than the Fast Forword program, and the company doesn't provide extensive data on your child's progress via the Internet. However, it's less expensive, currently retailing at $59 for a CD you can keep and use indefinitely and use with more than one child. Also you don't have to hire a trained professional to guide its use.

The Earobics program consists of six listening games with up to 114 levels, which increase in difficulty as the child improves. "The comprehensive training program includes skill development in auditory memory, phonemic synthesis, sound segmentation, auditory and phonemic identification, sound-symbol correspondence, rhyming and phonological awareness."[8] This program, like Fast Forword, uses computer-modified speech to help the child distinguish sounds that may be difficult at first.

Although we purchased it for Ryan, we became distracted with medical issues and never finished the program. Ryan easily understood most of the games, though he had difficulty with one that required him to imitate the beat of a drum. Overall, this seems like a tool that could benefit some children who struggle with phonics, auditory processing problems, or other language issues.

For Further Information
Cognitive Concepts, Inc.
990 Grove Street
Evanston, IL 60201
Phone: 888-328-8199 (orders) or
    847-328-8099 (customer service)
Fax: 847-328-5881
Web site: http://www.cogcon.com

Vision Therapies
Many of us struggle with vision problems that can usually be corrected with glasses or contacts. But what if your vision caused you to have a different *perception* of the world?

We assume some children with autism have visual disorders because of the multiple symptoms. Unfortunately, there aren't many options for therapy since we don't know much about the vision disorder. Currently there are three main approaches: Irlen lenses, ambient or prism lenses, and visual training.

Irlen lenses are named after Helen Irlen, who discovered a visual perception problem related to light sensitivity. This perception disorder is now known as Scotopic Sensitivity Syndrome (SSS) or Irlen Syndrome. In her article "The World of Misperception," Helen Irlen lists these symptoms of SSS:

- light sensitivity
- poor depth perception
- attention deficit disorders
- contrast and color sensitivity
- restricted span (difficulty in seeing groups of objects)
- inefficient reading
- distortions (images moving, changing, jumping, disappearing, or sparkling)[9]

The theory behind this intervention is that certain light frequencies can be disturbing or overstimulating. Helen Irlen at the Irlen Institute and Irlen specialists worldwide provide specially tinted lenses for glasses. These lenses, which come in a thousand different colors, filter out some of the frequencies to protect the individual from unpleasant input.[10] If the individual can't tolerate the overabundance of visual input, filtering out some frequencies may allow the brain to process the remaining visual information more easily.

Jacquelin Gorman, through her own struggles with vision, came to realize that her autistic brother, Robin, may have stumbled on this solution as a child. Robin would use an iced-tea-colored piece of broken glass to look through when he went to catch crabs. Jacquelin didn't make the connection between the tinted glass and better vision until she lost her sight and then began to regain it.

One day, after she had lost her brother in a car accident,

Jacquelin and her sister went through Robin's belongings. In a duffel bag he was carrying when he died, they found the old broken glass. She went on to make this startling discovery.

> Later, at home, I picked up Robin's seeing glass and walked upstairs to catch the last rays of sunset. I held the glass before my eyes, but it made the colors outside almost too bright. I turned around and wandered through the house, up and down the hallways, still holding the glass before my eye.
>
> I noticed that in the dimmer light, looking through the glass, I saw things I hadn't been able to see before. Shadows appeared, colors sharpened. I was amazed.[11]

Besides Irlen lenses, some people have found that ambient or prism lenses can help visual distortions. Melvin Kaplan, O.D., from the Center for Visual Management, explains that abnormalities of ambient vision are frequently found in children with autism. Ambient vision is "involved in spatial organization—related to body posture, locomotion, and the perception of self-motion."[12] These types of lenses can enhance depth perception as well as assist in centering the vision.[13] One study has shown that ambient lenses can help a child with autism improve his posture, head tilt, and coordination.

Along with ambient lenses, Dr. Kaplan recommends vision exercises, the third option for therapy. Dr. Kaplan strives to retrain the visual system, helping the brain to understand and function with the altered visual input. Others state that the lenses can help change an individual's perception of his environment, but the exercises "are required for full visual motor adaptation…and a higher level of functioning."[14]

For Further Information

Irlen Institute

5380 Village Road

Long Beach, CA 90808

Phone: 562-496-2550

Fax: 562-429-8699

E-mail: Irlen@Irlen.com

Web site: http://www.irlen.com

Change of Heart

In the beginning I didn't consider Ryan's sensory issues as very important, but I do now. It is amazing to watch his demeanor change as he bounces on our trampoline after being frustrated or overly excited. I've also seen how planning sensory breaks throughout his day helps him concentrate and focus better at school. I no longer consider sensory therapy as merely a bonus for Ryan—it is a need.

Chapter 11

Education and Communication Needs

The direction in which education starts a man will determine his future life.

PLATO

Before we began treating Ryan's autism, he was not able to learn. He didn't observe the world as my daughter did, drinking in every experience with delight. So with each passing month, he was falling further behind. This was true for his language as well. A two-year-old without language may not be greatly hindered, but a three- or four-year-old who can't communicate suffers frustrations you and I can only imagine.

These two important needs—the ability to learn and to communicate—are more difficult for a child with autism, but they can and *must* be met.

Public Educational Services

Birth-to-Three
Often the first resource used by parents with special-needs children is Birth-to-Three, a government-funded, early intervention

program that provides services to children up to age three. After a child turns three, he is transferred into the early childhood program provided by the school district.

Before we knew about Ryan's autism, we contacted them to do a series of evaluations. From that we developed a treatment plan called an IFSP (Individual Family Service Plan). Depending on the child's needs, the IFSP may include occupational therapy, physical therapy, speech and language therapy, and family support services. Occupational therapy focuses on small-muscle movement (fine motor), while physical therapy works on the large muscles (gross motor). Speech and language therapy addresses not only verbal speech but other forms of communication as well. Family support services may include educational programs, support groups, and coordinating services.

Many families start with these public services and then assess the benefit of each to determine which to continue. Unfortunately, the child's needs often go beyond what the services offer, leaving parents to seek additional therapists in private practice. Depending on the provider, these additional services may be covered by insurance or Medical Assistance.

Early Childhood/School Services

In a perfect world the public school system would meet all our children's educational needs, but that isn't usually the case. Funding is tight, and the special needs of children are great, so you and the schools may have to work to reach an agreement on services for your child.

When Ryan first received his diagnosis, he was offered one hour a week of combined speech and occupational therapy. When he turned three, they increased the therapy to one hour a week *each* of speech, occupational therapy, physical therapy, and "early child-hood," which targets preschool skills. Though school services can be beneficial, had we been satisfied with these minimal services, Ryan wouldn't have made the gains he has. Even with good services, four hours a week of therapy will not bring dramatic changes.

The basic school services usually include an educational learn-ing environment, either in a special class or in an integrated regu-lar class, along with speech, occupational, and physical therapy as needed by the child. Other services may be negotiated as well. However, before any therapies can be provided to a child, an M-Team (Multidisciplinary Team) conducts an evaluation. Then, along with the parents, the team writes an Individualized Edu-cation Plan (IEP), spelling out the services to be offered and the goals to be targeted.

Before writing an IEP for your child, talk with other parents and, if they're willing, read their IEPs to get ideas on what to expect. When you make an agreement with the school on services, get everything in writing. Verbal promises may not always be upheld, but an agreement written into the IEP is legally enforceable. Two books that may help prepare you are *Creating a Win-Win IEP for Students with Autism* by Beth Fouse and *What Do I Do When…: The Answer Book on Special Education Law* by Susan Gorn.

School districts are required to provide "free and appropriate" education for all children, including those with special needs, but what they consider appropriate may not match a parent's expecta-tions. You will need to evaluate the school system to determine if the services they offer meet your needs. If not, you can fight the school district, which many people do, or you can find supple-mental or alternative therapies. Because we were able to find fund-ing for our ABA (Applied Behavior Analysis) program outside the school district, we chose to use what was most effective for Ryan and turn down what was not.

How did we decide which services to use? First we asked ourselves what Ryan needed. Since we believed Ryan needed intensive ABA, that was our priority. Could he use both ABA and the school-offered services? For the first year we said yes, and we did both, but we were careful not to rob time from ABA for anything else—even a good thing—that might be less effective. After a while we felt the school services weren't benefiting Ryan as much, so we discontinued them. Later, when he entered kindergarten, we resumed some services as we saw best.

We've found the best approach is to work with the public schools if at all possible, not against them. Having been to a number of parent meetings where school officials were labeled as mean, uncaring bureaucrats, we were pleasantly surprised to find that the school personnel were generally eager to help us do what was best for Ryan. Treating school officials with professional respect has paid huge dividends down the road.

However, at some point a parent may have to fight to receive the services his child requires. A "no" doesn't have to remain a "no" if you're willing to be a persistent advocate for your child. Many people fight the school to receive appropriate services and win! After all, if you don't press for what your child needs, no one else will. But starting off combative inevitably causes problems.

Alternatives to ABA Therapy

From my experience and research, I believe ABA is the therapy of choice for many children with autism. However, there may come a time when you want to supplement ABA or transition into an alternative method. I can't cover all the possibilities in one chapter, nor am I an expert in these educational options. I've researched them, but I've not lived with them for the last four years as I have ABA. I offer the information as a steppingstone for your own investigation if you believe they might help your child. As you investigate the options, I caution you to research any claims for a therapy so that you make the most informed decision possible.

The Greenspan Method

Dr. Stanley Greenspan, child psychiatrist and professor of psychiatry, behavioral sciences, and pediatrics, is well known for his approach to treating children with autism and other developmental disorders. His method centers on relationships and interaction, while taking into account underlying sensory issues.[1]

In his book *The Child with Special Needs,* Dr. Greenspan specifies "six functional milestones" of development in this order: self-regulation and interest in the world, intimacy, two-way communication, complex communication, emotional ideas, and emotional thinking.[2] He believes these lay a foundation for more advanced learning since they are based upon emotional interactions usually developed early in life.

Dr. Greenspan encourages the D.I.R. (Developmental, Individual-Difference, Relationship-Based) model. "The primary goal of the D.I.R.-based intervention is to enable children to form a sense of themselves as intentional, interactive individuals and develop cognitive language and social capabilities from this basic sense of intentionality."[3]

Part of the Greenspan method uses "floor time," which is "an intensive, one-on-one experience" during a "20-to-30-minute period when you get down on the floor with your child and interact and play."[4] The focus is on relationships, since he believes that "the more intellectual functions of the brain—logic, judgment, abstract thought—don't develop without a constant source of relating."[5] During floor time, the adult follows the child's interest, even if the interest is merely a self-stimulatory behavior, in order to encourage interaction. For example, if the child lines up toys, the adult sits near him and helps line up the toys. The adult, whether a parent or therapist, might limit the number of toys available so the child has to interact in order to get more toys. The goal is not just to follow the lead of the child but to help the child expand his interactions. According to Dr. Greenspan, the four goals of floor time are two-way communication, logical thought, attention and intimacy, and the expression and use of feelings and ideas.[6]

About two and a half years into ABA treatment, Ryan became increasingly aggressive and agitated during therapy sessions. He ran away when the therapist came into our home and was becoming more downcast daily. When Dr. Glen Sallows, our ABA consultant, came to help us deal with the aggression, he realized Ryan was burned out with drills and desperately needed a change. Starting that day, Dr. Sallows stopped drills and initiated some of Greenspan's floor time methods with Ryan. For nine months we did no drills but focused on interacting with Ryan, primarily to show him that being with other people is more fun than being alone.

Dr. Sallows's instincts were right; Ryan's behaviors changed dramatically. Within weeks we regained our happy boy, and after the nine months we reinstated drills, this time with very positive responses from Ryan.

I believe Greenspan's techniques were the right approach for our son at that time. However, I also believe this method wouldn't have worked for Ryan in the beginning. He needed the structured learning in bite-size pieces that ABA offers. Although play and interaction are important parts of ABA in addition to the drills, we had focused on the drills without integrating *enough* play into Ryan's program, which led to his burnout.

I know many people who incorporate Greenspan's floor time into their child's daily play activities. To learn more about Dr. Greenspan's methods, I recommend *The Child with Special Needs: Encouraging Intellectual and Emotional Growth.*

For Further Information

Dr. Stanley I. Greenspan
4938 Hampden Lane, Box 229
Bethesda, MD 20814
Phone: 301-320-6360
Web site: http://www.stanleygreenspan.com

TEACCH

TEACCH (Treatment and Education of Autistic and Related Communication Handicapped CHildren) is a state-funded program in North Carolina, although cities throughout the world use it. Established in the early 1970s by Dr. Eric Schopler, TEACCH uses "structured teaching" in a variety of settings, including the child's home or school. TEACCH doesn't have a specific technique of therapy, but proponents claim their structured teaching considers the needs of each child and develops a treatment plan using a variety of techniques. Their goal is increasing the child's skills and functioning ability, not recovery from autism.[7]

TEACCH uses an evaluation tool called the Psycho Educational Profile (PEP) in order to begin therapy at the appropriate level and structures the teaching in the best way to promote learning. "Organizing the physical environment, developing schedules and work systems, making expectations clearer and explicit, and using visual materials have been effective ways of developing skills and allowing people with autism to use these skills independently of direct adult prompting and cueing."[8] In other words, TEACCH adapts the learning environment and schedule to be effective and stress free for the child. "While the Lovaas program is based on the premise that the child must overcome his autistic characteristics so as to adapt to the world around him, in TEACCH the child is provided with an environment designed to accommodate the characteristics of autistic children."[9] Whether it's better to adapt the child or the environment may depend upon the ability of the child.

I've not seen TEACCH in action, so I'm not qualified to evaluate their techniques. However, one thing struck me as peculiar when I read about "Outcome Data" in an article by Dr. Gary Mesibov, director of Division TEACCH. Several examples of TEACCH's effectiveness are given, but they are *subjective* examples, not scientific data.[10] The studies he cites don't document specific gains. To evaluate this therapy, I'd like to review pre- and post-therapy data that show IQ, language, level of functioning, and socialization gains.

Shirley Cohen, professor of special education at Hunter College of the City University of New York, expressed similar concerns.

Given the long number of years that TEACCH has been in operation...it is surprising that TEACCH has not pursued comprehensive studies of child performance outcomes.

The data that are available on children served by TEACCH come largely from studies focused on stability of IQ rather than the effects of treatment per se. Based on these studies, Lord and Schopler report that substantial increases in IQ are common among children first evaluated at ages three or four.... However, most of these children still had IQs in the range considered to indicate mental retardation.... Moreover, while a substantial number of children had increases of 20 points or more in IQ, decreases of this magnitude were found with equal or greater frequency among children first assessed after age three.[11]

Besides educating children with autism, TEACCH offers family counseling, parent training, and vocational training and job placement for the adult with autism.

To learn more about TEACCH, you can read Dr. Schopler's three-volume set of books titled *Individualized Assessment and Treatment for Autistic and Developmentally Disabled Children* or contact:

Division TEACCH Administration and Research
CB# 7180
310 Medical School Wing E
The University of North Carolina at Chapel Hill
Chapel Hill, NC 27599-7180
Phone: 919-966-5156
Fax: 919-966-4003
Web site: http://www.unc.edu/depts/teacch

The Option Program

The Son-Rise program, offered through the Option Institute, is probably the hardest therapy to explain because it doesn't view treatment in a conventional way. The Son-Rise method was developed by Barry and Samahria (Suzi) Kaufman, whose son Raun was diagnosed as autistic and mentally handicapped with an IQ level under thirty. They say, "After working with him intensively for three and a half years, Raun emerged completely from autism. Today he is the graduate of an Ivy League university and bears no trace of his former condition."[12]

Unlike ABA, the Son-Rise program doesn't set an agenda of teaching specific skills. Instead, the parents and therapists follow the lead of the child and join what he's doing, including self-stimulatory behavior, in order to show the child love and approval. When they receive any response from the child, they try to expand the activity and encourage more responses. The Son-Rise program believes that the best teacher is the child.

> Often, parents and professionals helping children with special needs have specific agendas: Teach my child or student how to walk, talk, use the toilet, eat with utensils, read or perform any number of other practical and useful skills.
>
> Certainly, we want every child to realize those capabilities: yet, in the Son-Rise Program, we give up the demand that we control the agenda. It is much less important that we teach a child specific skills than that we encourage them to become a fully participating and motivated person.[13]

The Kaufmans say their "intention is to enter and understand their world, to create a bonding so special, so loving that the young person will want to know more and learn more from us."[14] While that is a worthy goal, it seems to imply that our children haven't been learning because we haven't bonded with them, a contention with which I disagree.

Since the Son-Rise program doesn't record data on changes in the individual, what are the results of using this method? "According to

Barry Kaufman, the Son-Rise approach has 'facilitated deep-seated and lasting change in hundreds of children and their families.'"[15] What does that mean? Did the changes occur in the children through improved language, intelligence, and relational abilities, or did the changes occur in the families as they learned to accept their children's autism? In her book *Autism: Handle with Care!* Gail Gillingham says, "The Family Program at the Option Institute in Massachusetts does not claim to effect changes in the individual child, but focuses on training the family to work with the child and to train other volunteers in this method once the family returns home.... In fact, parents and professionals...claim that the Option Method does much more for the parents and other family members than it does for the child with autism."[16] Yet there are several anecdotes of children who reportedly overcame their autism using this approach.

As with TEACCH, I would like to see before-and-after test results of the children in this program. All therapies, including Son-Rise, need to provide parents more than just their word to base our decisions upon, because our children's futures are at stake.

The Kaufmans have three books about children who are said to have benefited from their methods: *Son-Rise, A Miracle to Believe In,* and *Son-Rise: The Miracle Continues.*

For Further Information
The Option Institute
2080 S. Undermountain Road
Sheffield, MA 01257-9643
Phone: 413-229-2100
Fax: 413-229-8931
E-mail: happiness@option.org
Web site: http://www.option.org

Communication

Speech and Language Therapy

Since language delays are a hallmark of autism, many parents employ a private speech and language pathologist (SLP) in addition to the services of the Birth-to-Three program or the school district. A good SLP can be an invaluable member of your therapy team.

Many SLPs focus merely on helping the child produce verbal sounds. Although important, that's only a small part of communication. Our SLP, Marge Blanc, pointed out that "intentionality"—communicating on purpose because something matters to the child—is key in language development. Prelanguage or preverbal intentionality starts with simply having an interest, desire, or even disinterest in something: A child crawls toward a favorite toy, takes your hand to direct you to a cookie, or pushes away an unwanted food. An experienced SLP will assess intentional behavior first, determining what a child wants. Only then will the SLP look for preverbal means of expressing those wants, which is a step toward using words to communicate.

Some children with autism eventually learn to imitate language, and many imitate it almost effortlessly, a pattern called echolalia. Immediate echolalia is when the child repeats what was just said to him. If asked, "What's your name?" he answers, "What's your name?" Delayed echolalia is when a child repeats phrases he has heard previously. When Ryan began to speak, he picked up delayed echolalia. He often quoted full sentences from movies, using them to express his needs. As his speech developed, his delayed echolalia diminished.

Speech and language pathologists consider echolalia to be a "gestalt" language learning style, where learners say whole phrases and sentences first and only later break them down into words. It is at this point that the children learn to form original sentences.

According to Gail Richard, an SLP and author of *The Source of Autism,* half of the children with autism do not develop verbal language. She and other SLPs attribute this to a condition known as "apraxia of speech" or "verbal apraxia," which means the inability to talk when you *want* to. Some children with apraxia are almost silent until they ride in a car or jump on a trampoline. Then, when they aren't trying to talk, they can. The sounds they make seem unrecognizable, but an experienced SLP can pick out attempts at real communication. Our SLP feels that with increased understanding of apraxia among children with autism, many more of our "quiet" kids will one day be talkers.

Speech and language pathologists are also trained in augmentative communication like sign language and electronic communication systems. When looking for an SLP, you may want to ask these questions:

1. How do you approach communication (as opposed to "speech" or "language")?
2. How do you approach children with autism in their communication development?
3. How do you approach the preverbal precursors of language?
4. How do you approach apraxia (if it is applicable to your child)?
5. How do you feel about augmenting speech with other means of communication?

One of my regrets is that we didn't seek a good speech therapist earlier. Ryan was learning language quickly through ABA, but since the ABA therapists were not trained in speech and language, they weren't able to point out deficits or make appropriate suggestions for language development. Once we hired Marge, she was able to pinpoint Ryan's language deficits and give us excellent direction on targeting his needs.

We've also learned that sensory issues may need to be addressed for language to develop. Therefore, your SLP may need to work closely with someone trained in sensory integration.

Language Augmentation

Some words that other parents hear frequently and may even take for granted, like a child speaking his name or telling his parents he loves them, painfully elude many parents of children with autism. When Ryan was diagnosed, he was almost three, yet he couldn't speak to us. He couldn't share his wants, his frustrations, or even his most basic needs. It grieved and frustrated us as we tried to read his mind.

Many children with autism will develop verbal language with time and hard work, but others won't ever develop it, regardless of the effort. *That doesn't mean they can't learn to communicate!* Alternative methods can give nonverbal children the power to express themselves.

As a guideline, if your child isn't speaking after several months of intensive intervention, you might consider integrating a form of augmented communication. This doesn't mean you're giving up on your child speaking. Augmentation may be a steppingstone to verbal communication, and if your child develops cognitively yet can't express himself, withholding augmentative methods may, in fact, hinder further development. As you work with your child for a few months, you'll learn his capabilities and be better equipped to help him communicate.

Sign Language

Sign language is probably the best known form of augmentative communication and usually the first tried. I know a family in which the parents teach sign language to their toddlers, since it's easier to learn than verbal language, even though the children don't have special needs. Over time, their children transition into spoken language. Maybe this would work with some of our children as well.

Sign language may prove beneficial, since a child often finds it easier to pay attention to people's hands than their faces. However, many children with autism have trouble imitating, which may prevent them from learning the signs. Also, touching the child's hand to help him form the word or gesture may be difficult if the child has tactile sensitivities.

Picture Exchange Communication System

A popular and effective form of augmentative communication is the Picture Exchange Communication System or PECS. Though the system is designed for nonverbal individuals, many young children who begin with PECS later develop verbal language.

The title indicates the nature of the system: the use of pictures to communicate. In the beginning a child may learn to exchange a picture of a cookie for a real cookie. He not only learns to express his desires but also becomes motivated to interact with other people, taking his turn in communication by initiating an exchange. Teaching the child to initiate is a key component of PECS.

As the child learns more, he's taught to make "sentences" out of the pictures. When I was visiting a friend of mine over dinner, her son got up from the table and with two pictures made a sentence on a Velcro strip of his notebook. The first said "I want" and the second said "chicken." With two pictures he communicated that he didn't want what was being served but instead wanted chicken.

If your child might destroy the picture cards, try laminating the pictures and attaching them to the round metal tops from frozen-juice containers or small wooden discs available at craft stores. To save yourself time and hassles, make three copies of each picture—one for home, one for school, and a spare.

Through the six phases of PECS, children learn how to ask questions, make comments, and express their desires. Many families find that PECS works well when combined with behavioral therapies. It can also be used to create a daily schedule for a child so he can understand more clearly what his day will be like.

A nice feature of PECS is that it doesn't require expensive materials or equipment. Trained consultants and training workshops for parents and professionals are available, and the PECS training manual, along with communication books and other materials, can be ordered through Pyramid Educational Consultants at the following address:

Pyramid Educational Consultants, Inc.
226 W. Park Place, Suite #1
Newark, DE 19711
Phone: 888-PECS-INC or 302-368-2515
Fax: 302-368-2516
E-mail: pyramid@pecs.com
Web site: http://www.pecs.com

Electronic Devices
A more advanced form of communication allows a nonverbal individual to "speak" verbally through an electronic device. The simplest

device is actually a toy called Yak Bak, which can be purchased in toy stores for less than $10. The Yak Bak allows one recording to be made at a time, which can be repeated by pushing a button. One mother bought two of them and sewed them into a vest for her son. Her son couldn't nod or shake his head to respond to yes/no questions, so on one Yak Bak she recorded "yes" and on the other she recorded "no." When her son wanted to respond, he pressed his answer on the Yak Bak.

Moving up a step from a one-cell recording is the Time Frame Four (currently $39), which has four cells, and the Attainment Five Talker (currently $299), which has five. Each cell can be individually recorded to offer more choices of responses. At home a child can use the device to communicate whether he wants milk or water. In therapy it can be used with any drill where five choices would reveal mastery of a task. For example, each cell could "say" a different color—red, yellow, purple, green, blue. Then you would ask your child the color of the sun. If he consistently chooses yellow, you know he's mastered that. (Be sure to change the order of the colors so you know he's learning the color, not just which cell to choose.) The Attainment Fifteen Talker, which sells for under $500, obviously offers even more choices since it has fifteen cells to program. All three of these devices can be purchased from the Attainment Company.

Much more sophisticated tools are the DynaVox and DynaMyte, synthesized speech devices that can be used with preprogrammed materials or with messages you create. Although versatile, at this time they cost from $6,000 to $8,000.

You can also purchase software to make a regular computer a tool for communication. One program, Speaking Dynamically, transforms a touch-screen Macintosh into a portable augmentative communication device. It's available from the Mayer-Johnson Company and costs about $300.

Hundreds of devices probably exist, but finding out about them is the trick. If you want to learn what your options are, consider attending a yearly conference in Minneapolis called "Closing the Gap," which focuses solely on augmentative communication devices. There is also a "Closing the Gap" publication that may give added direction. You can find information on this in Appendix C.

A major university or hospital in your area can be another source of information on new technology. Ask the personnel where they would direct you if you lost your ability to speak as the result of a serious illness or accident. They may be able to suggest a clinic or developmental department. If so, ask them if they work with children and if they would work with a child with autism, because many such clinics work only with adults and only with those who have lost their speech. There also may be a waiting list to get into such a clinic, but it could be worth the wait.

If your child is school age and needs one of the more sophisticated devices, the school may pay for it. By showing he needs it to participate in school activities, you may be able to write it into the IEP (Individualized Education Plan). If the school does purchase one for your child, make sure the teachers agree to your using it at home as well so your child can have consistency in his communication.

If your child isn't school age yet and you believe he needs such a device, you might seek funding through Medical Assistance (MA). Each state has its own regulations on applying for financial assistance to purchase an augmentative device, but investigating this avenue could be worth your time.

Whichever avenue you pursue, be prepared with the necessary

information. Why does your child need the device? How will it be used? How much does it cost? Ask a professional to write a recommendation, explaining why your child needs it. Those who receive funding do their homework ahead of time.

Retailers

Attainment Company
P.O. Box 930160
Verona, WI 53593-0160
Phone: 800-327-4269 or 608-845-7880
Fax: 800-942-3865 or 608-845-8040
E-mail: info@attainmentcompany.com
Web site: http://www.attainmentcompany.com

CAMA (Communication Aid Manufacturers Association)
P.O. Box 1039
Evanston, IL 60204
Phone: 800-441-CAMA (2262)
E-mail: cama@northshore.net
Web site: http://www.aacproducts.org
This site lists dozens of manufacturers of augmentative communication devices.

DynaVox Systems Inc.
2100 Wharton Street, Suite 400
Pittsburgh, PA 15203-1942
Phone: 800-344-1778 or 412-381-4883
Fax: 412-381-5241
E-mail: sales@dynavoxsys.com
Web site: http://www.dynavoxsys.com

Enabling Devices/Toys for Special Children (catalog)
385 Warburton Avenue
Hastings-on-Hudson, NY 10706
Phone: 800-832-8697
Fax: 914-478-7030
Web site: http://www.enablingdevices.com

Mayer-Johnson Company
P.O. Box 1579
Solana Beach, CA 92075-7579
Phone: 800-588-4548 or 858-550-0084
Fax: 858-550-0449
E-mail: mayerj@mayer-johnson.com
Web site: http://www.mayer-johnson.com

Facilitated Communication

Probably the most controversial method of communication with nonverbal individuals is Facilitated Communication (FC), which uses a keyboard or letter board so the person can "type" messages with the physical assistance of a facilitator. The facilitator often assists the hand that is typing, but in some cases the facilitator just touches the arm or shoulder to give support. Proponents of FC claim that many people with autism have normal or superior intelligence and can spell their thoughts if given the opportunity and help.

However, studies have cast doubts on such claims. Temple Grandin, a successful woman with autism, commented on Facilitated Communication:

Fifty scientific studies have now shown that in the vast majority of cases, the teacher was moving the person's hand.... The teacher was communicating, instead of the person with autism. A summary of forty-three studies in the Autism Research Review showed that 5 percent of nonverbal, severely handicapped people can communicate with simple one-word responses. In the few cases where facilitated communication has been successful, someone has spent many hours teaching the person to read first.[17]

Dr. John W. Jacobson and associates published their views in the *American Psychologist,* views that echo Grandin's statements.

Controlled research using single and double blind procedures in laboratory and natural settings with a range of clinical populations with which FC is used have determined that, not only are the people with disabilities unable to respond accurately to label or describe stimuli unseen by their assistants, but that the responses are controlled by the assistants.[18]

Four respected professional organizations—the American Academy of Child and Adolescent Psychiatry, the American Association of Pediatrics, the American Association on Mental Retardation, and the American Psychiatric Association—have made statements rejecting the efficacy of Facilitated Communication.[19] The statement released by the American Academy of Child and Adolescent Psychiatry expresses its position.

Facilitated communication (FC) is a process by which a facilitator supports the hand or arm of a communicatively impaired individual while using a keyboard or typing device. It has been claimed that this process enables persons with autism or mental retardation to communicate. Studies have repeatedly demonstrated that FC is not a scientifically valid technique for individuals with autism or mental retardation. In particular, information obtained via FC should not be used to confirm or deny allegations of abuse or to make diagnostic or treatment decisions.[20]

Despite the research, if you feel Facilitated Communication might benefit your child, Dr. Bernard Rimland from the Autism Research Institute suggests using a "Four Object Test," which can be done without special equipment or facilities.

How does one conduct the "four object" test? The parent (or judge, or experimenter) requests that the facilitator go to another part of the building, so that he or she can not hear what is going on. The parent then selects 4 objects from his or her person, or from the room, and shows these objects, dramatically, one at a time, to the autistic person. For example:

1. Pull a comb out of your pocket or purse. Say, very clearly, "This is a comb." Comb your hair with it a few times. Comb the child's hair with it a few times, saying the word "comb" very clearly. Replace the comb in purse or pocket.

2. Open a desk drawer. If you find scissors, look delighted and say, "Here are some scissors!" Use the scissors to cut a few strands of your own hair, saying, "I'm giving

myself a haircut with the scissors." Then do the same to the autistic person, laughingly saying, "I'm using the scissors to give you a haircut." Cut some scraps of paper, clearly demonstrating the scissors before they are replaced in the drawer.

Continue with two more objects or even pictures of objects, making sure you explain and use each item in such a way that the child has the best chance of remembering it. Be dramatic in your presentation and let the child interact with the item if possible, touching it or using it in some way.

Call the facilitator back into the room, and ask what was discussed or shown to the autistic person during the facilitator's absence. If the handicapped person types things such as…"scissors," "comb," "haircut," etc. that suggest[s] real communication.

If the facilitator tells you that autistic people don't like to be tested, or that an autistic person has "word finding problems" or whatever…, you can decide for yourself whether to accept those reasons.[21]

If your child can't "pass" this test using FC, make sure he is able to read before you give up hope of communicating with him. If he can learn to read, even if he is mute, then one of the augmentative forms of communication may greatly empower him to communicate. The Autism Research Institute has a free publication called *Teaching a Mute Autistic to Read.*

For Further Information

Facilitated Communication Institute

Syracuse University

370 Huntington Hall

Syracuse, NY 13244-2340

Phone: 315-443-9657

Fax: 315-443-2274

E-mail: fcstaff@sued.syr.edu

Web site: http://soeweb.syr.edu/thefci/

A Final Thought

As with any child, the educational and communication methods used with an autistic child will need to be reevaluated and changed periodically as his needs and skills change. Helping our children learn and communicate may require a lot of extra effort, but it is worth it.

They are worth it!

Chapter 12

Family Matters

BY ROGER S. HAMILTON

Genuine love is honor put into
action regardless of the cost.
GARY SMALLEY

When Ryan's therapy program was just getting off the ground, at times the collective pressures of everyone else's needs seemed too much for me to bear. But when I stopped to look at our situation objectively, it was clear Lynn was bearing much more of the burden than I was. She was the one trying to run the home and meet our needs, while investigating and implementing treatment options for Ryan.

I asked to write this chapter because we husbands are often tempted to run the minute the going gets tough. And we don't have to leave home to run; many of us escape by overcommitting to our careers or hiding away in our hobbies.

Years after beginning Ryan's therapy, the daily joys we share as a family make the perseverance and commitment all worth it. My hope is that the following lessons we learned together as a family regarding marriage, sibling issues, and preparing for your child's future will help you to experience those same joys.

Keeping Your Marriage Strong

Marriage under normal circumstances is tough enough, but factor in a child with special needs, and the pressure on a marriage can be overwhelming. The devastation and grief from shattered dreams for your child, the daily strain of caring for one who has significant limitations and paying for that care, and the uncertainty of the future—all take an enormous toll even on healthy relationships. However, not only is it possible to keep our marriages intact as we battle autism in our children, but our marriages can even be strengthened.

This begins with choosing to give top priority to your relationship with your spouse, no matter what. Autism need not and should not rule our lives. Neither spouse can afford to let the child and his autism become more important than the marriage.

Does that mean we shouldn't invest a significant amount of time, energy, and money in the fight against autism? Not at all. It does mean that the needs of the marriage and other family members must not be overlooked while tending to the child with autism.

So how do you balance the needs of your marriage with the needs of your child? How do you give your other children the time and nurture they deserve? What does this mean for one or both of your careers? How can you reconcile the need for more time with your child and the need to earn enough to pay for the tests and treatments? While it isn't easy, we believe there are answers to these questions, answers that can keep your marriage and family together —even when your world is torn apart.

Sacrificial Love

Regardless of the severity of a child's autism, the parents' love drives them to put their child's needs above their own. The same attitude is needed in our marriages. In fact we can learn a lot about how to love our spouse from the way we love our kids. In caring for his disabled daughter, Bob Dale discovered this secret of self-sacrificing love.

> Jessica has taught me what true love is. Poets and preachers, young lovers, and idealists have professed a knowledge of this elusive concept for years. But, in Jessica's silence, I have learned the real essence of love: you give everything and expect nothing in return.
>
> Even husbands and wives give kisses expecting kisses in return. Not so with Jesse. You give for the pure love of it, knowing that she is unable to reciprocate. You watch her face as you tend to her, looking for any sign of pleasure or happiness, and when you catch a glimpse, real or imagined, you repeat what you are doing, because you found something that makes her happy. The joy of loving her is its own reward. This could quite possibly be the purest love I've ever felt, untainted by worldly expectations, unaffected by demands, cause or effect. It simply surrounds you.[1]

This same unselfish love can hold our marriages and families together during difficult times. Marriage and family counselor Gary Smalley echoes Bob Dale's sentiments. "Real love means a sacrificial, courageous commitment—especially when the other person may not be able to give back to you."[2] And right now because of your child's needs, your spouse may not be able to invest as much in the marriage as you would like. Your job is to continue to love him or her sacrificially, regardless of what you receive in return.

It may help to take a close look at the sacrifices your spouse is making for the sake of your child.

Husbands, has your wife given up a successful career to focus her attention at home, or is she balancing the demands of a career with working overtime at home? Our friend Susan has put a successful law career on hold in order to care for her son Franke. Lynn has sacrificed a fruitful ministry to college students in order to ensure on a daily basis that Ryan receives his special diet, that therapists are hired and scheduled to work, that they actually show up and know what to do once they're here. What personal interests has your wife given up in order to devote more time to the family?

Wives, do you understand the tremendous burden placed on your husband, perhaps requiring extra responsibilities at work in order to meet the financial burdens? How is that robbing him of precious time and energy for the family? What personal hobbies has he put aside to be with the family? My brother-in-law, Rob, added a monthly rotation at a hospital in another state to his already grueling schedule as a director of an emergency room in order to finance my nephew's ABA therapy. Although minor by comparison, I gave up playing trumpet in a brass quintet, as well as attending various sporting events, so I could spend more time with my family. I miss performing with the quintet and going to football games, but these are truly tiny and, I hope, temporary sacrifices that serve my family greatly.

The fact remains: *You need each other.* As difficult as it is to face the challenges together, the task is much more daunting for a parent alone. Personal dreams and desires may have to be sacrificed or put on hold for a time, but your marriage and your family are much more valuable than anything a career, money, or another relationship can offer.

Understanding

Though a husband may not be particularly skilled at expressing his emotions, the pain of seeing his precious child struggle with a disability cuts like a knife to the heart. In her book *Siblings of Children with Autism,* Dr. Sandra Harris recounts a conversation with a father who was wrestling with his emotions concerning his son's autism.

> He felt unable to share these feelings with his wife, because he knew how upset she was over their son's diagnosis. As her husband he believed he needed to be strong and protect her from his sorrow. Ironically, a few weeks before, his wife had told me how upset she was by her husband's apparent lack of distress about their son. She could not understand why he did not seem to care very much about the boy's problems. His being unemotional made her feel all the worse, because she felt all alone with her sadness. In this particular case, a bit of encouragement to the father to share some of his feelings with his wife allowed them both to feel better. He realized that his wife respected his feelings of sorrow, and she discovered she was not alone in her pain.[3]

Perhaps the greatest strain on our marriage in the early days of Ryan's therapy was that Lynn didn't feel that I understood the world in which she was living. I *said* I understood, but I really had no clue. Until we made the effort to sit down and discuss what her daily life was really like, I didn't truly appreciate all she was going through.

Understanding and appreciating the unique pressures on your partner is another key to keeping your marriage strong. Now is the time to sit down with your spouse and share openly the hardships you're facing. If possible, find a baby-sitter, go to a park or a nice restaurant, and talk heart to heart about what you can do to lift each other's burdens, physically and emotionally. Consider seeking help from a trained counselor. There's no shame in gaining a fresh perspective from a professional in helping people make it through stressful times.

Forgiveness

Parents often ask themselves how their precious child became affected by autism, and in wrestling with their grief, they often blame each other. Do you blame your spouse for contributing faulty genes? Did your wife take a drink during pregnancy, or was she too active? Did your husband play too roughly with your child when he was a baby? Did you let your child watch too much TV?

Lynn followed every rule during her pregnancy with Ryan and couldn't point to any wrongdoing, but she did have morning sickness twenty-four hours a day for four and a half months. Did that cause Ryan's autism? What about our genes? For a long time Lynn blamed herself—without reason. Then when my sister's son was diagnosed with autism, Lynn mentally transferred the "gene blame" to me. Both perspectives were wrong. Neither my genes nor hers alone were at fault, although a combination of our genes *may* have affected Ryan.

I struggled with self-blame for an accident in Siberia. While I was taking Ryan for a walk in his stroller one day, a car came driving down the sidewalk—an accepted practice in our area. As I moved the stroller out of the way, Ryan stood up and, with the sudden movement of the stroller, fell out and hit his head on the cement. As he cried, we grabbed him and ran to an American friend who was a nurse. She checked Ryan's eyes and head and saw no sign of damage. We watched him over the next few days and saw no delayed ill effects.

But when Ryan was diagnosed with autism, I blamed myself. What if Ryan's brain was injured by that fall? Even though the neurologist didn't think it caused Ryan's problems, I struggled with guilt.

Who do you blame? We eventually realized that asking these questions wouldn't help Ryan. It's not your fault or your spouse's fault that your child has autism, and *the sooner you stop blaming yourself or each other and start working together toward a solution, the better off you will be.* Don't let bitterness and a lack of forgiveness—either toward your spouse or yourself—distract you from helping your child.

Addressing Sibling Issues

Just as our response to our child's autism can either strengthen or break the marriage, how we help siblings cope with this challenge can give them either bitter memories or wonderfully positive ones.

Cassie, age eighteen, writes of her sister: "Jennifer has probably achieved more than I have. She's been through so much. She couldn't even talk when she started school; now she can, and she can understand others. She's really fulfilling her potential."[4] Another woman says of her sister, Martha: "She taught me how to love without reservation; without expectation of returned love. She taught me that everyone has strengths and weaknesses. Martha is no exception. She taught me that human value is not measured with IQ tests."[5]

Helping Siblings Understand Autism

Explaining the diagnosis to your other children will be an ongoing process. Sandra Harris observes that though a four- or five-year-old child may acknowledge that his brother or sister has autism, he won't fully understand what that means. "This seeming understanding may create a false sense of security for parents who believe…the children are fully informed about autism. It may be puzzling when they discover that their children seem misinformed and confused about the disorder."[6] A parent has to explain the complexities of autism in age-appropriate language, which will involve covering various aspects of autism in stages over the child's lifetime. Dr. Harris traces these stages and the appropriate explanations in detail in her thorough book *Siblings of Children with Autism*.

Meeting Needs of Siblings

Dr. Harris points out that siblings may struggle with anger, jealousy, embarrassment, and lack of attention. Anger is often symptomatic of one of the other issues. It may start with a child being angry at his autistic sibling for monopolizing the TV or wrecking a block tower he's worked hard to build. But if these feelings of anger are allowed to fester, they may turn into bitterness and resentment.

Siblings are often jealous of the extra attention given to special-needs children, especially if they are undergoing an intensive therapy program. Our daughter, Tori, is drawn like a magnet to any therapist who comes to the door. She has no idea that Ryan is getting "therapy." In her mind big brother is having fun with a friend, and she wants in on the action. We allow her to play with them for a few minutes at the beginning of the day, then we gently lead her out of his room so they can focus on Ryan. As Ryan's program moved toward peer play and socialization, Tori proved to be a key part of his therapy, since she was a ready-made peer for playing games and practicing "school."

With so much attention given to your child with autism, it's critical to give your other children special attention as well. Lynn observed that whenever our family was in the car, I would eagerly point out signs or cows to Ryan, since I wanted him to notice these things and learn to talk about them, but I often acted as if Tori weren't there. Now I try to make observations that are significant to both of them, and I use both of their names to draw their attention to something. I also regularly have a "date" just with Tori, going to McDonald's or taking a walk while Ryan is at school or in therapy.

Families in our city have come up with some creative ways to help siblings cope. Mary Alice found a college student who volunteers a couple of hours each week to come and play with her older daughter, since her daughter with autism gets so much attention from therapists during the week. Susan and her family see a family counselor and have arranged for their daughter, Lucy, to receive individual counseling to help her relate to her brother, Franke. We allowed Tori to start preschool two mornings a week at age three, instead of four, because she desperately needed the social interaction with other children.

As children become more social, especially during the teen years, they may be embarrassed around their friends because of their sibling's "weird" behavior or lack of friends. Dr. Harris stresses the importance of open communication between the parents and the "typical" sibling, however awkward or difficult it may be, and suggests ways siblings can discuss the situation frankly with their friends.[7]

In addition to Dr. Harris's book, we found a Web site that provides excellent resources and encouragement for siblings of children with special needs. Donald Meyer, editor of *Uncommon Fathers: Reflections on Raising a Child with a Disability*, is director of the Sibling Support Project in Seattle. The Sibling Support Project home page, which can be accessed at http://www.chmc.org/departmt/sibsupp, provides encouraging quotes from siblings, newsletters, and directories of helpful materials and workshops.

Each member of the family brings a unique personality and special gifts to the family. It is important to help our children see the blessings that a child with special needs can bring, while allowing them to express openly their feelings of hurt or disillusionment.

A colleague of mine, Brian Van Zante, describes the joys of growing up with a sister with special needs.

> Becky was an integral part of our family, not an inconvenience. Her life was as important as ours. I'll admit it was pretty embarrassing for me to endure temper tantrums, especially around nonfamily members. But there were benefits. Sincere hugs and expressions of joy. As often as she was cloudy, she was equally sunny. When she was cheerful, her smile lit up the table. Becky helped me learn that God doesn't measure my value by standards. Looks. Grades. Success. What did Becky have to offer to *Who's Who?* Does Becky care if I am a successful employee or if I climb the corporate ladder? She likes my wife but is unimpressed by the car I drive. She likes it when I call her to talk about her new living environment. She lets me know when she brushes her teeth and where she hangs up her

clothes. Life is fun for her, and small things are important. I'm learning to think a little like her.[8]

Shadow Syndromes

As more research reveals a wide variety of medical problems associated with autism, you may discover similar but less intense needs in your children who *don't* have autism. For example, if a child with autism suffers from a yeast overgrowth, then a sibling of that child may have a less severe yeast problem. If so, then treating a minor problem now may protect the sibling against a future of chronic illness.

You may want to test siblings for any abnormalities your child with autism has. Since Ryan has an immune problem, we tested Tori for an immune deficiency as well and discovered that she was borderline. When we're able, we plan to test her for yeast and possibly have a body chemistry workup done.

You would be wise also to watch for any emotional or mental illnesses a sibling may have, like depression, ADD (attention deficit disorder), ADHD (attention deficit hyperactivity disorder), OCD (obsessive-compulsive disorder), or even a very mild case of autism. If one child has autism, a problem like ADD in a sibling may go unnoticed.

Taking Care of Family Needs

Keeping your family strong will take extra effort, even if you feel as though you have no energy left. However, by taking time to strengthen our families, we actually have more emotional, physical, and mental energy to keep battling for our children with autism.

Take Time to Enjoy Each Other

When we began Ryan's ABA program, we stressed over every minute he wasn't in therapy. The clock was ticking, and every hour was absolutely critical to his recovery. How could we think about spending an afternoon in the park to play as a family? Ryan was only three years old, but he was "working" as much as an adult, and Lynn was overseeing Ryan's programs with every ounce of energy at every waking moment. Fortunately, we realized that this attitude was backfiring; there was so much stress in our house we were driving each other crazy.

We all needed a break from the pressure cooker of Ryan's therapy schedule, but our options for family fun were limited because of his behaviors. Rather than venturing out into the "world," we played in our yard or took Ryan and Tori to the park around the corner. As Ryan improved, we got a bit bolder, going to the playland at McDonald's at strategic times when Ryan's screams would scare the fewest children.

Thankfully, we are now at a point where we can go anywhere with our kids and enjoy our time as a family. No matter what stage you're in, creating memories with your family and having fun are not frivolous activities; they are essential.

Perhaps the greatest challenge, yet the most strategic, is planning time away as a couple. Early on, we wouldn't consider leaving Ryan with anyone, not even Lynn's mom. But within a few months of starting therapy, Ryan had improved to a point we could leave him with Gram. In time, close friends could baby-sit. We haven't yet managed a weekly date night, but our semi-regular evenings away have been essential to our marriage and have given us the emotional energy to keep going.

Sometimes opportunities have come as pure serendipities.

We were shocked when we were notified one day that we had been selected to spend a night at the fanciest hotel in Madison as part of its Hotel with a Heart program. Our local respite program, which helps parents with special-needs children to cover baby-sitting expenses, had a lengthy waiting list when we first applied. Because of the long wait, they drew names from the waiting list each month, with the winner receiving a free hotel room and dinner.

We walked into our room to find a fancy gift basket of gourmet chocolates and coffees. Then we went down to the restaurant for dinner, where the waiter insisted that we order anything we wanted, compliments of the hotel.

Taking time for each other need not be extravagant or expensive. A walk around the block can be just as valuable as a nice dinner out. Whatever you decide is best, keep each other accountable to following through.

Physical Needs

As with setting aside time for your spouse or children, carving out time for exercise takes effort and creativity. Finding someone to watch your kids is a limiting factor. As Ryan has gotten older, we've found it possible to join a health club or the YMCA, where they provide childcare as part of the monthly fee. If this isn't possible for your family, consider watching the kids while your spouse takes an aerobics class or goes for a run. It's a nice way to give your spouse a break and a chance to get some exercise.

Financial Needs

Of all the challenges and pressures associated with raising a child with autism, the financial concerns generally loom the largest.

When you add the costs of starting and maintaining a home ABA program, special dietary needs, toys and other equipment, extra childcare expenses, and myriad other variables, it's tempting to give up before you start. But just as your child has hope in battling autism, so you can overcome the financial obstacles.

The single biggest decision is whether one parent needs to stay home or both parents should work outside the home. We know families in every possible situation, and each solution can be valid. The following scenarios are *not* listed in any priority.

Choosing to have one parent stay home is one option. Most often the mother stays home while the father works, but this doesn't have to be the case. We made the decision for Lynn to stay home long before having children, so it wasn't related to having a child with special needs. Some of you may already be "stay home" moms or dads, and now that you've seen the extra responsibilities combating autism brings, your decision may be confirmed even more.

After several months of both parents working, Susan and Mark decided that she would leave her job in order to stay home and care for their autistic son, Franke, and their daughter, Lucy. Susan sacrificed a well-paying job as an attorney but felt the challenges of Franke's treatment necessitated it. As a result of this decision, Mark continues in a job that requires a lot of travel and time away from home in order to cover the additional financial needs.

Others choose for both parents to work. Since an ABA program or comparable therapy program can be incredibly expensive, two incomes may be essential. Imposing an extra two to five thousand dollars on an already tight budget may settle the question rather coldly and definitively.

Still another option is for one parent to rejoin the work force after staying home initially. We know a mother of a child with chronic health problems who has gone back to work part-time because the constant strain of caring for her child was causing significant emotional and physical problems. By working part-time she got a break from home pressures and renewed her energy for the tasks at home.

If you're a single parent, you may not have any other choice than to work full-time. I know two mothers in this position who arranged for ABA therapists to go to the day-care center and perform therapy there. Although it wasn't easy for the mothers to transfer the needed materials back and forth from home to day care, they managed, and their children received the help they needed.

Once the choice is made regarding job status, then you have to decide how the money will be spent. What are the priorities? What expenses—especially those on your wish list—can be postponed or eliminated? I can't justify regularly spending twenty-five or thirty dollars to play golf when we're struggling to pay a speech therapist or to afford a secretin infusion for Ryan. Is cable TV worth thirty dollars a month when I don't have time to watch it anyway? We've gone back and forth on this issue, since there are some wonderful shows we enjoy, and we can relax watching an old movie or a football game. But in the end we canceled the cable because the money could be used for more pressing needs.

Please don't misunderstand. It's easy to go overboard in reducing expenses. Don't entirely eliminate your entertainment budget, because you and your spouse need to go out occasionally for a nice dinner or to the theater to maintain your balance and your marriage. But you may have to be more strategic and thoughtful about how you spend your money. A generous couple from our church allowed me to use their lake home for a tenth anniversary getaway.

For less than fifteen dollars I took Lynn away for a memorable evening, complete with a candlelight dinner I cooked and a couple of sappy old movies that we watched while curled up by a warm fire. The point is, you don't have to spend two hundred dollars for a memorable evening.

Talk with other families and share ideas on solutions for the difficult financial issues you face. In addition to the practical help, the empathy and encouragement of others who understand the unique pressures you're facing will be a great help to you and your spouse.

Future Needs

Though no one likes to prepare for his death, it's imperative that parents of a child with a disability provide for the child after they're gone. Many shortcuts and "Easy Will" kits are available, but they don't take into consideration the serious legal questions you have to face. You can't just leave your children to your brother's family. It's worth the investment to have a good attorney help you sort through the complex legal issues surrounding a child with special needs.

Having a good will is the first step. In your will you need to designate the executor of your will and also your children's guardian, which can be the same person or two different people. Considering the tremendous responsibility of this guardianship, it's best to have frank discussions with whomever you choose.

Next you need to decide how to allocate your assets, for your autistic child and your other children. A special-needs trust is a key aspect of your will, no matter how well your child is doing in therapy. (Remember you can always change it later.) This trust is designed to protect assets that will be used to provide for a person who is unable to manage his own assets. It will also protect your child from losing essential services. If this trust isn't set up right, your child will first deplete the money left him before the government will pay for anything, so he won't have any extra money for things he wants, such as phone calls, special trips, or extra clothes.

Our will outlines this trust in detail, but one paragraph gives the gist of what a special-needs trust should accomplish.

> My son, Ryan, has a disability that can be expected to continue indefinitely and that substantially impairs his ability to support and care for himself, which disability constitutes a substantial handicap to him. My purpose in creating this trust is to provide the funds necessary for his happiness over and above the essential, primary support and services which may be provided to him by public aid. It is my wish and hope that his trust will enable Ryan to have the opportunity to develop his full potential and to enjoy as pleasant, comfortable and happy a life as is possible. This trust is not to replace or make unnecessary the public aid that Ryan would otherwise be qualified to receive. It is my intent that his trust only provide those resources considered beneficial to Ryan's happiness over and above the essentials which may be available to him from government aid.

The main issue of concern is to keep your child from losing his financial assistance, but you also may want to have your attorney check into the income tax implications of the special-needs trust, which may be significant and may vary based on current legislation. Retaining an attorney who is well informed on these issues could save you lots of money and headaches down the road.

A Letter of Intent

A letter of intent is a private letter to friends or relatives outlining your desires on issues and concerns not covered in the will. "For example, it might express in great detail your hopes and concerns about how to take care of your son or daughter financially and personally. Unlike the provisions of your will, however, these hopes and concerns, even when stated as instructions, are not legally enforceable."[9]

The letter of intent should address seven major areas:

1. Residence: Where do you want your child to live?
2. Education: Are there unique educational goals or settings for your child's education that you want to enumerate?
3. Employment: What goals, desires, special skills, or limitations does your child have that would impact the kind of job he might have?
4. Medical concerns: Include a list of your child's physicians past and present and their phone numbers, his current medications or supplements, what treatments he has and why, and how to follow through with the treatments and testing that may still be needed.
5. Social issues: What activities does your child enjoy? Where does he like to go? Does he have friends he enjoys playing with or favorite toys?
6. Religious: What church or synagogue do you wish your child to attend? Are there programs within that church or synagogue you wish your child to participate in?
7. Behavior management: Outline what discipline works best for your child, how he might be redirected during difficult situations, and positive rewards that motivate him.[10]

Though none of us likes the idea of planning ahead for the time when we won't be around, it is foolish not to do so, especially when a special-needs child is concerned.

A Look Back

These early years struggling to help Ryan overcome autism have been much like climbing Mount Everest. Hazards and obstacles presented themselves every inch of the way. One step would move us slightly forward, the next sideways or even backward. Though the journey has been difficult and exhausting, with many setbacks along the way, every member of our family has made a significant contribution and has sacrificed in order to help us all "make it to the top."

For us, the summit is in sight. Many times we've paused and looked down the mountain to see how far we've come and have celebrated as a family that we have done it *together.*

Chapter 13

A Word to Family and Friends

A favour well bestowed
is almost as great an honour to him who
confers it as to him who receives it.

RICHARD STEELE

Since the day we found out about Ryan's autism, we have been humbled by the support of our friends and family. So many people have taken the initiative to walk alongside us through all the ups and downs, and we are extremely grateful. Because of their out-pouring of love and support and what it has meant to us, practically and emotionally, I pass along these suggestions to you who have a friend or relative living with autism and who want to help. (For you parents of a child with autism, you might consider these ideas when friends ask, "What can I do to help?") Decide what is feasible for you and then act upon it. The thought is nice, but the follow-through is even better.

Personal Support

Learn

The day that Ryan was diagnosed, we called Sandy and Rick. Sandy and I spoke for only a minute, and I knew she cared, but what she did next touched me deeply. When we hung up, Sandy went to the library and checked out several books on autism. By the time she came to visit on Monday, she had already read two books and was working on her third! At that point she knew more about autism than I did. Because she understood, she could talk with me in greater depth and was even able to answer some of my questions based on the books she'd read. You don't have to become an expert, but learn what you can.

Listen

Whether you talk with the parents of a child with autism in person or on the phone, take time to listen. Ask how they're doing and *really* listen. They may need to process their thoughts and feelings and concerns with an objective friend. No matter what's going on in my life, good or bad, I can call my dear friend Ruth Ann, and she will listen. She doesn't offer me answers or try to fix my problems; she just listens. By doing so she provides great support.

Encourage

In addition to listening, you can encourage struggling parents in many other ways. If they share choices they're making, let them know you have faith in their ability to do what is best for their child. Do you respect or admire all their work and persistence? Let them know. Have you been encouraged by how they have handled the struggles? Tell them. Any family can easily become overwhelmed with negatives. Encourage them about the good you see in their lives. Your words might revitalize them and give them courage to face the next day.

Pray

Because of the newsletters we send out regularly, people around the world have been aware of Ryan's autism, and we have been touched by their prayers. This year we received a phone call from a family asking how Ryan was doing—a family we had met only once. Three years ago they received one of our newsletters, asking them to pray for us, and they took up the challenge. Beginning that night, they have prayed *daily* for Ryan to recover. Their daughter is only six years old, but she has diligently prayed for Ryan for three of those years!

For us, the most beautiful words are "I pray for Ryan." Will you take up the challenge to pray for the family you know? You may want to pray that they will find comfort and strength from God and that He will give them wisdom and insight for making good decisions about treatment options. You can also pray that God will provide for their needs and then ask if He wants you to fill any of them. Of course, be sure to ask the family what they would like you to pray for.

Expect Your Relationship to Change

Much has changed in your friends' lives that will affect every relationship. Right now they have more responsibilities than they ever imagined, and their priorities are shifting. Expect your relationship to change also.

When you call, be flexible. If they can't talk right then, understand that it isn't a reflection on your friendship. One mother told me that if she talks on the phone for more than five minutes, she risks her children getting into trouble and physically hurting themselves. Friends she used to talk with for hours now get only a few minutes at a time.

Your friends actually need you more than ever, but they may not be able to reciprocate in kind. You may be the one initiating everything, and you may be turned down often, but don't give up. Let your friendship adapt to their new situation.

Tangible Support

Baby-Sit
Finding a good, trustworthy baby-sitter for a special-needs child is particularly difficult. Although your friends need time away from the pressures of daily life, they may have limited opportunities. Consider baby-sitting for them so they can run errands or go to dinner. You will need to spend time beforehand learning what to do and allowing their child to get to know you. *Ask* if you can help in this way; chances are they won't ask you.

Help with Housekeeping
I love a clean house, but with Ryan's crazy therapy schedule, that isn't always realistic. Especially in the early stage of Ryan's therapy, we had to keep his room neat and organized so the therapists could find the toys and equipment they needed for each session. I spent hours putting toys in plastic boxes and organizing files with ther-

apy cards, just to find them messed up within days. The times that friends came over and helped me clean or reorganize materials lifted one more task from my load.

Cook a Meal

I remember one day as I was running around trying to keep my head above water, a friend called to see how I was doing. We talked for just a few minutes, and I shared my day with her. An hour later she showed up at my door with dinner. It wasn't fancy—sloppy joes, carrots, chips, and cookies for dessert—but to me it was a feast! That night I didn't have to think about cooking or cleaning up. When Roger got home from work, we could eat and relax, thanks to my friend.

One word of caution: Before you show up at their door with food, find out what they can eat. If their diet excludes gluten or casein and requires special ingredients, you might offer to come over and cook for them since they already have the necessary ingredients. Either way, it will be a blessing.

Enable Them to Go Out

During Ryan's first years, I felt like a prisoner in my home. Going anywhere alone with the kids was more than two hands could handle. One day I tried to take the kids to Wal-Mart to pick up a few things we needed. With Tori in the seat of the cart and Ryan in the back, I wheeled down the first aisle. Immediately, Ryan jumped out and ran to the men's clothing section, where he darted in and out of the racks. With Tori in one arm, I chased him, all the while telling him to stop. People's stares pierced me, each one saying, "Why can't you control your child? You must not be a good parent if your child acts like that." Trying to ignore the stares, I finally caught up with Ryan, picked him up like a sack of potatoes, and carried the two children out of the store as he kicked and screamed. After several such trips, I quit venturing out alone.

Does your friend need to get out when her husband isn't available? Perhaps you could go with her to the park or McDonald's or to run some errands. Just being there to lend an extra hand will allow her to do what she may not be able or willing to do alone.

Treatment Support

Send Information

Having current information plays a critical role in treating autism. Have you read an encouraging article lately or heard of a treatment that may benefit your friends' child? Cut it out and send it. Is there a helpful program on television? Let them know when it's on, or tape it and send it to them. They may already know the information, but I'd much rather be told something twice than to miss out because someone assumed I already knew it.

Volunteer As a Therapist

Did you realize that anyone—grandparents, neighbors, friends— can be trained as a therapist to provide Applied Behavior Analysis? If you can consistently spare four to six hours a week, consider volunteering your time to work one-on-one with your friends' child. But before you volunteer, check your calendar and make sure you can be consistent for at least six months.

Send Money

Families not only have to pay therapists, they need to buy materials and supplies. Consider sending them a gift of money. How much should you send? As a guideline, you may want to sponsor a therapy session or a day of therapy, but any amount is helpful. Speaking as one who has received gifts from friends and relatives, I know whatever you decide to give will be put to good use.

Help with Lesson Preparation

As with any teaching situation, much preparation is needed. Do you have a spare hour? Ask your friends if they need help cutting pictures from magazines, making copies, or preparing crafts. When Ryan began therapy, we had to cut out dozens of pictures from a three-foot pile of catalogs and magazines in our living room. One afternoon my friend Chris came over and cut out pictures of everything from people to furniture. We glued them on cards, and they were ready for the therapist. Her afternoon saved me hours of valuable time.

Bring Your Children Over to Play

Although perhaps not immediately, at some point your friends will need children to come over and play during therapy times in order to teach social skills. This may sound easy, but it wasn't for us. First of all, we needed children who were slightly older than Ryan who were *willing* to play with him even though he didn't have good play skills or comparable language skills. Then, once we found the peer and set up a play date, we often needed to transport him to or from our house. This isn't a big deal for the typical family who may have play dates only once a week, but we had to set up play dates every day. If your child might be a good peer, volunteer to bring your child over.

Bottom Line—Ask

Although it's common sense, people often fail to ask their friends what would be most helpful. Some of my suggestions may be good for them, while others might be inconvenient, depending on their personality and where they are in the therapy process. But please don't inquire out of mere politeness. If you ask, be ready to help, knowing that your assistance—big or small—will greatly impact your friends' lives and maybe yours as well.

Chapter 14

Remembering the Milestones

There is a time for everything,
and a season for every activity under heaven:…
a time to weep and a time to laugh,
a time to mourn and a time to dance.

ECCLESIASTES 3:1,4

It has been more than four years since we began our quest to rescue Ryan. Looking back at the *Operation Rescue Ryan* newsletters we have sent out during this time, I am reminded of how far we have come from those first devastating days. Ryan has reached many milestones that would have seemed absolutely impossible in the beginning. As you look back with us, may it encourage you to persevere and to believe in your journey to reclaim your child as well.

Sleeping Through the Night

As we learned more about autism, we discovered that sleeping problems were common, though knowing that didn't lessen my frustration. Every night Ryan needed me to lie down next to him until he fell asleep. When he awoke in the middle of the night, which happened several times each night, he needed me next to him to get back to sleep. He would either climb into our bed or scream until I lay next to him in his bed. Roger tried to be Ryan's comfort, but it didn't work; Ryan wanted Mommy. Needless to say, we were exhausted.

After Ryan's first week of ABA therapy, we decided to try an experiment. When we tucked Ryan in bed, we told him he needed to stay in bed. We were firm with our words but not angry. Ryan did stay in bed, but he cried. However, after a few minutes he fell asleep.

To our great surprise, Ryan stayed in his bed all night! He woke up once but didn't get out of bed, and he went back to sleep without me. After that night Ryan began sleeping through the night, perhaps as a result of being totally exhausted from his therapy sessions or perhaps because of the compliance required in the drills. Whatever the reasons, he was *finally* getting a good night's sleep and, thankfully, so were we.

Operation Rescue Ryan—May 10, 1995

Two months ago, Ryan...

- *had three words ("ma ma," "wa wa," and "up"), none of which he used appropriately. He wouldn't imitate any sounds and wasn't learning any new words.*

- *lined up or stacked his toys and didn't play with them appropriately. He didn't have any pretend play and didn't play any games with others.*

– would respond to his name only about 30 percent of the time and wouldn't follow simple commands. He wouldn't imitate any actions and screamed when he was shown how to do a task.

– couldn't point out an object if we named it (e.g., "touch chair").

Now, Ryan...

– has over thirty words and uses them appropriately. He can answer the question "What's this?" for fifteen different objects. He is able to imitate certain sounds and syllables and is picking up words in and out of therapy. He doesn't say all the words clearly, and most are only one syllable, but he is learning.

– has learned to build with blocks, play with cars, and pretend to feed a doll. He has also learned to play "Ring Around the Rosy," which has become a favorite activity.

– can imitate over sixty actions and can obey over forty commands (e.g., stand up, turn around, clap, wave). Now he will usually respond to his name when called. He still throws tantrums, but less frequently than before.

– can point out over eighty objects, all the letters of the alphabet, the numbers 1-7, and twenty-five action pictures (e.g., "touch sleeping"). He can also verbally name many of these objects, as well as twelve letters and four numbers.

Singing His First Song

Ryan's first song was "Pop Goes the Weasel," which he learned with Dawn, one of his therapists. Ryan was just beginning to speak, so he said only one word of the song, but it was wonderful.

Dawn had been working on this song with Ryan, singing it to him over and over, without our knowing it. One night at a team meeting she said Ryan had a surprise for us. She sang quietly into his ear, "All around the cobbler's bench the monkey chased the weasel. The monkey thought 'twas all in fun…" Then she stopped. Ryan, who was sheepishly hiding behind Dawn's legs, got a big smile on his face, popped his head out from behind her, and yelled out, "Pop," as Dawn finished, "goes the weasel."

To our thunderous applause he jumped around the room with pride. Within weeks, Ryan was singing all the words to this song, as well as songs like "Itsy Bitsy Spider" and "Ring Around the Rosy."

Saying "Daddy"

After being called "Mama" for so long, Roger really longed for the day when Ryan would call him Daddy, so he made a deal with our therapy team. The first person to get Ryan to say the magic word would be taken to lunch. Michelle set up the drills to work toward it, and the race was on. We started by trying to get him to say "Dada," which took awhile, but it came. Although pleased, Roger was still waiting for that wonderful word "Daddy." For days Michelle and the others drilled Ryan with "Say, 'Dah-dee.'" They emphasized the syllables to make it clearer to Ryan. Again and again they repeated the drill, until one day in May it came! Who won? It was such a team effort that they could all take credit. No words can describe the joy on Roger's face as he told the world about his son's latest word.

In those early days, simple words that seem insignificant to the rest of the world came as a result of hours of effort, but in the months that followed, Ryan's language snowballed. And we celebrated each new word out of his mouth as if he had just won a Nobel Prize.

In July of that first year, Roger wanted to surprise me with a special phrase of my own, so he asked Michelle to add it to Ryan's verbal imitation program. One day when I said, "I love you, Ryan," to my total surprise he answered, "I woo, Mommy." Ryan smiled, and my heart melted. At that moment *nothing* could hold a candle to hearing "I love you" from my son for the first time.

Expressing Desires

As Ryan's language began to bloom, he found the power of words for expressing his desires. More significantly, Ryan began to *have* desires. That may sound strange, but Ryan's desires were limited to his needs, like food and water, and specific wants, like movies.

One day Ryan received a package from his great-aunt and great-uncle—a snap-up sweatshirt with Thomas the Tank Engine on it. When the gift came, Ryan didn't really notice it, but several days later he went to his drawer and picked it out. He chose an item of clothing for the first time in his life! Soon he fell in love with that shirt and wore it often. From that, he developed a love for trains, especially the Thomas collection.

Most parents struggle with teaching their children not to be greedy and want too many things. For us, developing desires for items was a great joy. The boy who used to show no reaction to new items was now beginning to have preferences.

Learning to Spell

About five months into therapy, Bohdanna, one of the therapists, came running downstairs to the kitchen. With panic in her voice she cried out, "Lynn, come here, quick!" I ran upstairs to Ryan's room, fearing the worst. When I walked in, she pointed to the floor, tears forming in her eyes. On the floor Ryan had spelled "DUMBO" with his magnet letters. He apparently had noticed the title on his Disney video and remembered it well enough to spell it. Bohdanna had turned her back on Ryan to take notes, and when she faced him again, she saw it. Although a three-year-old child being able to spell isn't earth-shattering, it gave us insight into his high visual and memory skills.

Starting that week, we put a spelling program into his therapy and began to use more visual word cues to teach Ryan typical auditory information. For example, he didn't understand the concept of "I have" as well as he understood "I want," so he continually said, "I want have cup." Focusing on his visual strengths, we typed out the words "I" and "have" in big letters. We taught him what these words were by saying, "Touch 'I'" and "Touch 'have,'" until he knew the words. Then we asked him, "What is it?" and he would reply, "I" or "have." When he learned the words, we put them next to each other and had him read them.

Next, we handed Ryan an object, then pointed to the words we had placed on the table as he said the sentence. By seeing it, he was able to understand what he was supposed to be saying, and we got "I have cup" versus "I want have cup." This worked on a number of new verbal drills that we tried over the years.

Operation Rescue Ryan—August 11, 1995

Last month we found out some very exciting news! The children who participate in this ABA therapy program are tested after three months to check their progress. Of the children who have recovered in the past, all of them scored at least 90 percent in three out of five categories. Ryan scored 100 percent in three categories and over 90 percent in the other two! It does not guarantee he will recover, but it means he has a great chance!

Ryan's programs now include receptive and expressive labels, receptive commands, nonverbal imitation, animal sounds, verbal imitation, puzzles, block imitation, "I want...," "I see...," receptive letters and numbers, expressive letters and numbers, prepositions, action labels, colors, emotions, matching and sorting, and reading. (Yes, Ryan is learning to read! Autistic children often have very strong visual skills.)

Ryan's language is developing very well, but he doesn't converse. He will point out objects and make his needs known to us but usually in one or two words only. He is beginning to answer the question "What do you want?" He says, "I whop ice wasee," which means "I want ice water." He's doing so well from only five months ago when his main communication was "wa wa," which meant almost anything. Miracles are happening daily!

Playing Duck-Duck-Goose

Within the first year, Ryan learned to play a few games—Ring Around the Rosy, London Bridge Is Falling Down, and Duck-Duck-Goose—but Duck-Duck-Goose was my favorite to watch. When it was Ryan's turn, he would smile from ear to ear as he went around the circle. "Duck...duck...duck," he would say as he carefully scrutinized whom to pick. If Roger was playing, Ryan would scream out "Goose!" as soon as he reached him. Then he would run as fast as he could, laughing all the while. The rest of us cheered him on as Roger chased but never caught him. Such a simple game, but a year earlier it would have been unthinkable for Ryan.

Having His Picture Taken

Ryan had been a photogenic child who loved to smile and have his picture taken. We had a wonderful photo taken on his first birthday, with him wearing suspenders and a bow tie and smiling handsomely from ear to ear.

A few months later, as Christmas approached, we took Ryan in for a Christmas photo, only to come away frustrated and disappointed as Ryan screamed, unwilling to enter the room. As if an invisible fence guarded the doorway, Ryan would throw himself backward at the threshold and lie on the floor in a tantrum. Although we didn't realize it, this was one of the early signs of his regression. We left the studio without a photo, wondering what had happened to our little boy who had loved to have his picture taken. As the deluge of Christmas cards brought scores of beautiful family photos with happy, smiling kids, our hearts ached for a family photo of our own.

After many unsuccessful attempts, when Ryan was three and a half, I decided to try once more to get a Christmas photo of Ryan and Tori together. While having a picture of your children doesn't seem like a big deal, to me it was. On the day of the appointment, I dressed the kids in coordinating outfits and headed to the studio. I explained to the sympathetic photographer that Ryan had autism and getting a good picture wouldn't be easy.

To my surprise Ryan walked into the room without any prompting. He wanted to touch *everything,* so we let him, not wanting to hinder his cooperation. The photographer didn't try to make

Ryan sit on a table, since that hadn't worked in the past. Instead she set two wooden horses on the floor for the children to sit on.

What caught me completely off guard was that Ryan was willing to sit on the horse and smile, but now *Tori* was afraid! She didn't throw a tantrum as Ryan had, but no matter what we did, she looked uncertain and fearful. Even without Tori smiling, the pictures came out nicely, and we proudly sent them to our relatives and friends and placed one on our living room wall to remind us of a simple, yet meaningful milestone.

Our house is now full of family photos that obscure the memory of those "dark years." Once again we can go into a studio and have Ryan's picture taken, although his hyperactivity makes sitting still and smiling "just right" a challenge. Yet, more important than the photos themselves is what they illustrate: Ryan is happy again and greatly enjoys being a kid.

Operation Rescue Ryan—March 22, 1996

One year ago, Ryan...

- *scored 53 on an IQ test designed for normal children, though he scored 100 on a test for nonverbal children.*

- *spoke three words, but he didn't use them appropriately. He scored 0 on a language test.*

- *didn't play with toys appropriately. He would line them up in a row or stack them. He didn't know how to pretend, imitate, or play with other kids.*

– wouldn't come to the table, sit down, or pay attention at all. He made very little eye contact and didn't acknowledge most people.

– didn't know the names of any objects. He didn't understand the concept that objects had names.

Now, Ryan. . .

– has scored 101 on the IQ test designed for normal children. There was no need to do the special IQ test this time.

– has over three hundred words. He is beginning to speak in sentences and is learning rote conversation.

– has gone from 0 to the skills of a twenty-three-month-old child in language.

– plays with cars, toy food, dolls, building blocks, play clay, and trains, though he still doesn't tolerate others directing or intruding on his play.

– comes to the table when he's called, sits down, and pays attention better. He still has a very short attention span for his age and doesn't always listen when he should, but his eye contact has improved greatly.

– has learned the names of over 150 objects and is able to learn new objects more naturally outside of therapy.

— is working on these programs: "I see...," occupations, rote conversation, verbal imitation, functions of objects, what's missing?, reading, pretending, circle games, and expressive action labels.

Physical Skills

For nearly a year Ryan received supplemental therapy provided by the Madison school district. When Ryan began treatment, he was clearly behind children his age in both gross and fine motor skills, being unable to jump, hop, ride a tricycle, draw, or color.

We worked every week on a variety of exercises to build his confidence in his physical abilities. Our physical therapist, Cyndy Smith, brought a foam balance beam to walk on, a small scooter to ride on, and other devices. We also used speech, occupational, and early childhood therapies through the school district.

As Ryan made gains in his ABA therapy, we saw him make gains in his gross motor skills as well. One day in the spring of 1996, Cyndy showed up at our house and confessed, "I can't justify coming here anymore. This kid doesn't need my help!" What beautiful words to our ears.

Operation Rescue Ryan—June 14, 1996

I'd like to share with you a wonderful highlight of last month — Ryan's fourth birthday. We invited five of Ryan's friends over to help us celebrate. Before the party, we decorated the house with lots of balloons and streamers and placed his toy trains around the room for atmosphere. He got a kick out of everything! (Ryan is very much into Thomas the Tank Engine, so all the decorations had Thomas on them.)

When the kids arrived, Ryan ran to the door, opened it, and said, "Come in!" The kids played together, and Ryan interacted well with all of them. When it was time for presents, the kids sat around Ryan, and he opened them! Ryan had never opened presents before; he didn't even understand the concept until now. It was amazing! He even sat at the table for the ice cream cake.

To an outsider he would not have seemed different from any other child, except for his language deficiencies. Roger and I were overwhelmed at God's gracious gift of this party. In the midst of the daily work, it was nice to be able to see how far Ryan has come and get a glimpse of what the future might hold.

Bathroom Break at McDonald's

By the time Ryan turned four, he had become partially toilet trained, but he was still extremely afraid of public bathrooms. One weekend when Roger was out of town, my mother and I drove three hours to visit my brother Mark and his wife, Karen, for their daughter's birthday party. When we stopped at McDonald's for lunch, I tried to take Ryan to the bathroom. Terribly afraid, he began screaming at the top of his lungs, "Don't hurt me! No, don't hurt me!"

I'd been through this before, so it didn't faze me. I picked him up and walked toward the rest room. My mom, not used to this display, stayed with Tori and restrained herself from hiding under the table. The workers at the counter leaned over to watch, and every customer in the restaurant unashamedly stared. I smiled at them as my son continued to scream, "Don't hurt me!"

His screams continued, ricocheting off the tile bathroom walls, until he was finished. Then his whole demeanor changed. He was proud of himself. We washed his hands, and he ran out of the bathroom, singing just as boldly as he had screamed, "I went potty at McDonald's! I went potty at McDonald's!"

Operation Rescue Ryan—November 27, 1996

Ryan started preschool at the end of August with nineteen other children in his class, and he loves it! We were hoping he could attend without the teachers knowing his diagnosis, but that wasn't the case. Ryan is still not fully potty trained, his language is lacking, and his social and attentive skills need work. Two weeks before he started, we decided to meet with the teachers and tell them everything. This proved to be a good decision, because they were very open-minded and excited to work with him.

At first, Ryan stayed only an hour and a half in the morning, but within a few weeks he could make it successfully through the whole morning. He has made wonderful progress in circle time, interactive play, and attentiveness. We are praying that he will continue to grow in his school readiness so he can go to kindergarten next fall undetected.

Ups and Downs at Preschool

We were so excited about Ryan going to preschool and equally excited that his teachers were glad he was there. Ryan enjoyed school and talked often about the trains and blocks and playing in the pretend kitchen, and he usually cooperated with the teachers.

Since we had a therapist with him, we assumed everything was fine.

However, halfway into the school year, Connie, the clinic's school coordinator, observed Ryan at preschool and pointed out how much work was still ahead. She noticed that Ryan played nicely by himself, but when another child came near him, within ten to fifteen seconds he would quietly move to a different toy area.

The teachers were encouraged that Ryan enjoyed school and wasn't disruptive, but our standards were higher. We weren't as concerned about Ryan's academic ability as his ability to play and make friends with his classmates. He had no interest in playing with the other kids, so something had to be done.

Connie and Dr. Sallows advised us to pull Ryan out of preschool completely and use the time to focus on developing the skills for socializing and making friends. Though Ryan enjoyed preschool, they pointed out that wasn't the best use of his time. He needed one-on-one help in learning social skills.

We wanted to do whatever was necessary to help Ryan succeed, but our hearts were slow to agree. This seemed like a major setback. All along, Ryan's progress had been two steps forward and one backward, and with every step back we worried about his future prospects. Yet, we knew Ryan would never integrate fully into a regular classroom until he could develop the necessary social skills, so we agreed and took one step back.

Understanding Cause and Effect

As we targeted more complex language concepts in therapy, I began working with Ryan to help him understand cause and effect. When I would drive past a school on weekends, I would ask, "Ryan, why aren't the kids at school today?" hoping he would answer, "Because it's Saturday." Instead he would say, "I don't know," and I would have to prompt him with the right answer. This went on day after day, and even though we were addressing it in his therapy, he never seemed to catch on.

One day as the rain poured down, I tried again, asking, "Ryan, why aren't there any kids in the park?"

"Because it's raining," he said as naturally as if we'd had this conversation a dozen times. I swooped him up in my arms and twirled him around. Yes, he understood!

The next step was teaching him to wonder and ask why. We targeted *why* by asking him questions, but one day he turned the tables on us. He wanted to go to the park, and I told him no. He looked at me and said, "Why not?"

Stunned and excited, I grabbed his hand, and we dashed out the door for the park!

Most parents become frustrated when their youngsters constantly ask "Why?" Not us. We smile and find joy in the simple things because they mark great progress.

Operation Rescue Ryan—March 29, 1997

Two years have come and gone quicker than I expected. March 6 marked the two-year anniversary of Ryan's therapy, and with that came two-year testing. Ryan's IQ has remained in the normal range, and his language has increased to that of a forty-month-old. (By comparison, two years ago he had no language, and last year he had the language of a twenty-three-month-old.) One encouraging result from the testing is that Ryan's scores are evenly distributed among the four categories (which is typical for "normal" children) versus last year when he had varied highs and lows (which is typical for autistic children).

Preschool at Kid's Express

While Ryan spent the summer doing play therapy with his therapists, I busily prepared for a second try at preschool. A couple from our church had begun a preschool on their small farm within a mile of our house. Sandy Dahl, who has her Ph.D. in education, had established Kid's Express as a school with a good mix of structure and free time, well-qualified teachers, and a fun environment complete with animals. When I discussed with her the possibility of Ryan attending there for the year, Sandy was genuinely interested in helping Ryan develop socially as well as cognitively.

From day one Ryan had a great experience. He loves animals, so the thought of feeding the goats and llamas made it seem like anything but school. The therapists that went into his class looked for signs of social progress in Ryan but were instructed to stay away from him and help only when he really needed it. At first this was quite often, as many adjustments were made, but before long Ryan was functioning well in the class without a therapist. On days when a therapist couldn't be with him, he and the teachers did just fine. We were so encouraged to see him thriving in school once again that it gave us great hope for his chances in kindergarten the following year.

Operation Rescue Ryan—November 14, 1997

Last week we had a specialist, Connie, come to Ryan's preschool to observe him. She was the one who recommended we pull Ryan out seven months ago. This time she was very excited to see the changes in Ryan. Not only is Ryan staying when children approach him, he is even joining other children as they play! She mentioned that Ryan has gone from 0 percent in socialization with other children to about 10 percent. That might not seem like much, but it is tremendous! It means we have gotten over the first hump of learning in this area. Now that he has started, progress is much easier. For the first time, Ryan has become interested in "circle time" at school. He still has difficulty sitting for the entire time and paying attention, but he will need to learn this before kindergarten next fall.

We are extremely excited about the progress in Ryan's language. He is speaking more than ever, and his language becomes more complex daily. He talks continually, which brings us much joy. He initiates comments and questions with anyone who will listen. He has even learned how to tell jokes. Although he remains behind other five-and-a-half-year-olds, he is learning. However, his language needs to progress in more complex areas, such as abstract thinking, reasoning skills, and "circles of communication," not only for the sake of his language but for his socialization. It's hard to socialize if you can't communicate!

Operation Rescue Ryan—April 20, 1998

Three years have come and gone since we started therapy with Ryan, and so much has happened in that time. Our little boy, who then could not speak, learn, or play, has blossomed.

Preschool is the highlight of Ryan's day. He loves going to school and is doing so well there. He now attends preschool four hours a day, five days a week. His socialization has been increasing by leaps and bounds since last fall! He will greet adults enthusiastically but doesn't greet kids yet. However, he will join kids in playing or ask them to play with him.

Yet, there is still room for improvement. He needs to learn more tolerance in his play when things aren't exactly as he wants, and he needs to develop some good friends who enjoy his company. Ryan understands the concept of friends and knows if people like him. When a new boy started at school, Ryan came home and told me that this boy liked him and they were friends. A couple of weeks later I asked him about his friend. Ryan said, "He doesn't like me anymore. He has a new friend." My heart sank.

Although still significantly behind, Ryan's language improves daily. Yesterday Ryan said something I'll never forget. We had some of the neighborhood girls over to play with Tori, and Ryan wanted to go outside and join them. As he opened the door, I went to follow. He stopped me in my tracks and said, "Wait! I'm going to play with the kids. I'm a kid. You're a grownup. Your job is to stay here!" So I remained inside and watched through the windows. It was great! He was playing and laughing with them, just like any other kid.

Operation Rescue Ryan—September 7, 1998

On August 24, Ryan eagerly went to his first day of kindergarten. For weeks Ryan had asked, "Is it August 24 yet? Can it be August 24?" He even changed the calendar from July to August, thinking that might make kindergarten come sooner.

On that day he ran to his room and greeted his teacher enthusiastically. The other kids were arriving too, so I wasn't able to stay long, but as I peeked in the room before leaving, joy radiated through my entire being. How can I find words to convey the gratefulness I felt that day? There was Ryan, looking no different than any other child attending kindergarten.

When we were planning for the school year, we suggested to the school that we send one of our therapists as a transitional aid for Ryan. But after the teacher and special education teacher met Ryan and watched him at preschool, they felt he didn't need one. After discussing this at length, we fully agreed. We decided to have a person in the room "for Ryan" but that Ryan and the children wouldn't know she was there for him. She would help any child who needed it but would keep an eye on Ryan. After the first two weeks they said the aid needed to help the other children much more than Ryan.

All the teachers are thrilled with Ryan and how well he is doing. He is completely integrated in his room without the parents or children knowing he is any different, and at no time will Ryan need to be pulled from the class for special help.

Kindergarten

For the most part, Ryan has done very well in kindergarten, though we've had our share of setbacks. From the first day he has loved to take animals for show and tell, loved to bring books home to read, and loved the school computer lab. He has made friends and requires little help from classroom aids. He needs help mostly for behavioral issues that arise when he tries to push the limits of the classroom rules or doesn't understand what is expected of him.

In particular, his progress in socialization and speech has been remarkable to us. One day in the fall as the class was running under a parachute in gym class and everyone's hair stood on end, Ryan shouted out, "Hey look! We're all having a bad hair day!" The whole class laughed at Ryan's joke, and he enjoyed being the center of attention. A small episode marking a huge step for Ryan.

How Is Ryan Today?

On May 14, 1999, Ryan celebrated his seventh birthday. He's a very active, affectionate, and playful boy who is learning and growing daily. His IQ has continued to be in the normal range, and his language tests only nine months behind his peers. He learns everything at school that the other children learn without requiring preteaching or extra learning sessions. His reading is well above grade level, and he can add, subtract, write, and spell. He still struggles with fine motor skills, so writing is the most difficult subject for him, which shows in his frustration level during journal time.

Ryan loves to laugh, play, and pretend. He especially loves animals. He has friends from school and the neighborhood who come to our house to play and who invite him to their houses. He still requires more guidance in his play than his sister, Tori, but neither he nor his friends seem to mind.

This summer he is learning to ride a two-wheeler and to play on a T-ball team. He loves to swim at the beach and at the pool, and if you were there, you probably couldn't pick him out from the rest of the crowd.

Is Ryan recovered? That depends on the eye of the beholder. Many parents can't distinguish Ryan from typical children, but we know residual symptoms still need to be addressed. We also believe Ryan has some underlying biomedical issues that need to be identified and dealt with in the coming years. He still prefers things done in a particular way, though he is now more easily redirected. He is also hyperactive and therefore has a shorter attention span than others his age. In terms of language, he can say whatever he wants, but he needs to learn more complex ways to express his thoughts, and then he needs to *listen* while others express theirs. We worked so hard to get him to talk. Now we can't get him to stop long enough for anyone else to speak!

What *has* happened over these past four years is that Ryan is no longer confined by his autism. His life has been reclaimed, and he is enjoying it to the fullest. It's as if he has been set free and he's now ready to experience everything. This hasn't been an easy road, but it has been worth every tear and every sacrifice.

Will Ryan live a "normal" life? We think so. Judging from where he is now, we believe he will enjoy his life and become a productive member of society. With his love for animals, I predict he will either be a zookeeper or a zoologist, depending on his continuing development.

We don't know what the future holds for Ryan, but we continue to take each day one step at a time, thankful for every milestone he reaches—thankful to have our son back.

Chapter 15

Maintaining Hope

You see things; and you say "Why?"
But I dream things that never were; and I say "Why not?"
GEORGE BERNARD SHAW

From the very beginning, hope has been a hallmark of our journey with autism. When Ryan began to regress, we hoped for answers. When his autism was diagnosed, we hoped for recovery. With each step of his therapy, we have hoped Ryan would progress a bit farther.

I hope that someday someone will find a cure for autism that will free all children from its devastating effects. More research is being done now. Organizations like the Autism Research Institute and its DAN! (Defeat Autism Now!) project, CAN (Cure Autism Now), and the NAAR (National Alliance for Autism Research) are paving the way, and internationally known researchers, like Drs. Karl Reichelt and Andrew Wakefield, are finding pieces to the puzzle. Although there is much yet to be learned, each new piece brings more promise that one day there will be a cure.

While that isn't a present reality, I believe *some* can completely overcome autism and *all* have the hope that the future holds something better than today. However, maintaining that hope as a parent doesn't come easily. Hope is a choice we make daily, and because of that hope we are motivated to pursue that better future.

Hope from Others

When I read Catherine Maurice's book *Let Me Hear Your Voice,* my outlook, motivation, and hope changed dramatically. Her journey that brought both of their children completely out of their autistic world gave me hope for Ryan's recovery.

I also urge you to get to know others who have progressed farther down the road than you to be encouraged by their successes. Our city has numerous children with autism, some more advanced than Ryan, some farther behind. I love hearing other parents' success stories. Several weeks into our ABA therapy, I went to the home of a woman I'll call Laura. Her son greeted me, looked me in the eye, pointed to a small imitation pine tree, and said, "This is a Christmas tree."

I looked at Laura with amazement! "That is so neat," I told her. "I can't imagine Ryan doing that!" At the time Ryan's speech was fragmented and not very spontaneous, but her son stretched my hope of what might come.

I also gleaned much hope from other parents on the Internet through the support group called the ME-LIST. When I read about a child who had recovered or was doing well, I placed the message in a folder. If I became discouraged, I turned to these letters and read them over and over. Some reminded me of our goal and the possibility of reaching it, while others just made me smile as I read a proud parent's words.

One caution, however. Hearing of other children's successes can stir feelings of disappointment and jealousy if your child doesn't "measure up." Consequently, some parents choose to isolate themselves, allowing their anger and jealousy to lead to bitterness. I encourage you to keep a positive, hopeful attitude and to stay connected with other people. Your attitude may not change the situation, but it will change how you deal with it.

Hope in the Midst of Setbacks

Over the last four years we've had our share of setbacks as well as victories with Ryan's progress. One summer after attending an autism conference in northern Wisconsin, I returned home eager to accelerate Ryan's program with the new things I'd learned. Unfortunately, Ryan didn't feel the same. We made too many changes too fast, and within a couple of weeks Ryan had a meltdown. His aggression went up, and his learning went down. We called our psychologist, Dr. Sallows, and when he came out to observe, he recommended we go back to where Ryan was in the program three months earlier. My heart cried out, "No! We'll lose three months of work!" But trusting Dr. Sallows, we followed his advice, and though it was really difficult to watch Ryan be taken backward, it ended up benefiting him.

It's like a football game. Before the quarterback throws the ball, he takes a few steps backward so his pass can make even greater gains. And while we all seek the thrill of the long pass for a touchdown, teams most often progress by a series of short plays that advance the ball a few yards at a time. As parents we think, *If we could only make the right connection, our child would make great, sudden strides and cross the goal line.* We would be wise to take the approach of a seasoned quarterback, not panicking when we encounter a setback but instead continually plotting to move forward, one step at a time.

If you find yourself facing many setbacks, you may need to rethink your plan. Do you have the right goals for your child? Are they really attainable? Are you moving too fast or too slow? Do you have the right people on your team? Don't be afraid to make changes if necessary.

Hope That You *Will* Survive

There were many days, especially in the beginning of treatment, that I thought I wouldn't make it through the day, much less through several months or years. I remember sitting alone in our home office one afternoon with tears streaming down my face. I'd had it with all the demands Ryan's therapy was putting on me, and I'd had my limit of people in my house. The very sound of my name made my skin crawl because if someone called my name, he needed something from me, and I had nothing left to give. As I sat there, the phone rang. It was another mother who has a child like Ryan. Although we didn't know each other well, we shared our pain and our stress. She had no answers on how to alleviate my pain, but she was, in fact, an answer. Just talking with her reminded me I wasn't the only one with these struggles. That empathetic conversation and that timely reminder made the stress more bearable, made me feel so much better.

Later, a friend told me that when she feels overwhelmed, she tries to figure out what she needs to do to make it through the day. If that seems too much, she looks at only an hour. If she can't foresee surviving even an hour, she asks herself what she can do to help herself and her family manage the next ten minutes. When ten minutes have gone by, she takes hold of another ten minutes. I think she's wise. Sometimes the uncertainty of the future can overwhelm us so much that it paralyzes us in the here and now. Break down the future into manageable pieces. Look ahead only as far as you are able.

Hope from the Lord

Roger and I have a strong faith in the Lord, which brings us the greatest hope. In the book of Romans we find this blessing: "May the God of hope fill you with all joy and peace as you trust in him, so that you may overflow with hope by the power of the Holy Spirit."[1] God is called a God of hope, not a God of despair. That doesn't mean I will never despair, but when I am in the midst of despair, God will give me hope if I choose to trust in Him. He has given me hope when people around me have tried to take it away. He has given me hope when the outlook was bleak, and He gives me hope today for Ryan's future.

Although my desire has always been for Ryan's full recovery, my *complete* hope is in the Lord. I know that whatever happens, He will be there with each of us.

Hope When Recovery Seems Out of Reach

Perhaps you're thinking it's easy to maintain hope when a child has improved as much as Ryan has, and it's true that every step Ryan takes forward brings us joy and stirs our faith and hope in his complete recovery. But hope and joy aren't dependent on success. Susan Wallitsch has devoted the last six years to her son, Franke, whom we've mentioned throughout the book. Although Franke is still quite affected by autism, Susan and Mark exude hope and joy. Susan explains:

> No matter what diagnosis our children are given, no matter how profoundly our children are affected by autism, this syndrome cannot take away our ability to choose to live splendidly. Our son, Franke, will probably remain severely limited by his autistic symptoms, yet there is happiness in our day-to-day activities and eager anticipation for the future. We never, ever stop hoping that one day Franke will be able to speak his own name.

Our journey with autism began when Franke, our first-born, was administered an MMR vaccination at seventeen months of age. Franke exhibited the classic signs of a vaccine reaction followed by encephalopathy and loss of developmental skills. Our pediatrician told us it was just another ear infection and prescribed more antibiotics. My husband, Mark, and I accepted the judgment of the pediatrician and continued to treat Franke for recurrent ear infection and unspecified viral illness. As Franke's developmental losses became more difficult to deny, we sought explanations from an ENT (Ear, Nose, and Throat physician), an audiologist, a pediatric neurologist, a speech therapist, and finally from the Department of Child and Adolescent Psychiatry at the University of Chicago. At twenty-two months, Franke was diagnosed with autism. As Dr. Catherine Lord completed the interview informing us that our dear and perfect child was autistic, she said, "Remember, Franke has not changed because of this diagnosis; only your perception of him has changed."

We grieved. There are simply no words to describe the crushing pain that followed Franke's diagnosis. I was working as a public-interest attorney, a career I had found exciting and fulfilling. For six months, on the forty-five-minute drive to and from my office, I would weep. When I reached my destination, I would wipe off my face, compose myself, and numbly prepare for the tasks ahead. When I was with Franke at home, it was a little better. I could hold him, I could dance with him in my arms, and we could go for walks. I consoled myself by loving him more. Mark and I comforted each other in the absolute certainty that we

supported one another and would cherish and protect
Franke no matter what happened. To the world he might
be a child with autism, but to us he was still dear and perfect.

Slowly, the diagnosis became less painful. As the grieving eased, we began to reweave the fabric of our lives. We
promised each other that Franke's autism was not going to
be our "family tragedy." But we also acknowledged that we
could not continue to live the ambitious, two-career lifestyle
we had planned. Lovaas therapy, now called ABA, offered
hope of recovery. I chose to leave my career and devote all
my energy to Franke's therapy program. Mark continued to
work for a telecommunications company but used all of his
spare time to participate in Franke's therapy and to provide
me moral support. We were sustained in the conviction that
Franke would be one of the 47 percent to recover from
autism through Lovaas therapy.

After three years in an intensive behavioral modification program, Franke made many significant gains. His
tantrums were under control. His activities were more
appropriate and less bizarre. He enjoyed "school" and
could participate appropriately in a preschool classroom,
and most importantly he was a much more cheerful and
happy child. He now had a baby sister, Lucy, whom he tolerated and sometimes even kissed. But Franke was still not
talking and continued to be unable to perform any of the
expressive or receptive ABA drills. Franke's miracle recovery
was not happening.

What did we do? We grieved again. This time our grief
was not so violent, but it was, and is, a persistent ache.
There is so much Franke cannot communicate to us, so

much we know he wants to express. Will we ever know him as he wants to be known? Will he ever have the capacity to express his more complex choices and ideas? Franke was recently diagnosed with Landau-Kleffner Syndrome, and the specialists tell us it's unlikely he will ever speak. Yet, we refuse to accept that his inability to speak means a lack of desire or ability to communicate.

Once again, we are reweaving the fabric of our lives. Franke's behavioral program now focuses on socialization skills, daily living skills, and the use of augmentative communication aids of the Picture Exchange Communication System (PECS) and the DynaMyte (an augmentative communication device). When we concluded that Franke had reached a plateau with the ABA curriculum, we decided to use ABA techniques to help Franke with the daily activities that are most difficult for him and most challenging for us. Using ABA, we are teaching Franke to set and clear the table at mealtime, to prepare simple snacks for himself, to eat appropriately with utensils and a napkin, to dress and groom himself, to make his bed, to play with games and toys with his sister, to use the computer, and to express himself using PECS or the DynaMyte. Franke is not treated as helpless. He is expected to participate fully in the daily activities of our family. We are so proud of the progress he has made.

We are excited about the improvement Franke experiences with biological interventions such as the gluten-free/casein-free diet, treatment of yeast and fungal overgrowth in the GI tract, regular chiropractic care, and most recently, secretin infusions. As we learn more about emerging biological interventions in the treatment of autism, we remain hopeful that increasingly effective treatments will be available. With each of these interventions, Franke has become more healthy, focused, and socially appropriate. His cheerful engagement in family and school activities is enormously gratifying.

I remain at home with Franke, now seven years old, and Lucy, who is four. Each day we plan at least one "just for fun" activity in our schedule. We squeeze as much enjoyment as we can out of our daily routine, trying to turn even the most tedious tasks, such as laundry, cooking, and doctor visits, into interesting learning experiences. It is exhausting! But most of the time, we are calm and happy and really enjoy one another. There is richness in our days together, which blesses me. I remind myself not to regret the career I abandoned five years ago. I know I could not have chosen otherwise.

It's unlikely Franke will be able to live independently as an adult. With several of our friends who also have children who may not be able to live on their own, we are planning to create a farm community. The parents will live in private residences scattered across the property. Our children will share a residence with appropriate supervision. We feel that this setting will provide a safe environment and opportunities for meaningful labor and recreation for our children. We look forward to the natural beauty and peace of a rural retirement.

Dr. Lord initially offered us hope by assuring us that our child did not change with his diagnosis of autism. It was only our perceptions that were so painfully assaulted. Our perceptions are within our control. Over time, it was not our perception of Franke that changed; it was our perception of ourselves. We have become more accepting and forgiving, more sympathetic and compassionate, less self-absorbed and demanding. Our hope springs from the happiness and engagement we find in our daily activities with one another. It is nourished by the sweetness and goodness of our children. It is renewed by the splendid future we will create together.

Most of all, our hope resides in the deep, still, quiet faith that we are all loved completely and absolutely, just as we are.

Choosing Hope

If you have a specific hope in your heart for your child, don't throw it away. If you choose to give up your hope because others tell you it isn't possible, you will be defeated before you begin. We each must follow the hopes and dreams that we have been given. Someday your hopes may have to change as Susan's have, but she hasn't given up. She still hopes for big things for Franke, though her dreams are different from a few years ago.

Just as hope for the future is important, living within today is even more so. If we spend our lives longing for the results that will come "tomorrow," we may miss the pleasures of today. Enjoy your child where he is now. Celebrate the gains that have been made no matter how small they seem. When I take time to look back and reflect on the changes that have occurred in Ryan, my hope is refreshed, and my motivation to continue is renewed.

Each day we hear Ryan laughing and playing with his sister as they pretend to be different animals. Tori chooses to be basic animals, but Ryan is more elaborate, pretending to be an Australian frilled lizard or a Jackson's chameleon. Each day he teaches me something new about his exciting animal kingdom. He recently explained to me what *cartilaginous* means. (In case you don't know either, it means having cartilage instead of bones.) Although Ryan can get "stuck" in his zoological world, with a small reminder he will move on to something else. I'm amazed that a child who couldn't say "dada" four years ago can now use words I can hardly pronounce—with understanding!

Each day we treasure the joys our precious son brings to us, and each night as we tuck him into bed, Roger and I talk with Ryan about his day, and we pray together, thanking God for His blessings. Ryan prays too, usually thanking God for his beloved animals. We kiss him good-night and tell him how much we love him. In days past he would have responded with silence or whines, but no longer. Now he looks us in the eyes, gives us a hug and a kiss, and says, "Good night, Mom. Good night, Dad. I love you!"

There *is* hope.

ABA Providers

Disclaimer: Providers listed here are intended only as a resource; this is *not* an exhaustive list. By including these providers, I am neither recommending them nor guaranteeing their experience or the quality of their services. The reader is responsible for checking all credentials carefully.

United States

California

Applied Behavior Consultants School (ABC)
4540 Harlin Drive
Sacramento, CA 95826
Phone: 800-435-9888 or 916-964-7800
Fax: 916-964-7888
E-mail: jmorrow223@aol.com
Web site:
    http://www.onlearn.com/abc.html

Autism Partnership
200 Marina Drive, Suite C
Seal Beach, CA 90740-6057
Phone: 562-431-9293
Fax: 562-431-8386
E-mail: autismptnr@aol.com

Behavior Analysts, Inc. / S.T.A.R.S. School (Strategic Teaching and Reinforcement System)
3329 Vincent Road
Pleasant Hill, CA 94523
Phone: 925-210-9378
Fax: 925-210-0436
E-mail: stars@corteks.com
Web site:
    http://www.corteks.com/stars

Behavior Therapy and Family Counseling Clinic
32123 Lindero Canyon Road, Suite 302
West Lake Village, CA 91361
Phone: 818-706-9913, ext. 4
Fax: 818-706-6093
E-mail: btfcc@best.com
Web site: http://www.btfcc.com

Center for Autism and Related Disorders (CARD)
2061 Business Center Drive, Suite 202
Irvine, CA 92612
Phone: 949-833-7736
Fax: 949-833-7566

Center for Autism and Related Disorders (CARD)
5677 Oberlin Drive, Suite 200
San Diego, CA 92121
Phone: 619-558-4567
Fax: 619-558-9250

Center for Autism and Related Disorders (CARD)
2400 Moorpark Avenue, Suite 206
San Jose, CA 95128
Phone: 408-280-1112
Fax: 408-280-1113

Center for Autism and Related Disorders (CARD)
23300 Ventura Boulevard
Woodland Hills, CA 91364
Phone: 818-223-0123
Fax: 818-223-0133
E-mail: cardla@aol.com
Web site: http://www.cardhq.com

Central Valley Autism Project
1518 Coffee Road, Suite C
Modesto, CA 95355
Phone: 209-613-7220
Fax: 209-578-4272
Web site:
　http://www.lovaas.com/cvap1.htm

Institute for Applied Behavior Analysis
5777 West Century Boulevard, Suite 675
Los Angeles, CA 90045
Phone: 310-649-0499
Fax: 310-649-3109
E-mail: iabala@attmail.com
Web site: http://www.iaba.com

Lovaas Institute for Early Intervention
2566 Overland Avenue, Suite 530
Los Angeles, CA 90064-3366
Phone: 310-840-5983, ext. 100
Fax: 310-840-5987
Web site: http://www.lovaas.com

UCLA Young Autism Project
Dept. of Psychology
1282A Franz Hall
Box 951563
Los Angeles, CA 90095
Phone: 310-825-2319
Fax: 310-206-6380

Valley Mountain Regional Center
P.O. Box 692290
Stockton, CA 95269
Phone: 209-473-0951
Fax: 209-473-0256

Connecticut
Innovative Developments for Educational Achievement (IDEA)
20 Washington Avenue, Suite 108
North Haven, CT 06473
Phone: 203-234-7401
Fax: 203-239-4348
E-mail: ideasb@cshore.com

Florida

Reaching Potentials, Inc.
7390 NW 5th Street, #9
Plantation, FL 33317
Phone: 954-321-7393
Fax: 954-321-1019
E-mail: RpforAutism@hotmail.com or info@reachingpotentials.org
Web site: http://www.reachingpotentials.org

Illinois

Illinois Early Autism Project
Linden Oaks Hospital
852 West Street
Naperville, IL 60540
Phone: 630-718-0313
Fax: 630-718-0314

Maryland

Community Services for Autistic Adults and Children (CSAAC)
751 Twinbrook Parkway
Rockville, MD 20851-1428
Phone: 301-762-1650
Fax: 301-762-5230
E-mail: csaac@csaac.org
Web site: http://csaac.org/index.htm

Massachusetts

The May Institute
940 Main Street
P.O. Box 899
South Harwich, MA 02661
Phone: 508-432-5530
Fax: 508-432-3478
E-mail: information@mayinstitute.org
Web site: http://www.mayinstitute.org

The New England Center for Children (NECC)
33 Turnpike Road
Southboro, MA 01772-2108
Phone: 508-481-1015
Fax: 508-485-3421
E-mail: ksenecal@necc.org
Web site: http://www.NECC.org

Michigan

The Association for Behavior Analysis
213 West Hall
Western Michigan University
1201 Oliver Street
Kalamazoo, MI 49008-5052
Phone: 616-387-8341 or 616-387-8342
Fax: 616-387-8354
E-mail: 76236.1312@compuserve.com
Web site: http://www.wmich.edu/aba/Autismwebfile.htm
This association deals with using ABA for autism as well as other disorders. They can provide direction on finding an ABA provider, and their Web site gives training guidelines for qualified ABA professionals.

Minnesota

Families for Effective Autism Treatment of Minnesota
1821 University Avenue
Suite 324 South
St. Paul, MN 55104
Phone: 612-927-0017
E-mail: elarsson@worldnet.att.net
Web site: http://208.210.146.138/abta/

Nevada

Early Childhood Autism Program
Department of Psychology / 296
University of Nevada
Reno, NV 89557
Phone: 775-784-1128
Fax: 775-784-1126

New Jersey

Alpine Learning Group
777 Paramus Road
Paramus, NJ 07652
Phone: 201-612-7800
Fax: 201-612-7710

Bancroft School
P.O. Box 20
Hopkins Lane
Haddonfield, NJ 08033-0018
Phone: 800-774-5516 or 856-429-0010
Fax: 856-429-4755
E-mail:
  inquiry@Bancroftneurohealth.org
Web site:
  http://www.Bancroftneurohealth.org

*Douglas Developmental Disabilities
  Center*
Rutgers, the State University of New Jersey
25 Gibbons Circle
New Brunswick, NJ 08901-8528
Phone: 732-932-9137
Fax: 732-932-8081
Web site: http://www.rci.rutgers.edu/
  ~gsapp/gsappweb/dddc.html

Douglas Outreach
Rutgers, the State University of New
  Jersey
30 Gibbons Circle
New Brunswick, NJ 08901-8528

Phone: 732-932-3902
Fax: 732-932-4469
E-mail: kdvorak@rutgers.edu

Eden Family of Services
One Logan Drive
Princeton, NJ 08540
Phone: 609-987-0099
Fax: 609-987-0243
E-mail: EdenSvcs@aol.com
Web site: http://members.aol.com/
  EdenSvcs/index.html

New Jersey Institute for Early Intervention
52 Haddonfield-Berlin Road,
Suite 4000
Cherry Hill, NJ 08034-3502
Phone: 856-616-9442
Fax: 856-616-9454

Partners in Therapy, Inc.
804 Park Avenue
Collingswood, NJ 08108
Phone: 856-858-3673
Fax: 856-869-9469
E-mail: partner1@ix.netcom.com

Princeton Child Development Institute
300 Cold Soil Road
Princeton, NJ 08540-2002
Phone: 609-924-6280
E-mail: njpcdi@earthlink.net
Web site: http://www.pcdi.org

Rutgers Autism Program
41 Gordon Road, Suite A
Piscataway, NJ 08854
Phone: 732-445-1141
Fax: 732-445-7970
Web site:
  http://www.rci.rutgers.edu/~rapsite

New York

Center for Autism and Related Disorders (CARD)
280 North Central Avenue, Suite 314
Hartsdale, NY 10530
Phone: 914-683-3833
Fax: 914-683-3836

Eden II Programs / Genesis School
150 Granite Avenue
Staten Island, NY 10303
Phone: 718-816-1422
E-mail: eden2si@aol.com
Web site: http://www.eden2.org

Fred S. Keller School
1 Odell Plaza
South Westchester Executive Park
Yonkers, NY 10701
Phone: 914-965-1152
Fax: 914-965-1419

North Carolina

Building Blocks Children's Group
1102 North Main Street, Suite 202
High Point, NC 27262
Phone: 336-886-8019
Fax: 336-886-8661
E-mail: BBlkChldGr@aol.com

Center for Autism and Related Disorders (CARD)
3711 W. Market Street, Suite B
Greensboro, NC 27403
Phone: 336-855-1700
Fax: 336-855-1787

Meredith Autism Program
Meredith College—Department of Psychology
3800 Hillsborough Street
Raleigh, NC 27607-5298
Phone: 919-760-8080
Fax: 919-760-2303

Oregon

Project PACE, Inc.
9725 SW Beaverton Hillsdale Highway
Suite 230
Beaverton, OR 97005
Phone: 503-643-7015
Fax: 503-641-3640
E-mail: hred@projectpace.com
Web site: http://www.projectpace.com

Pennsylvania

The Childhood Learning Center
98 Fairview Street
Reading, PA 19605
Phone: 610-929-9459
Fax: 610-929-4066
E-mail: cynthia@tclc.com or info@tclc.com
Web site: http://www.tclc.com

Pittsburgh Young Autism Project
Intercare—Brentwood Office
4411 Stilley Road / Route 51
2nd Floor, Suite 202
Pittsburgh, PA 15227
Phone: 412-881-3902
Fax: 412-881-3599

South Carolina

Autism Research Center, S.C.
P.O. Box 1066
Anderson, SC 29622
Phone: 864-260-9005
Fax: 864-226-8902
E-mail: drbmetzger@aol.com

Texas

Texas Young Autism Project
Department of Psychology
University of Houston
Houston, TX 77204-5341
Phone: 713-743-8610
Web site: http://www.uh.edu/tyap

Virginia

*Center for Autism and Related Disorders
(CARD)*
5105-P Backlick Road
Annandale, VA 22003
Phone: 703-256-6383
Fax: 703-256-6384

Washington

Northwest Young Autism Project
Department of Psychology
Washington State University
P.O. Box 644820
Pullman, WA 99164
Phone: 509-335-7750
Fax: 509-335-2522

Wisconsin

Autism and Behavioral Consultants
349 Winnebago Drive
Fond du Lac, WI 54935
Phone: 920-926-1255
Fax: 920-921-1798

*Families with Autism Counseling and
Resource Center*
6333 University Avenue, Suite 202
Middleton, WI 53562
Phone: 608-218-9790
Fax: 608-218-9794

Integrated Developmental Services
14 Ellis Potter Court
Madison, WI 53711
Phone: 608-441-0123
Fax: 608-441-0126

Wisconsin Early Autism Project (W.E.A.P.)
727 East Walnut Street
Green Bay, WI 54301
Phone: 920-431-3380
Fax: 920-431-0256
E-mail: weapgb.jobs@wiautism.com

Wisconsin Early Autism Project (W.E.A.P.)
6402 Odana Road
Madison, WI 53719
Phone: 608-288-9040
Fax: 608-288-9042
E-mail: weap@wiautism.com

Wisconsin Early Autism Project (W.E.A.P.)
2433 North Mayfair Road, Suite 102
Wauwatosa, WI 53226
Phone: 414-479-9798
Fax: 414-479-9805
E-mail: weapmil.jobs@wiautism.com

International

Center for Autism and Related Disorders (CARD)
Suite 69A
Royal Randwick Shopping Centre
73 Belmore Road
Randwick, NSW 2031 AUSTRALIA
Phone: 011-612-931-00022
Fax: 011-612-931-00233

Center for Autism and Related Disorders (CARD)
Unit 17—1st Floor
Ivanhoe 3079
Melbourne Victoria, AUSTRALIA
Phone: 011-613-949-99885
Fax: 011-613-949-99885

Geneva Centre for Autism
200-250 Davisville Avenue
Toronto, Ontario M4S 1H2 CANADA
Phone: 416-322-7877
Fax: 416-322-5894
E-mail: info@autism.net
Web site: http://www.autism.net

Center for Autism and Related Disorders (CARD)
The Chislehurst Business Centre
Sunnymead
1 Bromley Lane
Chislehurst, Kent BR7 6LH UNITED KINGDOM
Phone: 011-44-181-295-2424
Fax: 011-44-181-295-2414

London Early Autism Project
699 Fulham Road
London, SW65UJ UNITED KINGDOM
Phone: 011-44-171-736-6689
Fax: 011-44-181-956-2529
E-mail: LEAP@btinternet.com

Parents for the Early Intervention of Autism in Children (P.E.A.C.H.)
School of Education
Brunel University
300 St. Margaret's Road
Twickenham
Middlesex TW1 1PT ENGLAND
Phone: 44-0-181-891-0121, ext. 2348
Fax: 44-0-181-891-8209
E-mail: peach@brunel.ac.uk
Web site: http://www.peach.uk.com

Iceland Young Autism Project
Digranesvegur 5
200 Kopavogur
ICELAND
Phone: 011-354-554-5462
Fax: 011-354-564-1753

Center for Children with Autism (Comunidad Los Horcones)
Carretera a Yécora Km. 63 (Highway 16)
Apartado Postal # 372
Hermosillo
Sonora 83000 MEXICO
Phone/fax: 52-62-14-72-19
E-mail: walden2@infosel.net.mx

Web site (English):
  http://www.loshorcones.org.mx/
  autism.html
Web site (Spanish):
  http://www.loshorcones.org.mx/
  autismo.html

Akershus College
P.O. Box 372
1301 Sandvika, NORWAY
Phone: 011-67-11-74-22
Fax: 011-67-11-74-01

*Norwegian Research Institute for Children
  with Developmental Disabilities
  (NFBU)*
Glenne Center
3184 Hortew, NORWAY
Phone: 0047-33-078800

Barcelona Autism Project
Paseo San Gervasio
90, Local 2
08022
Barcelona, SPAIN
Phone: 011-3493-418-4850
Fax: 011-3493-418-4850

State Resource Centers

Alabama

Alabama's Early Intervention System
2127 East South Boulevard
P.O. Box 11586
Montgomery, AL 36116-0586
Phone: 800-543-3098 or 334-613-2394
TTY phone: 800-548-2546
Fax: 334-613-3494

Alaska

Healthy Alaskans Info Line
701 East Tudor Road, Room 280
Anchorage, AK 99503-7445
Phone: 800-478-2221 or 907-343-6718

Arizona

Arizona Children's Information Center
Arizona Department of Health Services
411 North 24th Street
Phoenix, AZ 85008
Phone: 800-232-1676 or 602-220-6570

Arkansas

Arkansas Early Intervention
Department of Human Services
Developmental Disabilities Services
P.O. Box 1437, Slot 2520
Little Rock, AR 72203-1437
Phone: 800-643-8258 or 501-682-8699
TTY phone: 501-682-1332
Fax: 501-682-8687

California

Early Start
California Department of Development
 Services
1600 9th Street, Room 310
Sacramento, CA 95814
Phone: 800-515-BABY or 916-654-2773
TTY phone: 916-654-2054
Fax: 916-654-2271

Colorado

Birth to Age Three (El Paso County Only)
Resources for Young Children and
 Families
201 East Colfax, Room 305
Denver, CO 80203
Phone: 888-777-4041 or 303-866-6667
Fax: 303-866-6662

Connecticut

Birth-to-Three Info Line
1344 Silas Dean Highway
Rocky Hill, CT 06067
Phone: 800-505-7000 or 860-571-7556
TTY phone: 860-571-7556
Fax: 860-571-7525

Delaware

Child Development Watch
2055 Limestone Road, Suite 201
Wilmington, DE 19808
Phone: 800-671-0050 or 302-995-8617
New Castle: 800-671-0050
Kent and Sussex Counties:
    800-752-9393
Fax: 302-995-8363

District of Columbia

DC Early Intervention Program—
    Department of Human Services
609 H Street NE, 5th Floor
Washington, DC 20002
Phone: 202-727-1839
Fax: 202-727-9709

Florida

Florida Children's Forum
2807 Remington Green Circle
Tallahassee, FL 32308
Phone: 800-654-4440 or 850-921-5444
TTY phone: 800-654-4440
Fax: 850-681-9816

Georgia

Parent to Parent of Georgia, Inc.
2872 Woodcock Boulevard
Suite 230
Atlanta, GA 30341
Phone: 770-451-5484
Voice/TTY phone: 800-229-2038
Fax: 770-458-4091

Hawaii

Hawaii Keiki Information Service System
Zero to Three Hawaii Project (H-Kiss)
1600 Kapiolani Boulevard
Suite 1401
Honolulu, HI 96814

Voice/TTY phone: 800-235-5477 or
    808-955-7273
Fax: 808-946-5222

Idaho

Idaho Careline
P.O. Box 83720
Boise, ID 83720-0036
Phone: 800-926-2588
TTY phone: 208-332-7205
Fax: 208-334-5531

Illinois

Help Me Grow Helpline
2501 North Kirksen Parkway
Springfield, IL 62702
Voice/TTY phone: 800-323-4769 or
    217-557-3887
Fax: 217-557-3777

Indiana

Bureau of Child Development
402 West Washington Street, Room
    W386
Indianapolis, IN 46204
Phone: 800-441-7837 or 317-232-2429
Fax: 317-232-7948

Iowa

Iowa Compass
S277 Hospital School
100 Hawkins Drive
Iowa City, IA 52242-1011
Voice/TTY phone: 800-779-2001 or
    319-353-8777
Fax: 319-356-1343
E-mail: iowa-compass@uiowa.edu
Web site: www.medicine.uiowa.
    edu/iowacompass

Kansas

Kansas Make a Difference Info Network
Kansas Department of Health and
   Environment
Landon State Office Building, 10th Floor
900 SW Jackson Street
Topeka, KS 66612-1290
Phone: 800-332-6262
Voice/TDD phone: 785-296-1317
Fax: 785-296-8616

Kentucky

First Steps
Kentucky Early Intervention System
Division of Mental Retardation
100 Fair Oak Lane 4E-E
Frankfort, KY 40621-0001
Phone: 800-442-0087 or 502-564-7722
Fax: 502-564-0438

Louisiana

Louisiana Disabilities Info Access Line
200 Lafayette, 4th Floor
Baton Rouge, LA 70801
Phone: 800-922-3425 or 225-342-7700
TTY phone: 225-342-5704 or
   800-256-1633
Fax: 225-342-1970
Web site: http://www.laddc.org

Maine

Department of Education
Child Development Services, State
   House Station 146
Augusta, ME 04333
Phone: 207-287-3272
Fax: 207-287-3884

Maryland

*Governor's Office for Children, Youth, and
   Families*
301 West Preston Street, 15th Floor

Baltimore, MD 21201
Phone: 800-535-0182 or 410-767-4027
TTY phone: 410-767-8117
Fax: 410-333-5248

Massachusetts

Early Intervention Services
Department of Public Health
250 Washington Street, 4th Floor
Boston, MA 02108-4619
Phone: 617-624-5969
Fax: 617-624-5990

Michigan

Early On
Michigan 4C Association
2875 Northwind Drive, Suite 200
East Lansing, MI 48823
Voice/TTY phone: 800-327-5966 or
   517-351-4171
Fax: 517-351-0157

Minnesota

Pacer Center
4826 Chicago Avenue South
Minneapolis, MN 55417-1098
Voice/TTY phone: 800-537-2237 or
   612-827-2966
Fax: 612-827-3065

Mississippi

Parent Partners
1900 North West Street, Suite C-100
Jackson, MS 39202
Phone: 800-366-5707 or 601-714-5707
Fax: 601-714-4025

Missouri

Missouri Parent's Act (MPACT)
2100 South Brentwood, Suite G
Springfield, MO 65804
Phone: 800-743-7634 or 417-882-7434

Montana

Family Support Services Info Network—
Parents, Let's Unite for Kids
516 North 32nd Street
Billings, MT 59101-6003
Voice/TTY phone: 800-222-7585 or
406-255-0540
Fax: 406-255-0523

Nebraska

Nebraska Child Find
5143 South 48th Street, Suite C
Lincoln, NE 68516-2204
Voice/TTY phone: 888-806-6287 or
402-471-0734
Fax: 402-471-6052

Nevada

Nevada Project Assist
P.O. Box 70247
Reno, NV 89570-0247
Phone: 800-522-0066 or 775-688-2819
TTY phone: 775-688-2818
Fax: 775-688-2558

New Hampshire

Infants and Toddlers Program
State Office Park South
105 Pleasant Street
Concord, NH 03301
Phone: 800-298-4321 or 603-271-7931
Fax: 603-271-6826

New Jersey

Early Intervention Program
State Office on Disability Services
P.O. Box 364
Trenton, NJ 08625-0364
Voice/TTY phone: 888-285-3036 or
609-292-7800
Fax: 609-292-3580

New Mexico

Baby Net
Info Center for New Mexicans with
Disabilities
435 St. Michaels Drive, Building D
Santa Fe, NM 87505
Phone: 800-552-8195 or 505-827-7596
TTY phone: 800-552-8195
Fax: 505-827-7589

New York

New York State Office of Advocates for
Persons with Disabilities
One Empire State Plaza, Suite 1001
Albany, NY 12223-1150
Phone: 800-522-4369 or 518-474-5567
TDD: 518-473-4231
Fax: 518-473-6005

North Carolina

Family Support Network of NC
CB #7340
UNC at Chapel Hill
Chapel Hill, NC 27599-7340
Voice/TTY phone: 800-852-0042 or
919-966-2841
Fax: 919-966-2916

North Dakota

Developmental Disabilities Unit
Department of Human Services
600 South Second Street, Suite 1A
Bismarck, ND 58504-5729
Phone: 800-755-8529 or 701-328-8930
Fax: 701-328-8969

Ohio

Ohio Coalition for the Education of Children with Disabilities
Bank One Building
165 West Center Street, Suite 302
Marion, OH 43302-3741
Voice/TTY phone: 800-374-2806 or 740-382-5452
Fax: 740-383-6421

Oklahoma

Oklahoma Areawide Service Information System (OASIS)
Oklahoma Univ. Health Sciences Center
4545 North Lincoln Boulevard
Suite 284
Oklahoma City, OK 73105
Voice/TTY phone: 800-426-2747 or 405-271-6302
Fax: 405-521-1452

Oregon

Oregon Department of Education
Public Services Building
255 Capitol Street NE
Salem, OR 97310
Phone: 503-378-3598, ext. 637
TTY phone: 503-378-2892
Fax: 503-373-7968

Pennsylvania

Parent to Parent
150 South Progress Avenue
Harrisburg, PA 17109
Phone: 800-986-4550 or 717-540-4722
Fax: 717-540-7603

Rhode Island

Division of Family Health
State Department of Health
Three Capitol Hill
Cannon Building, Room 302
Providence, RI 02908-5097

Phone: 800-464-3399 or 401-222-4612
Fax: 401-222-1442

South Carolina

South Carolina Babynet Central Directory
Center for Disability Resources
USC School of Medicine
Columbia, SC 29208
Voice/TTY phone: 800-922-1107 or 803-935-5300
Fax: 803-935-5279

South Dakota

South Dakota Part C Central Directory
Dept. of Education and Cultural Affairs
700 Governors Drive
Pierre, SD 57501-2291
Phone: 800-529-5000 or 605-773-4478
Fax: 605-773-6846

Tennessee

Tennessee Early Intervention System
2147 Belcourt Avenue, Suite 200
Nashville, TN 37212
Phone: 800-852-7157 or 615-936-1849
Fax: 615-936-1852

Texas

Texas Interagency Council on Early Childhood Intervention (ECI)
Intervention Program
4900 N. Lamar Boulevard
Austin, TX 78751
Phone: 800-250-2246 or 512-424-6785
Fax: 512-424-6799

Utah

Access Utah Network
555 East 300 South, Suite 201
Salt Lake City, UT 84102
Voice/TTY phone: 800-333-8824 or 801-533-4636
Fax: 801-533-5305

Vermont

Family, Infant, and Toddlers Program
Vermont Department of Health
108 Cherry Street
P.O. Box 70
Burlington, VT 05402
Voice/TTY phone: 800-660-4427 or
    802-863-7338
Fax: 802-863-7635

Virginia

Autism Program of Virginia
1116 Floyd Avenue
Richmond, VA 23220
Phone: 800-649-8481, ext. 304 or
    804-649-8481, ext. 304
Fax: 804-649-3585
E-mail: autismva@aol.com
Web site: http://www.autismva.org

Washington

Answers for Special Kids (ASK)
300 Elliott Avenue West, Suite 300
Seattle, WA 98119
Phone: 800-322-2588

TTY phone: 800-833-6388
Fax: 206-270-8891

West Virginia

Family Matters
P.O. Box 1831
Clarksburg, WV 26302-1831
Phone: 888-983-2645 or 304-623-6183
Fax: 304-623-6683

Wisconsin

Wisconsin First Step
c/o Lutheran Hospital—La Crosse
1910 South Avenue
La Crosse, WI 54601
Voice/TTY phone: 800-642-STEP
    (7837)
Fax: 608-791-4766

Wyoming

Division of Developmental Disabilities
Herschler State Office Bldg. West
Cheyenne, WY 82002
Voice/TTY phone: 307-777-7115
Fax: 307-777-6047

U.S. Provinces

American Samoa

American Samoa Government
Pago Pago, AS 96799
Phone: 011-684-633-4929
Fax: 011-684-633-2167

Guam

*Early Childhood, Department of
    Education*
Division of Special Education
Box DE
Agana, GU 96910
Phone: 011-671-647-4400 or
    011-671-475-0555
Fax: 011-671-646-8052

Puerto Rico

Infants and Toddlers with Handicaps
Department of Health
P.O. Box 70184
San Juan, PR 00936
Phone: 787-274-5660

Virgin Islands

Charles Harwood Complex
3500 Richmond
St. Croix, VI 00803-4370
Phone: 809-773-1311, ext. 3006
Fax: 809-774-2820

Autism Resources

United States

Access to Respite Care and Help (ARCH)
Chapel Hill Training–Outreach Project
800 Eastowne Drive, Suite 105
Chapel Hill, NC 27514
Phone: 800-473-1727 or 919-490-5577
Fax: 919-490-4905
E-mail: YLayden@intrex.net
Web site: http://www.chtop.com/arch-
broc.htm

ACRES National Headquarters
(American Council on Rural Special
Education)
Kansas State University
2323 Anderson Avenue
Suite 226
Manhattan, KS 66502
Phone: 785-53-ACRES
Fax: 785-532-7732
E-mail: acres@k-state.edu
Web site: http://www.ksu.edu:8000/
acres/contact.html

Autism Autoimmunity Project
45 Iroquois Avenue
Lake Hiawatha, NJ 07034
Phone: 973-299-9162
Fax: 973-299-2668
E-mail: truegrit@gti.net

Autism Research Institute
4182 Adams Avenue
San Diego, CA 92116
Phone: 619-281-7165
Fax: 619-563-6840
Web site: http://www.autism.com/ari

The Autism Society of America
7910 Woodmont Avenue, Suite 300
Bethesda, MD 20814-3015
Phone: 800-3AUTISM, ext. 150 or
301-657-0881
Fax: 301-657-0869
Web site: http://www.autism-society.org

Center for the Study of Autism
P.O. Box 4538
Salem, OR 97302
Phone: 503-538-9045
Web site: http://www.autism.org

COSAC (Center for Outreach and
Services for the Autism Community)
1450 Parkside Avenue, Suite #22
Ewing, NJ 08638
Phone: 609-883-8100
Fax: 609-883-5509
E-mail: NJautism@aol.com
Web site: http://members.aol.com/njautism

The Council for Exceptional Children
1920 Association Drive
Reston, VA 20191-1589
Phone: 888-CEC-SPED or 703-620-3660
TTY phone: 703-264-9446
Fax: 703-264-9494
Web site:
 http://www.cec.sped.org/index.html

The Doug Flutie Jr. Foundation for
 Autism
c/o The Giving Back Fund
54 Canal Street, Suite 320
Boston, MA 02114
Phone: 617-556-2820
Fax: 617-973-9463
E-mail: giveback@ma.ultranet.com
Web site: http://www.dougflutie.org

The HANDLE Institute (Holistic
 Approach to NeuroDevelopment and
 Learning Efficiency)
1530 Eastlake Avenue East, Suite 100
Seattle, WA 98102
Phone: 206-860-2665
Fax: 206-860-3505
E-mail: support@handle.org
Web site: http://www.handle.org

Indiana Resource Center for Autism
Indiana Institute on Disability and
 Community
2853 East Tenth Street
Bloomington, IN 47408-2696
Phone: 812-855-6508
TTY phone: 812-855-9396
Fax: 812-855-9630
E-mail: bowman@indiana.edu
Web site:
 http://www.isdd.indiana.edu/~irca

International Rett's Syndrome Association
9121 Piscataway Road
Clinton, MD 20735
Phone: 800-818-RETT or 301-856-3334
Fax: 301-856-3336
E-mail: irsa@rettsyndrome.org
Web site: http://www.rettsyndrome.org

The National Fragile X Foundation
P.O. Box 190488
San Francisco, CA 94119
Phone: 800-688-8765 or 510-763-6030
Fax: 510-763-6223
Web site: http://www.nfxf.org

National Organization for Rare Disorders,
 Inc. (NORD)
P.O. Box 8923
New Fairfield, CT 06812-8923
Phone: 800-999-6673 or 203-746-6518
Fax: 203-746-6481
E-mail: orphan@rarediseases.org
Web site: http://www.rarediseases.org

STOMP (Specialized Training of Military
 Parents)
6316 South 12th Street
Tacoma, WA 98465-1900
Voice/TTY phone: 800-5-parent or
 253-565-2266 (Military parents can
 call collect from anywhere in the U.S.
 or overseas.)
Fax: 253-566-8052
E-mail: wapave9@washingtonpave.com
Web site: http://washingtonpave.org/
 stomp.html

International

Allergy induced Autism (AiA)
8, Hollie Lucas Road
King's Heath
Birmingham B13 0QL UNITED
   KINGDOM
Phone: 44-0-173-333-1771
Fax: 44-0-121-444-6450
E-mail: aia@kessick.demon.co.uk
Web site: http://www.kessick.demon.
   co.uk/aia.htm

Autisme France
182 avenue des Jasmins
06250 Mougins
FRANCE
Phone: 04-93-46-00-48
Numero azur: 0810-179-179
Fax: 04-93-46-01-14

Autism-Europe
Avenue E. Van Becelaere 26B, Bte 21
B-1170 Brussels, BELGIUM
Phone: 32-0-2-675-75-05
Fax: 32-0-2-675-72-70
E-mail: autisme.europe@arcadis.be
Web site: http://osiris.sunderland.ac. uk/
   autism/eur.html

Autism Society of British Columbia
Suite 200—3550 Kingsway
Vancouver, B.C. V5R 5L7 CANADA
Phone: 888-437-0880 or 604-434-0880
Fax: 604-434-0801
E-mail: autismbc@istar.ca
Web site: http://www.enet.ca/autism

Autism Society of Canada
129 Yorkville Avenue, #202
Toronto, Ontario M5R 1C4 CANADA
Phone: 416-922-0302
Fax: 416-922-1032

Autism Society of Ontario
1 Greensboro Drive, Suite 306
Etobicoke, Ontario M9W 1C8
   CANADA
Phone: 416-246-9592
Fax: 416-246-9417
E-mail: mail@autismsociety.on.ca
Web site: http://home.tct.net/autism/

Gateway Provincial Resource Program
4812 Georgia Street
Delta, B.C. V4K 259 CANADA
Phone: 604-946-3610

The Geneva Centre for Autism
200-250 Davisville Avenue
Toronto, Ontario M4S 1H2 CANADA
Phone: 416-322-7877
Fax: 416-322-5894
E-mail: info@autism.net
Web site: http://www.autism.net

The National Autistic Society
393 City Road
London, EC1V 1NG UNITED
   KINGDOM
Phone: 44-0-20-7833-2299
Fax: 44-0-20-7833-9666
E-mail: nas@nas.org.uk
Web site:
   http://www.oneworld.org/autism_uk

PAPA Resource Centre (Parents and Professionals and Autism)
Graham House
Knockbracken Healthcare Park
Saintfield Road
Belfast BT8 8BH IRELAND
Phone: 44-0-1232-401729
Fax: 44-0-1232-403467

Pro Aid Autisme (AFPPA)
42 rue Benard
75014 Paris FRANCE
Phone/fax: 01-45-41-52-93

Sesame Autisme
53 rue Clisson
75013 Paris, FRANCE
Phone: 01-44-24-50-00
Fax: 01-53-61-25-63

Autism Publications

The Advocate
Published by the Autism Society of America
7910 Woodmont Avenue, Suite 300
Bethesda, MD 20814-3015
Phone: 800-3AUTISM, ext. 150 or 301-657-0881
Fax: 301-657-0869
Web site: http://www.autism-society.org

Autism Autoimmunity Project Newsletter
Published by the Autism Autoimmunity Project
45 Iroquois Avenue
Lake Hiawatha, NJ 07034
Phone: 973-299-9162
Fax: 973-299-2668
E-mail: truegrit@gti.net

Autism Research Review International
Published by the Autism Research Institute
4182 Adams Avenue
San Diego, CA 92116

Phone: 619-281-7165
Fax: 619-563-6840
Web site: http://www.autism.com/ari

Closing the Gap
526 Main Street
P.O. Box 68
Henderson, MN 56044
Phone: 507-248-3294
Fax: 507-248-3810
E-mail: closingthegap.com
Web site: http://www.closingthegap.com/index.html
This newsletter is about hardware and software products for the disabled.

Exceptional Parent
555 Kinderkamack Road
Oradell, NJ 07649-1517
Phone: 201-634-6550
Fax: 201-634-6599
E-mail: vieprnt@concentric.net
Web site: http://www.eparent.com
Included in the yearly subscription is an annually updated resource guide.

FEAT Daily Online Newsletter
To subscribe (no cost):
  http://www.feat.org/FEATNews
This on-line newsletter will send only
  two e-mail messages per day concerning features and breaking news in the
  world of autism.

Journal of Autism and Developmental
  Disorders
Published by Plenum Publishing Co.
233 Spring Street
New York, NY 10013-1578
Phone: 212-620-8000
Fax: 212-463-0742
E-mail: info@plenum.com
Web site: http://www.plenum.com

The MAAP
Published by MAAP (More Advanced
  Individuals with Autism, Asperger's

Syndrome, and Pervasive
  Developmental Disorder)
MAAP Services, Inc.
P.O. Box 524
Crown Point, IN 46307
Phone: 219-662-1311
Fax: 219-662-0638
E-mail: chart@netnitco.net
Web site: http://www.netnitco.net/
  users/chart/maap.html

NAARRATIVE
Published by the National Alliance for
  Autism Research (NAAR)
414 Wall Street
Research Park
Princeton, NJ 08540
Phone: 888-777-NAAR or 609-430-9160
Fax: 609-430-9163
E-mail: naar@naar.org
Web site: http://www.naar.org

Research

Autism Genetic Resource Exchange
  (AGRE)
5225 Wilshire Boulevard
Los Angeles, CA 90036
Phone: 888-AUTISM2
Fax: 831-684-0240
E-mail: familyagre@aol.com
Web site: http://www.hbdi.org/
  autismresearch2htm.htm

Autism Research Foundation
P.O. Box 1571 GMF
Boston, MA 02205
Phone: 617-414-5286
Fax: 617-414-7207

E-mail: tarf@ladders.org
Web site: http://ladders.org/tarf/

Autism Research Unit
School of Health Sciences
University of Sunderland
Sunderland SR2 7EE
UNITED KINGDOM
Phone/fax: 44-0-191-510-8922
E-mail: aru@sunderland.ac.uk
Web site: http://osiris.sunderland.ac.uk/
  autism/index.html

The Cure Autism Now Foundation
(CAN)
5225 Wilshire Boulevard, Suite 226
Los Angeles, CA 90036
Phone: 888-8AUTISM or 323-549-0500
Fax: 323-549-0547
E-mail: CAN@primenet.com
Web site: http://www.canfoundation.org

Medical Investigation of
Neurodevelopmental Disorders
(M.I.N.D.)
UC Davis Medical Center
4860 Y Street, Room 3020
Sacramento, CA 95817
Phone: 888-883-0961 or 916-734-5153
E-mail:
andrea.verdon@ucdmc.ucdavis.edu
Web site: http://mindinstitute.ucdmc.
ucdavis.edu

Mount Sinai School of Medicine
Seaver Autism Research Center
Department of Psychiatry, Box 1230
1 Gustave L. Levy Place
New York, NY 10029
Phone: 212-241-2994
Fax: 212-987-4031
E-mail:
E_Hollander@smtplink.mssm.edu
Web site: http://www.mssm.edu/
psychiatry/seaver.html

National Alliance for Autism Research
(NAAR)
414 Wall Street
Research Park
Princeton, NJ 08540
Phone: 888-777-NAAR or
609-430-9160
Fax: 609-430-9163
E-mail: naar@naar.org
Web site: http://www.naar.org

National Institute of Child Health and
Human Development
P.O. Box 3006
Rockville, MD 20847
Phone: 800-370-2943
Fax: 301-984-1473
E-mail: NICHDClearinghouse@
iqsolutions.com
Web site: http://www.nichd.nih.gov/

Southwest Autism Research Center
1002 East McDowell Road, Suite A
Phoenix, AZ 85006
Phone: 602-340-8717
Fax: 602-340-8720
E-mail: schneider@autismcenter.org or
SARC@autismcenter.org
Web site: http://www.autismcenter.org

Support Groups

Autism Network International
P.O. Box 448
Syracuse, New York 13210-0448
E-mail: jisincla@mailbox.syr.edu (Jim
Sinclair, ANI Coordinator)
Web site: http://www.students.uiuc.edu/
~bordner/ani/
This organization is designed for and
operated by individuals with autism.

The Autism Society of America
7910 Woodmont Avenue, Suite 300
Bethesda, MD 20814-3015
Phone: 800-3AUTISM, ext. 150 or
301-657-0881
Fax: 301-657-0869
Web site: http://www.autism-society.org

Families Working Together
12400 Cypress Avenue, Space 20
Chino, CA 91710
Phone: 909-627-4514
Fax: 909-627-6486
E-mail: javajive38@aol.com
Web site: http://www.ucddfam.com
This Christian Web site includes listings
of chapters of F.E.A.T. and the
Autism Society of America and
autism seminars around the country.

*F.E.A.T (Families for Early Autism
Treatment)*
P.O. Box 255722
Sacramento, CA 95865-5722
Voice mail: 916-843-1536
Web site: http://www.feat.org
They will be able to direct you to the
F.E.A.T. chapter nearest you.

NOTES

Chapter 2: Seeking Answers
1. Jeremiah 32:27

Chapter 3: Operation Rescue Ryan
1. Charles P. Hart, *A Parent's Guide to Autism* (New York: Pocket Books, 1993), 86-7, 194-5.

Chapter 4: Understand What You're Facing
1. American Psychiatric Association, *Diagnostic and Statistical Manual of Mental Disorders,* 4th ed. (Washington, D.C.: American Psychiatric Association, 1994), 66.
2. American Psychiatric Association, *Diagnostic and Statistical Manual of Mental Disorders,* 70-1.
3. Simon Baron-Cohen et al., "Psychological Markers in the Detection of Autism in Infancy in a Large Population," *British Journal of Psychiatry* 168 (1996): 159.
4. Simon Baron-Cohen, Jane Allen, and Christopher Gillberg, "Can Autism Be Detected at 18 Months? The Needle, the Haystack, and the CHAT," *British Journal of Psychiatry* 161 (1992): 842.
5. Michael D. Powers, ed., *Children with Autism: A Parent's Guide* (Bethesda, Md.: Woodbine House, Inc., 1989), 10.
6. Loretta Green, "Autism Epidemic," *San Jose Mercury News,* 24 May 1999. Located at http://www.mercurycenter.com/premium/local/docs/green23.htm.
7. Bernard Rimland, "Huge Increase in Autism Incidence Reported in California; Autism Cluster Investigated in Brick, New Jersey," *Autism Research Review International* 13, no. 1 (1999): 1.
8. California Health and Human Services Agency, "Changes in the Population of Persons with Autism and Pervasive Developmental Disorders in California's Developmental Services System: 1987 through 1998" (a report to the California state legislature, 1 March 1999), 8, 10. From the Web site maintained by the Autism Research Institute: http://www.autism.com/ari/dds/dds.html.

9. Bernard Rimland, "Is There an Autism Epidemic?" *Autism Research Review International* 9, no. 3 (1995): 3.

10. American Psychiatric Association, *Diagnostic and Statistical Manual of Mental Disorders,* 72-3.

11. American Psychiatric Association, *Diagnostic and Statistical Manual of Mental Disorders,* 74-5.

12. American Psychiatric Association, *Diagnostic and Statistical Manual of Mental Disorders,* 77.

13. American Psychiatric Association, *Diagnostic and Statistical Manual of Mental Disorders,* 77-8.

14. Shirley Cohen, *Targeting Autism* (Berkeley: University of California Press, 1998), 15.

15. Bernard Rimland, "More 'Autistic' Children Now Diagnosed with Treatable Landau-Kleffner Syndrome," *Autism Research Review International* 9, no. 2 (1995): 1.

16. Rimland, "More 'Autistic' Children Now Diagnosed," 2.

17. Colwyn Trevarthen et al., *Children with Autism* (London: Jessica Kingsley Publishers, 1996), 63.

18. Betty B. Schopmeyer and Fonda Lowe, *The Fragile X Child* (San Diego: Singular Publishing Group, 1992), 34.

19. Temple Grandin, *Thinking in Pictures and Other Reports from My Life with Autism* (New York: Vintage Books, 1996), 60.

20. Donna Williams, *Somebody Somewhere* (New York: Times Books, 1994), 238.

Chapter 5: Ten Things to Do First

1. Autism Research Institute Web site, http://www.autism.com/ari/dan.html, 9 December 1998.

2. Autism Research Institute Web site, http://www.autism.com/ari/dan.html, 9 December 1998.

3. Bernard Rimland, "Vaccinations: The Overlooked Factors," *Autism Research Review International* 12, no. 1 (1998): 3.

Chapter 6: Applied Behavior Analysis

1. O. Ivar Lovaas, *Teaching Developmentally Disabled Children: The ME Book* (Austin, Tex.: PRO-ED, 1981), x.

2. Gary Beck and Victoria Beck with Bernard Rimland and the Autism Research Institute, *Unlocking the Potential of Secretin* (San Diego: Autism Research Institute, 1998), 6.

3. O. Ivar Lovaas, "Behavioral Treatment and Normal Educational and Intellectual Functioning in Young Autistic Children," *Journal of Consulting and Clinical Psychology* 55 (1987): 3-9.

4. B. F. Skinner, *The Behavior of Organisms* (New York: Appleton-Century-Crofts, Inc., 1938).

5. O. Ivar Lovaas, *Behavioral Treatment of Autistic Children,* Huntington, N.Y., Focus International, 1988, videocassette.

6. Catherine Maurice, *Behavioral Intervention for Young Children with Autism: A Manual for Parents and Professionals* (Austin, Tex.: PRO-ED, 1996), 66-9.

7. O. Ivar Lovaas, foreword to *Autism: From Tragedy to Triumph,* by Carol Johnson and Julia Crowder (Boston: Brandon Books, 1994).

8. O. Ivar Lovaas, "Interview with Ivar Lovaas," interview by Catherine Johnson, on the Autism Society of America Web site: http://www.autism-society.org/packages/dtt_lovaas.html, 8.

9. Lovaas, "Behavioral Treatment and Normal Educational and Intellectual Functioning in Young Autistic Children," 8.

10. Lovaas, "Behavioral Treatment and Normal Educational and Intellectual Functioning in Young Autistic Children," 3,6-7.

11. Maurice, *Behavioral Intervention for Young Children with Autism,* 7.

12. Lovaas, "Behavioral Treatment and Normal Educational and Intellectual Functioning in Young Autistic Children," 3-9.

13. J. J. McEachin, T. Smith, and O. I. Lovaas, "Long-Term Outcome for Children with Autism Who Received Early Intensive Behavioral Treatment," *American Journal on Mental Retardation* 4 (1993): 359-372.

14. McEachin, Smith, Lovaas, "Long-Term Outcome for Children with Autism," 360.

15. R. Perry, I. Cohen, and R. DeCarlo, "Case Study: Deterioration, Autism, and Recovery in Two Siblings," *Journal of the American Academy of Child and Adolescent Psychiatry* 34 (1995): 236.

16. Maurice, *Behavioral Intervention for Young Children with Autism,* 10.

17. *Collier's Standard Dictionary,* international edition, s.v. "cure."

18. Catherine Maurice, *Let Me Hear Your Voice* (New York: Fawcett Columbine, 1993), back cover.

19. Lovaas, "Behavioral Treatment and Normal Educational and Intellectual Functioning in Young Autistic Children," 3.

20. Lovaas, *Behavioral Treatment of Autistic Children.*

21. Wisconsin Early Autism Project, *Employee Orientation Manual and Policy Handbook,* 17.

22. Charles A. Hart, *A Parent's Guide to Autism* (New York: Pocket Books, 1993), 86-7.
23. Hart, *A Parent's Guide to Autism,* 87.
24. Hart, *A Parent's Guide to Autism,* 88.
25. Shirley Cohen, *Targeting Autism* (Berkeley: University of California Press, 1998), 179.
26. Sabrina Freeman and Lorelei Dake, *Teach Me Language: A Language Manual for Children with Autism, Asperger's Syndrome and Related Developmental Disorders* (Langley, B.C., Canada: SKF Books, 1996).

Chapter 7: Dietary Intervention

1. David Le Vay, *Human Anatomy and Physiology* (Chicago: NTC Publishing Group, 1993), 232.
2. William Shaw, *Biological Treatments for Autism and PDD* (Overland Park, Kans.: self-published, 1998), 18.
3. P. D'Eufemia et al., "Abnormal Intestinal Permeability in Children with Autism," *Acta Paediatrica* 85 (1996): 1076.
4. Paul Shattock et al., "Role of Neuropeptides in Autism and Their Relationships with Classical Neurotransmitters," *Brain Dysfunction* 3 (1990): 328.
5. Shaw, *Biological Treatments for Autism and PDD,* 126.
6. Shaw, *Biological Treatments for Autism and PDD,* 127.
7. E. D. London et al., "Morphine-Induced Metabolic Changes in the Human Brain: Studies with Positron Emission Tomography and [Fluorine 18] Fluorodeoxyglucose," *Archives of General Psychiatry* 47 (1990): 73-81.
8. M. S. George et al., "Cerebral Blood Flow Abnormalities in Adults with Infantile Autism," *Journal of Nervous and Mental Disorders* 180 (1992): 413-7. J. M. Mountz, "Functional Deficits in Autistic Disorder: Characterization by Technetium-99mHMPAO and SPECT," *Journal of Nuclear Medicine* 36 (1995): 1156-62.
9. Lisa Lewis, *Special Diets for Special Kids* (Arlington, Tex.: Future Horizons, Inc., 1988), 38.
10. Stephen M. Edelson, "Allergies and Food Sensitivities" (Salem, Ore.: Center for the Study of Autism). Taken from the Web site at http://www.autism.org/allergy.html.
11. James Braly, M.D., *The Role of Food Allergy, the Brain and Hormones in Children's Illness,* audiotape of lecture presented at the DAN! Conference, Cherry Hill, N.J., October 1998.

12. Shaw, *Biological Treatments for Autism and PDD*, 125, and Lewis, *Special Diets for Special Kids,* 22.
13. Shaw, *Biological Treatments for Autism and PDD,* 18.
14. Edelson, "Allergies and Food Sensitivities," 2.
15. Bruce Semon, M.D., "Treating Yeast in Children with Autism: Typical Results of Anti-Yeast Therapy," in Shaw, *Biological Treatments for Autism and PDD,* 166.
16. Lewis, *Special Diets for Special Kids,* 26-7.
17. Lewis, *Special Diets for Special Kids,* 27.
18. Lisa S. Lewis, "Dietary Intervention for the Treatment of Autism: Why Implement a Gluten- and Casein-Free Diet?" in Shaw, *Biological Treatments for Autism and PDD,* 221.
19. Lewis, *Special Diets for Special Kids,* 13.
20. Sidney M. Baker, "Food Allergies and Autism Spectrum Problems in Children," *Autism Research Review International* 10, no. 4 (1996): 3.
21. Baker, "Food Allergies and Autism Spectrum Problems," 10.
22. Baker, "Food Allergies and Autism Spectrum Problems," 12.
23. Lewis, *Special Diets for Special Kids,* 43.
24. Lewis, *Special Diets for Special Kids,* 21.
25. Lewis, *Special Diets for Special Kids,* 18.
26. John M. Freeman, M.D., "Statement of the Child Neurology Society Regarding the Ketogenic Diet" (Child Neurology Society). Published on the Internet (2/18/97) at http://www.umn.edu/cns/ketodiet.htm.
27. Semon, "Treating Yeast in Children with Autism," in Shaw, *Biological Treatments for Autism and PDD,* 163-7.
28. Bruce Semon, M.D., personal communication, July 1999.
29. Shaw, *Biological Treatments for Autism and PDD,* 135.
30. Semon, "Treating Yeast in Children with Autism," in Shaw, *Biological Treatments for Autism and PDD,* 173.
31. Karl L. Reichelt, M.D., *Autism and ADD: Physiological Opposites and Overlapping Similarities,* audiotape of a lecture presented at the DAN! Conference, Cherry Hill, N.J., October 1998.
32. Shaw, *Biological Treatments for Autism and PDD,* 115.
33. Shaw, *Biological Treatments for Autism and PDD,* 116.
34. Mastering Food Allergies EPD Page (1998). Taken from the Web site at http://www.nidlink.com/~mastent/epdpage.html.
35. ANDI Web site at http://www.autismndi.com.

Chapter 8: Biomedical Intervention

1. Analogy based on the "Tacks Rules" by Sidney M. Baker, M.D., *Detoxification and Healing: The Key to Optimal Health* (New Canaan, Conn.: Keats Publishing, Inc., 1997), 1.

2. Bernard Rimland, flier for DAN! Conference, Cherry Hill, N.J., October 1998.

3. William Shaw, *Biological Treatments for Autism and PDD* (Overland Park, Kans.: self-published, 1998), 131.

4. Gary Beck and Victoria Beck, in cooperation with Bernard Rimland and the Autism Research Institute, *Unlocking the Potential of Secretin* (San Diego: Autism Research Institute, 1998), 5.

5. Beck and Beck, *Unlocking the Potential of Secretin,* 5-6.

6. Karoly Horvath, M.D., et al., "Improved Social and Language Skills After Secretin Administration in Patients with Autistic Spectrum Disorders," *Journal of the Association for Academic Minority Physicians* 9, no. 1 (January 1998): 9.

7. Autism Research Institute Web site: http://www.autism.com/ari/secretin2.html. Message dated 1 December 1998.

8. Sidney M. Baker, M.D., Secretin Information—updated 11-15-98. Weston, Conn. Web site: http://www.sbakermd.com/info/autism/Secretin.htm.

9. Paul M. Hardy, M.D., *Emerging Practices: The Use of Secretin As a Treatment for Autism,* audiotape of a lecture by Bernard Rimland, Walter Herlihy, Marie M. Bristol-Power, and Paul M. Hardy presented at the Autism Society of America Conference, Kansas City, Mo., July 1999 (Reno: Bill Stephens Productions, Inc., 1999).

10. Bernard Rimland, Ph.D., "Secretin Update: March 1999," *Autism Research Review International* 13, no. 1 (1999): 3.

11. Karl Reichelt, communication via e-mail, 4 January 1999.

12. Baker, Web site: http://www.sbakermd.com/info/autism/Secretin.htm, 6.

13. Bernard Rimland, "The Autism-Secretin Connection," *Autism Research Review International* 12, no. 3 (1998): 3.

14. Horvath, "Improved Social and Language Skills," 14.

15. Baker, Web site: http://www.sbakermd.com/info/autism/Secretin.htm, 3.

16. Beck and Beck, *Unlocking the Potential of Secretin,* 20.

17. Horvath, "Improved Social and Language Skills," 10.

18. Hardy, *Emerging Practices.*

19. Baker, Web site: http://www.sbakermd.com/info/autism/ Secretin.htm, 13.
20. Bernard Rimland, "The Use of Secretin in Autism: Some Preliminary Answers," *Autism Research Review International* 12, no. 4 (1998): 3.
21. Baker, Web site: http://www.sbakermd.com/info/autism/ Secretin.htm, 12.
22. Stephen M. Edelson, *The Candida Yeast-Autism Connection* (Salem, Ore.: Center for the Study of Autism). Taken from the Web site at http://www.autism.org/candida.html, 1.
23. William Shaw, "Yeast, and AD(H)D, Learning Disabilities, PDD, and Autism," *New Developments* 3, no. 4 (spring 1998): 1.
24. Shaw, *Biological Treatments for Autism and PDD,* 295.
25. Edelson, *The Candida Yeast-Autism Connection,* 1.
26. Bernard Rimland, "Our Children: Victims of Both Autism and Dogma," *Autism Research Review International* 11, no. 3 (1997): 3.
27. Shaw, "Yeast, and AD(H)D, Learning Disabilities, PDD, and Autism," 1.
28. Bruce Semon, M.D., personal communication, July 1999.
29. Semon, personal communication, July 1999.
30. Bruce Semon, "Treating Yeast in Children with Autism: Typical Results of Anti-Yeast Therapy," in Shaw, *Biological Treatments for Autism and PDD,* 168.
31. Shaw, *Biological Treatments for Autism and PDD,* 73.
32. Shaw, *Biological Treatments for Autism and PDD,* 75.
33. Semon, personal communication, July 1999.
34. Semon, personal communication, July 1999.
35. Semon, "Treating Yeast in Children with Autism," in Shaw, *Biological Treatments for Autism and PDD,* 170.
36. Semon, "Treating Yeast in Children with Autism," in Shaw, *Biological Treatments for Autism and PDD,* 89, and Shaw, *Biological Treatments for Autism and PDD,* 170-1.
37. Semon, personal communication, July 1999.
38. Bernard Rimland, "Vitamin B_6 (and Magnesium) in the Treatment of Autism," *Autism Research Review International* 1, no. 4 (1987): 3.
39. Bernard Rimland, "The Second Great Autism Watershed," *Autism Research Review International* 8, no. 1 (1994): 3.
40. Bernard Rimland and Sidney M. Baker, "Brief Report: Alternative Approaches to the Development of Effective Treatments for Autism," *Journal of Autism and Developmental Disorders* 26, no. 2 (1996): 238.

41. Rimland and Baker, "Brief Report: Alternative Approaches," 238.
42. Rimland, "Vitamin B$_6$ (and Magnesium) in the Treatment of Autism," 3.
43. Rimland, "Vitamin B$_6$ (and Magnesium) in the Treatment of Autism," 3.
44. Bernard Rimland, "Form Letter Regarding High Dosage Vitamin B$_6$ and Magnesium Therapy for Autism and Related Disorders," Autism Research Institute (1993, revised April 1996), 2.
45. Bernard Rimland, "Dimethylglycine (DMG), a Nontoxic Metabolite, and Autism," *Autism Research Review International* 4, no. 2 (1990): 3.
46. Bernard Rimland, "DMG and Obsessive-Compulsive Behaviors," *Autism Research Review International* 10, no. 3 (1996): 7.
47. Rimland, "Dimethylglycine (DMG), a Nontoxic Metabolite, and Autism," 3.
48. Bernard Rimland, "Dimethylglycine (DMG) for Autism," Autism Research Institute publication 110 (revised August 1996).
49. Bernard Rimland, *What Is the Right 'Dosage' for Vitamin B$_6$, DMG, and Other Nutrients Useful in Autism?* (1998), taken from the Web site maintained by the Autism Research Institute: http://www.autism.com/ari/editorials/dosage.html.
50. Rimland, *What Is the Right 'Dosage' for Vitamin B$_6$?*
51. Sidney M. Baker, M.D., personal communication, August 1999.
52. James F. Balch, M.D., and Phyllis A. Balch, *Prescription for Nutritional Healing*, 2nd ed. (Garden City Park, N.Y.: Avery Publishing Group, 1997), 17.
53. Mary N. Megson, M.D., F.A.A.P., *The Biological Basis for Perceptual Deficits in Autism: Vitamin A and G Proteins*, audiotape of a lecture presented at the DAN! Conference in Cherry Hill, N.J., October 1999.
54. Megson, *The Biological Basis*.
55. Mary N. Megson, M.D., F.A.A.P., "Form Letter from the Pediatric and Adolescent Ability Center," September 1999.
56. Donald R. Davis, Ph.D., "Using Vitamin A Safely," *Osteopathic Medicine* 3, no. 10 (October 1978): 40.
57. Lowell Ackerman, *Nutritional Intervention in Autism*, taken from the Web site sponsored by the Center for Autism Research and Education (C.A.R.E.), under the auspices of PHI, Inc. © 1997, PHI, Inc. Web site: http://www.autism-zone.com/autism/nutri.htm.
58. Bernard Rimland, *Vitamin C in the Prevention and Treatment of*

Autism, taken from the Autism Research International Web site: http://www.autism.com/ari/editorials/vitaminc.html.

59. James Braly, M.D., *Dr. Braly's Food Allergy and Nutrition Revolution* (New Canaan, Conn.: Keats Publishing, Inc., 1992), 139.

60. Lisa Lewis, *Special Diets for Special Kids* (Arlington, Tex.: Future Horizons, Inc., 1998), 62.

61. Balch and Balch, *Prescription for Nutritional Healing,* 58.

62. Bernard Rimland, *Parental Ratings of Behavioral Effects of Drugs and Nutrients,* Autism Research Institute publication 34 (July 1999).

63. Temple Grandin, *Thinking in Pictures and Other Reports from My Life with Autism* (New York: Vintage Books, 1996), 115.

64. Donna Shalala, *Health and Human Services News,* taken from the Web site of the U.S. Department of Health and Human Services at http://www.cdc.gov/nip/news/shalala.htm (Centers for Disease Control and Prevention, 1998). Press office phone: 404-639-3286.

65. Shalala, *Health and Human Services News.*

66. Bernard Rimland, "Vaccinations: The Overlooked Factors," *Autism Research Review International* 12, no. 1 (1998): 3.

67. Health Resources and Services Administration—HHS, National Vaccine Injury Compensation Program, *Vaccine Injury Table,* effective 24 March 1997. HRSA Web site: http://www.hrsa.dhhs.gov/bhpr/vicp/table.htm.

68. Bernard Rimland, "Editor's Notebook: The Autism Explosion," *Autism Research Review International* 13, no. 2 (1999): 3.

69. Bernard Rimland, "Children's Shots: No Longer a Simple Decision," *Autism Research Review International* 9, no. 1 (1995): 1.

70. Harold Buttram, M.D., "Daniel's Story: A Doctor's Concerns About Vaccination," *Autism Research Review Inernational* 10, no. 1 (1996): 3.

71. Rimland, "Vaccinations: The Overlooked Factors," 3.

72. A. Ekborn et al., "Perinatal Measles Infection and Subsequent Crohn's Disease," *The Lancet* 344 (1994): 508-10; and Hiroyuki Miyamoto et al., "Detection of Immunoreactive Antigen, with a Monoclonal Antibody to Measles Virus, in Tissue from a Patient with Crohn's Disease," *Journal of Gastroenterology* 30 (1995): 28-33; and N. P. Thompson et al., "Is Measles Vaccination a Risk Factor for Inflammatory Bowel Disease?" *The Lancet* 345 (April 1995): 1071-4.

73. A. J. Wakefield et al., "Ileal-Lymphoid-Nodular Hyperplasia, Non-Specific Colitis, and Pervasive Developmental Disorder in Children," *The Lancet* 351 (February 1998): 637-41.

74. Wakefield et al., "Ileal-Lymphoid-Nodular Hyperplasia," 637.
75. Wakefield et al., "Ileal-Lymphoid-Nodular Hyperplasia," 640.
76. Bernard Rimland, "Lancet Study Links Autistic Symptoms, MMR Vaccine," *Autism Research Review International* 12, no. 1 (1998): 1.
77. Laura J. Ruede, "New Study Shows Autism May Be Linked to Measles Vaccination," *Autism Autoimmunity Project Newsletter* 1, no. 1 (June 1999): 1.
78. Vijendra K. Singh, Sheren X. Lin, and Victor C. Yang, "Serological Association of Measles Virus and Human Herpesvirus-6 with Brain Autoantibodies in Autism," *Clinical Immunology and Immunopathology* 89, no. 1 (October 1998): 108.
79. Singh, Lin, and Yang, "Serological Association of Measles Virus," 107.
80. Rimland, "Lancet Study Links Autistic Symptoms, MMR Vaccine," 1.
81. Web site for the National Vaccine Information Center: http://www.909shot.com/question.htm.
82. Bernard Rimland, Ph.D., personal communication, October 1999.
83. William J. Hennen, *The Transfer Factor Report*, taken from the Web site: http://www.probiotics.net/studies.html (Woodland Publishing, 1998).
84. *Colostrum Gold*, taken from the Web site: http://www.kirkmanlabs.com, Kirkman Laboratories, 8, 10.
85. *Colostrum Gold*, taken from http://www.kirkmanlabs.com, 8, 10.
86. E. Gene Stubbs and Sarajini S. Budden, Denis R. Burger and Arthur A. Vanderbark, "Transfer Factor Immunotherapy of an Autistic Child with Congenital Cytomegalovirus," *Journal of Autism and Developmental Disorders* 10, no. 4 (1980): 451-8.
87. H. H. Fudenberg, "Dialysable Lymphocyte Extract (DLyE) in Infantile Autism: A Pilot Study," *Biotherapy* 9 (1996): 143.
88. Gay Langham-McNally, personal communication, September 1999.
89. Mike McDonald, ed., "The Goldenberg Family: After IGIV, the Autistic Behavior Began to Diminish," *Belonging* (summer 1995): 6.
90. Stephen B. Edelson, *Autism*, taken from the Web site: http://www.ephca.com/autism.htm, Edelson Center (1998), 17.
91. Sudhir Gupta, Sudeepta Aggarwal, and Cathy Heads, "Brief Report: Dysregulated Immune System in Children with Autism: Beneficial Effects of Intravenous Immune Globulin on Autistic Characteristics," *Journal of Autism and Developmental Disorders* 26, no. 4 (1996): 448.

92. Sujatha Ramesh, M.D., and Stanley A. Schwartz, M.D., "Therapeutic Use of Intravenous Immunoglobulin (IVIG) in Children," *Pediatrics in Review* 16, no. 11 (November 1995): 403.

93. Bernard Rimland, "IVIG Therapy Tested in Autism, Landau-Kleffner Syndrome," *Autism Research Review International* 12, no. 2 (1998): 1.

94. S. M. Baker, M.D., and Jon Pangborn, *Biomedical Assessment Options for Children with Autism and Related Problems* (San Diego: Autism Research Institute, 1997), 21-2.

95. Rosemary Waring, *The Sulfation Connection,* audiotape of a lecture by Rosemary Waring presented at the AiA (Allergy Induced Autism) Conference, Solihull, England, March 1999 (AiA, March 1999).

96. Baker and Pangborn, *Biomedical Assessment Options,* 22.

97. Baker and Pangborn, *Biomedical Assessment Options,* 22.

98. Waring, *The Sulfation Connection.*

99. Waring, *The Sulfation Connection.*

100. Baker and Pangborn, *Biomedical Assessment Options,* 23.

Chapter 9: The Parent-Doctor Balance

1. Victoria Beck, *Secretin—Discovering Its Potential in Treating Autism and Other Disorders,* audiotape of Victoria Beck and the secretin panel presented at the DAN! Conference, Cherry Hill, N.J., October 1998 (Coeur d'Alene, Idaho: INSTA-TAPES, 1998).

2. Jim Stovall, *You Don't Have to Be Blind to See* (Nashville: Nelson, 1996), 268.

3. *Autism Research Review International,* 1.

4. Dr. Andrew Wakefield, *Intestinal Pathology in Children with Autism: Clues to Environmental Causes,* audiotape of a lecture presented by Dr. Andrew Wakefield at the DAN! Conference, Cherry Hill, N.J., October 1998 (Coeur d'Alene, Idaho: INSTA-TAPES, 1998).

Chapter 10: Sensory Issues

1. Temple Grandin, *Thinking in Pictures and Other Reports from My Life with Autism* (New York: Vintage Books, 1996), 67.

2. Anne G. Fisher, Elizabeth A. Murray, and Anita C. Bundy, *Sensory Integration Theory and Practice* (Philadelphia: F. A. Davis Company, 1991), 3-4.

3. Bernard Rimland, "Sound Sensitivity in Autism," *Autism Research Review International* 4, no. 4 (1990).

4. Mary Sue Williams and Sherry Shellenberger, "An Introduction to 'How Does Your Engine Run?' The Alert Program for Self-Regulation" (Albuquerque: TherapyWorks, Inc., 1996).

5. Patricia Wilbarger and Julia Wilbarger, "Sensory Defensiveness in Children: An Intervention Guide for Parents and Other Caregivers" (Hugo, Minn.: PDP Products, 1990).

6. Bernard Rimland and Stephen M. Edelson, "Auditory Integration Training in Autism: A Pilot Study," Autism Research Institute publication 112 (June 1992): 1, 6.

7. Information provided by the Scientific Learning Corporation Web site: http://www.ScientificLearning.com.

8. Sally Brockett, Earobics Auditory Development and Phonics Program on the Web site: http://www.teleport.com/~sait/earobics.html maintained by the Society for Auditory Intervention Techniques, 1.

9. Helen Irlen, "The World of Misperception," Latitudes 2, no. 5 (1997). Produced by the Association for Comprehensive NeuroTherapy and reprinted on the Web site: http://www.latitudes.org/learn02.html, 2-3.

10. Irlen, "The World of Misperception," 3.

11. Jacquelin P. Gorman, The Seeing Glass (New York: Putnam, Inc., 1997), condensed in Reader's Digest, July 1997, 209-10.

12. Melvin Kaplan, "Ambient Lens for Autism and Other Types of PPD," Latitudes 2, no. 6 (1997): 2. Reprinted from the Association for Comprehensive NeuroTherapy at http://www.latitudes.org/amb_lens.html.

13. Audrey Bayer and Stephanie Brenner, "Seeing Is Not Always Believing," The Facilitator 2, no. 2 (fall 1992): 2. A newsletter produced by the Autism Directory Service.

14. Bayer and Brenner, "Seeing Is Not Always Believing," 1-2.

Chapter 11: Education and Communication Needs

1. Stanley I. Greenspan, M.D., and Serena Wieder, "An Integrated Developmental Approach to Interventions for Young Children with Severe Difficulties in Relating and Communicating," Zero to Three 17, no. 5 (April/May 1997): 5.

2. Stanley Greenspan, M.D., and Serena Wieder with Robin Simons, The Child with Special Needs: Encouraging Intellectual and Emotional Growth (Reading, Mass.: Addison-Wesley, 1998), 70-90.

3. Stanley I. Greenspan, M.D., "A Developmental Approach to Problems in Relating and Communicating in Autistic Spectrum

Disorders and Related Syndromes," *Spotlight on Topics in Developmental Disabilities* 1, no. 4 (summer/fall 1998): 5.

4. Greenspan, Wieder, and Simons, *The Child with Special Needs,* 121-2.
5. Greenspan, Wieder, and Simons, *The Child with Special Needs,* 122.
6. Greenspan, Wieder, and Simons, *The Child with Special Needs,* 125.
7. Shirley Cohen, *Targeting Autism: What We Know, Don't Know, and Can Do to Help Young Children with Autism and Related Disorders* (Berkeley: University of California Press, 1998), 104.
8. Gary Mesibov, "The TEACCH Approach to Working with People with Autism and Their Families," *Spotlight on Topics in Developmental Disabilities* 1, no. 4 (summer/fall 1998): 7.
9. Cohen, *Targeting Autism,* 104.
10. Mesibov, "The TEACCH Approach," 9-10.
11. Cohen, *Targeting Autism,* 105.
12. Barry Neil Kaufman and Samahria Lyte Kaufman, "The Son-Rise Program at the Option Institute," *Spotlight on Topics in Developmental Disabilities* 1, no. 3 (winter 1998): 7.
13. Son-Rise Web site: http://www.option.org/sonrise/heart.html, 5.
14. Kaufman and Kaufman, "The Son-Rise Program," 7.
15. Cohen, *Targeting Autism,* 169.
16. Gail Gillingham, *Autism: Handle with Care! Understanding and Managing Behavior of Children and Adults with Autism* (Arlington, Tex.: Future Horizons, 1995), 123.
17. Temple Grandin, *Thinking in Pictures and Other Reports from My Life with Autism* (New York: Vintage Books, 1996), 57.
18. John W. Jacobson, James A. Mulick, and Allen A. Schwartz, "A History of Facilitated Communication: Science, Pseudoscience, and Antiscience, Science Working Group on Facilitated Communication," *American Psychologist* 50, no. 9 (1995): 750-65. Article reprinted at http://www.apa.org/journals/jacobson.html, 1.
19. All four statements can be found at the Autism Society of America's Web site: http://www.autism-society.org/packages/ facilitated_ communication.html#statements.
20. Policy of the American Academy of Child and Adolescent Psychiatry, approved on 20 October 1993, and found at the Autism Society of America's Web site: http://www.autism-society.org/packages/ facilitated_communication.html#statements.

21. Bernard Rimland, text found at the Autism Society of America's Web site: http://www.autism-society.org/packages/facilitated_communication.html#statements.

Chapter 12: Family Matters

1. Donald J. Meyer, *Uncommon Fathers: Reflections on Raising a Child with a Disability* (Bethesda, Md.: Woodbine House, Inc., 1995), 2.
2. Gary Smalley with John Trent, *Love Is a Decision* (Dallas: Word Publishing, 1989), 113.
3. Sandra L. Harris, *Siblings of Children with Autism* (Bethesda, Md.: Woodbine House, Inc., 1994), 61.
4. B. Binkard, M. Goldberg, and P. F. Goldberg, eds., *Brothers and Sisters Talk with PACER* (Minneapolis: PACER Center, Inc., 1987), 17, quoted by Donald Meyer on the Sibling Support Project Web page at http://www.chmc.org/DEPARTMT/SIBSUPP/.
5. M. Westra, "An Open Letter to My Parents," *Sibling Information Network Newsletter* 8, no. 1 (n.d.): 4, quoted by Donald Meyer, on the Sibling Support Project Web site at http://www.chmc.org/DEPARTMT/SIBSUPP/.
6. Harris, *Siblings of Children with Autism,* 31-2.
7. Harris, *Siblings of Children with Autism,* 3.
8. Brian Van Zante, personal communication, July 1999.
9. H. Rutherford Turnbull III et al., *Disability and the Family* (Baltimore: Paul H. Brooks Publishing, 1989), 122. (See p. 123 for a sample Letter of Intent.)
10. Adapted from *National Information Center for Children and Youth with Disabilities News Digest* 2, no. 1 (1992) and *Special Child Magazine,* Online (www.specialchild.com/pourri.html).

Chapter 15: Maintaining Hope

1. Romans 15:13

INDEX

PERSONAL NOTES

PERSONAL NOTES

Autism Research Institute

4182 Adams Avenue
San Diego, California 92116
Fax: 619-563-6840
www.autism.com/ari
Bernard Rimland, Ph.D., Director

Information Request Form / Order Form

The Autism Research Institute conducts and facilitates research on the causes, prevention, and treatment of autism and similar severely handicapping conditions. The Institute is supported by donations from organizations and concerned people. Donations are needed and are tax deductible. Federal Exempt Designation: 501(C) (3)

If you would like to request information or order publications, please return the form below to our above address or fax number.

Please send me free of charge:

_____ Diagnostic E-2 Checklist

_____ Vitamin B$_6$/Magnesium information

_____ Dimethylglycine (DMG) information

_____ Sample copy of the *Autism Research Review International*

_____ **Parent/professional packet** (includes all of the above as well as several additional items)

If you fax your information request, please include your mailing address, because our information packet is too thick to fax back.

Other options:

_____ *Unlocking the Potential of Secretin,* $15.00 U.S., $16.00 foreign

_____ *Defeat Autism Now! Manual* (DAN! Protocol), $25.00

_____ Secretin Video (*Dateline* and *Good Morning America* footage), $12.00

_____ Tax: CA residents add 7.75% to above items

_____ One year subscription to the *Autism Research Review* ($18.00 U.S., $20 foreign)

_____ Back issues of the *Autism Research Review* ($10/year, not including current year)

_____ Donation to help with the work of the Autism Research Institute

_____ Total

Send form and check/money order in U.S. funds to the above address.
We also accept Credit Cards:

_____ Visa _____ MasterCard _____ American Express

Card # _____ _____ _____ _____ Expiration Date _____

Mail or fax to above address. No phone orders please.

Name _____

Address _____

City _____ State_____

Zip _____ Country _____

Phone _____ Fax _____

A nonprofit corporation established in 1967.